Facebook Democracy
The Architecture of Disclosure and the Threat to Public Life

JOSÉ MARICHAL
California Lutheran University, USA

Routledge
Taylor & Francis Group

LONDON AND NEW YORK

First published 2012 by Ashgate Publishing

2 Park Square, Milton Park, Abingdon, Oxon OX14 4RN
711 Third Avenue, New York, NY 10017, USA

Routledge is an imprint of the Taylor & Francis Group, an informa business

First issued in paperback 2016

British Library Cataloguing in Publication Data
Marichal, Jose.
Facebook democracy : the architecture of disclosure and the threat to public life.
1. Facebook (Electronic resource) 2. Online social networks–Political aspects. 3. Political socialization–Technological innovations. 4. Political participation–Technological innovations.
I. Title
303.3'8'02856754-dc23

Library of Congress Cataloging-in-Publication Data
Marichal, Jose.
Facebook democracy : the architecture of disclosure and the threat to public life / by Josi Marichalis.
   p. cm. — (Politics & international relations)
Includes bibliographical references and index.
ISBN 978-1-4094-4430-5 (hardback : alk. paper)
1. Political participation--Technological innovations. 2.Communication in politics—
Technological innovations. 3. Political participation—Data processing. 4. Facebook (Firm) 5. Disclosure of information. 6. Online social networks—Political aspects. I. Title.
JF799.M32 2012
323'.0402854678—dc23

2012002367

ISBN 978-1-4094-4430-5 (hbk)
ISBN 978-1-138-27466-2 (pbk)

FACEBOOK DEMOCRACY

Contents

Contents

Introduction
The Allure of Facebook

> It is best to erase all personal history because that makes us free from the
> encumbering thoughts of other people. I have, little by little, created a fog around
> me and my life. And now nobody knows for sure who I am or what I do. Not even
> I. How can I know who I am, when I am all this? Little by little you must create
> a fog around yourself; you must erase everything around you until nothing can be
> taken for granted, until nothing is any longer for sure, or real. Your problem now
> is that you're too real. Your endeavors are too real; your moods are too real. Don't
> take things so for granted. You must begin to erase yourself.
>
> Yaqui Indian shaman Don Juan in Carlos Castaneda's
> *The Teaching of Don Juan: A Yaqui Way of Knowledge* (1991: 17)

In *The Teachings of Don Juan,* Carlos Castaneda retells an account of his
experience as a young US graduate student in anthropology who was interested
in learning more about the plants of the Yaqui Desert in Mexico. He encounters a
Yaqui Indian shaman named Don Juan who, rather than teach him about botany,
dispenses life lessons. One of his key admonishments to the young Castaneda is to
forget about plants and focus on "erasing his personal history." Throughout their
hallucinogenic travels in the desert, Don Juan elaborates upon how to implement
his theory of erasure:

> Begin with simple things, such as not revealing what you really do. What's
> wrong is that once people know you, you are an affair taken for granted and
> from that moment on you won't be able to break the tie of their thoughts ... You
> see, we only have two alternatives; we either take everything for sure and real, or
> we don't. If we follow the first, we end up bored to death with ourselves and with
> the world. If we follow the second and erase personal history, we create a fog
> around us, a very exciting and mysterious state in which nobody knows where
> the rabbit will pop out, not even ourselves. (Castaneda 1991: 15)

In the hyper-connected world of 2010, this advice seems absurd. Growing up in
an era where, according to a recent Kaiser Family Foundation survey, teenagers
in the United States spend over seven hours a day engaged with some form of
information communication technology (ICTs), it would be inconceivable to these
kids that "eras(ing) your personal history" would be either viable or desirable
(Rideout et al. 2010). If ever such a point existed where we could "erase our
personal histories" and "create a fog around ourselves," that time is long past.

This is in no small part due to the advent of the Internet. The increase in processor speeds and point-to-point networking technologies has flattened what Giddens (1990) called *time/space distanciation*. This ability to connect with anyone anywhere has changed how we relate to other human beings. Most of us now live in a *network society* (Castells 2000) where our very identities are defined by our relationship to this network. Indeed, for many young people that have grown up in this network society, the salient question might be, "Do I have a self that is distinct from my Internet self"?

In this book, I argue there is a social and political benefit to being able to create "a fog around ourselves," not just for the outside world, but for ourselves as well. At the very least, our hyper-connected era makes it more difficult for us to be contingent, doubtful or uncertain in our online/public presentations of self. In addition, it makes it easier for us to retreat to our comfortable personal networks. The popularity of social networking sites (SNS), particularly the popularity of *Facebook*, makes it increasingly difficult to develop a *contingent self* that embraces and exhibits doubt, flexibility and uncertainty about the world around us.

Facebook encourages us to lift this fog around ourselves through an *architecture of disclosure* that compels us to provide more and more information about ourselves. On one hand, this *revelation* may make connect us more to those in our network, but it might also make us more rigid and fixed in our self-construct. Taking "everything for sure and real," is a formula for steadfastness and determination. It is also a formula for rigidity and intransigence, the latter poses serious problems for democratic societies.

The Social Networking Revolution

The network society (Castells 2000) remained largely theoretical until the development of social networking sites. Friendster, MySpace and others allowed individuals to organize themselves in ways not anticipated in the era of "one to many," mass media forms of communication. SNS sites allowed for sharing of content within one or more communities of interest. Shared interests could then be leveraged to co-produce content, a phenomenon Howe (2006) refers to as *crowdsourcing*. Things as innocuous as co-created restaurant reviews or where to find the cheapest version of a video game gave individual users a power they heretofore lacked.

In this Web 2.0 era, the *networked information economy* (Benkler 2006) empowered users to make better decisions by reducing information costs and reducing barriers to collective action. Sites popped up all over the Web that promised to improve a user's quality of life. Wikipedia entries, while oft maligned in academia, democratized the encyclopedia with only a marginal reduction in information quality. Sites like *e-Bay* reduced information asymmetries that had previously disadvantaged consumers in the market place. In the political arena, sites like *YouTube* allowed the sharing of political content in ways that reduced the costs of accessing political information.

However, despite all of these benefits, the Web initially functioned largely an external add-on to an individual's offline world. It took the advent of SNS sites, like Friendster and MySpace, to make an abstract online world of sharing with "avatar- ed." strangers meld with an individual's offline world. Donath and Boyd's (2004) definition of SNS's points to:

> on-line environments in which people create a self-descriptive profile and then make links to other people they know on the site, creating a network of personal connections. Participants in social network sites are usually identified by their real names and often include photographs; their network of connections is displayed as an integral piece of their self-presentation. (72)

The ability to do these three things – create profiles, build a network and grow that network – allowed users to organize the Web around their offline relationships. This innovation took the Web from an anonymous, fragmented environment to a *nomynous* space (Zhao et al. 2008) where one's persona was mediated through a self-selected profile and their networks were organized around their offline life. The growth of SNS sites has been explosive. In 2010, 43 percent of Internet users in the United States reported using social networking sites "several times a day," a sizeable increase from 2009 where only 34 percent reported using social networking at the same rate (Hampton et al. 2011). By contrast, a recent Pew survey found that only 14 percent of teens blog, compared to 28 percent in 2006 (Lenhart et al. 2010).

Boyd and Ellison (2007) trace the beginning of social networking sites in 1997 with the launch of a site called *sixdegrees.com*. Social networking sites evolved from the late 1990s – when SNSs existed primarily as groups around racial/ethnic communities (for example, *MiGente*, *Black Planet*, and *Asian Avenue*) – to the emergence of *Friendster* in the early 2000s, and then to an explosion of SNSs in the mid 2000s, with *MySpace* as the leader of the pack. *My Space*, Facebook's predecessor, started as a mechanism for musicians to promote their work. It quickly became "cool" and popular amongst US high school students throughout the late 2000s (Boyd and Ellison 2007).

As with many technological innovations, high-school and college students in the United States were among the first to adopt this technology en masse. Using the proximity of college life, students used sites to reconnect with old friends and to cultivate new relationships. In 2004, Harvard University undergraduate student Mark Zuckerberg launched a social networking application for the university's students called "the Facebook." Based on the tradition of printed college "Facebooks" that were similar to yearbooks, "the Facebook" restricted entry to those with a Harvard.edu address. Throughout 2004, Zuckerberg expanded the site to more US colleges and universities and, in 2005, made the application available to US high school students.

In late September of 2006, Facebook become publically accessible to everyone over 13 years of age with an email address. Boyd (2010) noted a distinct class and race division emerging around this time between MySpace and Facebook users, with MySpace popular among low-income minority groups and Facebook more popular among white, college-going, middle-upper income users. In the next few years, Facebook experienced explosive growth, overtaking MySpace in number of users by mid 2009, on its way to 500 million users worldwide in July 2010, a gain of 300 million users in 15 months (Sorkin 2010).

The key advantage Facebook had over its competitors was the ability to build applications that could expand the range of ways individuals could connect with those in their network (Boyd and Ellison 2008). Compared with blogs, social networking sites like Facebook have seen significant growth in the past year. As of July, 2010, Facebook had amassed 500 million users.

The Allure of Facebook

Zuckerberg began as a creator of dating websites *Coursematch* and *Facemash*, akin to the popular site *Rate my Professor* for fellow classmates because students could assess the attractiveness of fellow classmates or majors. Zuckerberg and two others, Dustin Moskowitz and Chris Hughes, founded "The Facebook", a precursor to the current site. As anyone familiar with the 2010 film *The Social Network* would attest, the launch was wildly successful attracting half of the undergraduate population at Harvard within a month.

Zuckerberg moved quickly, expanding the site to other elite colleges later in 2004 and moving to high schools and international schools in 2005 after leaving Harvard and moving to Silicon Valley, CA. In 2006 Facebook went public, allowing anyone with an email account to join up. Since then, the company has experienced unprecedented growth. Facebook has enjoyed a steady stream of venture capital since 2005. In 2007 Microsoft invested in Facebook, paying $240 million for a 1½ percent equity ownership of the company.

This site completely changed the paradigm of the Internet. Rather than see the Web as an anonymous site where folks could try on different identities, Facebook linked the public and the private. Users were encouraged to use their real names and share real facts about their lives. This helps to explain why this site has become so popular. Typically, SNS sites are used primarily to maintain relationships with old friends or to strengthen existing relationships with current friends and acquaintances (Ellison et al. 2007, Acquisti and Gross 2006, Dwyer 2007, Dwyer et al. 2007). Viewed from a rational perspective, there would seem to be little benefit to spending countess hours on Facebook reading about the minute details of the everyday lives of friends and acquaintances. Reading "status updates" about a friend's favorite movie hardly makes sense from a cost-benefit perspective. Sure, one might value friendship, but this investment of time would seem a high price to pay to maintain these ties.

This expenditure of time makes more sense if we recognize that the desire for social connection drives our behavior. The popularity of Facebook reinforces the notion that we are not atomistic models of human behavior that presume humans as "utility seekers" and community as a "means to an end." We are not rational actors who overcome emotion to act; rather we use emotions and the desire for connection frequently in decision-making.

Social networking sites appeal because they play into our human craving for connectedness. Human beings are a social species and, as such, we are driven to identify members of our *in-group* (Krienen et al. 2010). Recent neuroscience research suggests that, in many ways, we are "hooked" on community. Zak et al. (2004) found that humans release a chemical called *oxytocin* when they are in a "trusting" environment. Oxytocin, known colloquially as "the cuddle hormone," is made by the hypothalamus and is released primarily by mothers in preparation for labor. In addition, oxytocin is released when humans and mammals are in close, intimate contact with one another – breastfeeding, hugging one's children, and so on.

Some scholars suggest that we seek out social environments to receive boosts of oxytocin. While not tested on SNS users, Penenberg (2010) reported in *Fast Company* on unpublished research by Zak that suggests the *ambient awareness* created by constantly checking into SNS sites might trigger the same oxytocin release one finds in face-to-face interaction with intimate friends. While not conclusive evidence, Zak's early work poses the possibility that Facebook usage creates a warm and fuzzy feeling that "hooks" users into social connection.

Facebook facilitates this process of connection making and maintenance. Dunbar (1998) found that human beings maintain friendships through idle talk, gossiping, and so on, a process Dunbar calls "social grooming." This grooming process takes time and cognitive effort. As such, Dunbar (1998) posits an oft-cited "150 friends" proposition where human beings have an upper limit on how many friend relationships they can "groom" at a given time. Facebook also allows for the maintenance of non-proximate and/or new friendships in more affordable ways. Both of these types of friendships could have been maintained prior to the advent of Facebook, but neither could have been maintained with such little cost in terms of time and money.

This ability to "groom" those closest to us as well as our less intimate friendships is perhaps Facebook's greatest value. By being able to more easily "groom" *weak ties* (Granovetter 1973), or loose, informal affiliations of friends and acquaintances, users have access to a broader set of resources. These disparate, low-intensity networks serve as sources of social advancement. The knowledge of things like possible job opportunities available in "thin networks" can be valuable in improving the individual life chances of network members.

These contacts can be maintained at a reduced cost because Facebook represents a blurring of mass and personal communication. SNS sites like Facebook use a "public display of connections" as a primary means of communication (Boyd and Ellison 2007). As such, individuals can update their entire network of friends with one status update rather than having to engage in one-on-one contact with each friend. It is no accident that Facebook exploded as a cultural phenomenon once the company changed its interface by introducing a "news feed" in 2006 (Thompson 2008).

The "news feed" placed all of an individual's updates – status changes, photo updates, group membership, and so on – on a "news" format on the startup page for each member of the network. If a member joined a group, this fact would be shared with every other person in his/her network. The switch to this newsfeed format caused an uproar among Facebook's early subscribers (Hoadley et al. 2010). A number of users created Facebook groups to protest this seeming breach of privacy. However, today it is a critical component of Facebook's ability to use a mediated environment to promote low-cost social grooming.

Facebook as Mediated Communication

Users do not simply reproduce their offline networks on Facebook. It is more accurate to state that Facebook friends use their offline networks to craft an online network that resembles but does not replicate their offline world (Subrahmanyam et al. 2008, Zhao et al. 2008). Parks (2010) found that over half of Facebook friends consisted of "weak tie" friendships, including acquaintances, "lapsed" friendships and friends of friends. Only 10 percent of Facebook friends were regarded as "very close" or "strong" friendships. These networks emerge from offline contacts, but they are also larger than one's immediate offline networks. Facebook friend networks thus are spatially and temporally *extended* versions of offline networks.

Despite the fact that Facebook friend networks contain both strong and weak ties, they are networks we hand-pick. Facebook falls under what Walther (2007) calls *computer mediated communication*. Cathcart and Gumpert (1986) define *mediated communication* as "any person to person interaction where a medium has been interposed to transcend the limitations of time and space" (30).

This ability to self-select a community within which one can present an online self is key to Facebook's popularity. Facebook users have the ability to deny "friend requests" from strangers or acquaintances based on whatever grounds they choose. This mediated form of communication allows users to "hand pick" their interactions from those already vetted offline at a prior point in time, either individually or through friends. The ability to select photos for network display is a key element of impression management among college students (Manago et al. 2008). For instance, the ability to add photos to one's profile is a marker of friendship desirability. Wang et al. (2010) found that both male and female SNS users were more likely to "friend" opposite-sex persons with attractive profile photos. Users also were more willing to make friends with others who had no profile photos than those with unattractive photos: hence "anonymous" was preferable as a friend than someone perceived as ugly.

Facebook and Identity Performance

How does this mediated communication change the way we interact with one another? To understand this question requires us to understand human nature and how the architecture of Facebook plays to innate and socially constructed tendencies. A critical way it does this is by changing communication from instrumental or communicative to expressive. As Boyd and Ellison (2007) argue "SNSs constitute an important research context for scholars investigating processes of impression management, self-presentation and friendship performance" (10). These types of social performance are central to human identity. We connect by presenting each other with socially constructed selves. Facebook facilitates this construction of self by creating an *architecture of disclosure* that encourages users to share information about themselves.

Facebook's business model and company mission is predicated on encouraging users to share often. Founder Mark Zuckerberg claims to be guided by an ethos of *radical transparency* in designing the site (Kirkpatrick 2010). In a recent book about the early days of Facebook, Zuckerberg hints at his grand vision and value of a particular definition of *integrity*:

> You have one identity ... The days of you having a different image for your work friends or co-workers and for the other people you know are probably coming to an end pretty quickly ... Having two identities for yourself is an example of a lack of integrity. (Zuckerberg in Kirkpatrick 2010: 36)

This ethos of the virtues of radical transparency is mirrored by Facebook's business model: user identities are commodified by selling advertising on Facebook based on self-identified user interests. Facebook leverages this aspect of social networks to encourage advertisers to place non-intrusive ads tailored to individual preferences. Personal revelation is key to Facebook's existence. The business model depends on users actively revealing themselves to their network. As Cohen (2008) points out:

> By uploading photos, posting links, and inputting detailed information about social and cultural tastes, producer-consumers provide content that is used to generate traffic, which is then leveraged into advertising sales. By providing a constant stream of content about the online activities and thoughts of people in one's social networks, Facebook taps into members' productivity through the act of surveillance. In this model, rather than employing workers to create content, Web 2.0 companies or large media firms that own them profit from the unpaid labour time that producer-consumers spend working on their online identities and keeping track of friends. (5)

Facebook does not leave this process to chance. Thaler and Sunstein (2008) note that systems and policies can be designed to *nudge* users towards making desired choices by developing architectures that encourage a particular behavior. They refer to these types of systems as *choice architectures*. For example, you can encourage people to save and invest money if you design systems where a specific amount is automatically taken from their paycheck and placed in a retirement account by default, requiring the person to "opt out" if they choose not to invest.

Similarly, Facebook creates a choice architecture that encourages expressivity. Indeed Mark Zuckerberg claims as much: "*We always thought people would share more if we didn't let them do whatever they wanted, because it gave them some order*" (Zuckerberg in Kirkpatrick 2010: 100). This "order" is geared towards making Facebook a performative space. The newsfeed, for instance, allows users to share markers of identity: music preferences, favorite movies, photos from events in their lives, news of their achievements and failures, and so on to their hand-picked networks. This identity construction, however, is not a "made-up self." Back et al. (2010) found that users on Facebook create identities that largely mirror their offline personas. Part of the reason for this is the *nomymous* status of the application. Because most Facebook users have friendship networks derived from their offline lives, the self they present must meet a credibility test, lest they get accused of being inauthentic or untruthful about their online personas.

This performative aspect is not unique to mediated forms of communication, but it is exacerbated by Facebook. Valkenburg et al. (2006) suggests that this form of communication encourages users to be more revelatory to gain more attention from their network. In particular, the *newsfeed* format provides a constant stream on content that members can view at any time. If a goal of the medium is to remain relevant to friends *en masse*, then one has little choice but to post frequent updates in the hopes of "being seen." As a result, individuals reveal more and more of their selves to their network. From consumer preferences to political views, this breadcrumb trail of observations is invaluable to marketers. For one user, gaining the attention of an entire network of acquaintances is similar to a journalist who has written a news story. Similar questions arise. How does one attract interest? What is the Facebook post equivalent of a "snappy lead"? Users are driven by the architecture to become more revelatory, use humor, post unique or socially relevant content to gain the attention of their network.

This presentation is selective and constructed by the user. However, the amount of information a user volunteers is not willy-nilly, but heavily dependent on choice architectures. Boyle and Johnson (2010), for example, found that users on MySpace users were much warier about providing information when compared to Facebook users. While MySpace users were comfortable posting general information about themselves (gender, race, zodiac sign and hometown), they were much more averse to detailing information like income, whether they smoke or drank or groups to which they belonged.

However, on Facebook, users are more revelatory. By changing the choice architecture, Facebook changed this equation. Rather than be asked to provide sensitive information, users volunteered this information because Facebook, through innovations like the newsfeed, has provided a comfortable online environment where revealing information is seen as part of a natural process of relationship building.

Demographic variations play out in the amount of information shared on Facebook. Tufecki (2008b) finds that women are more likely to use Facebook for grooming (idle talk, gossiping to maintain social relations) than men and are thus more revelatory in their postings. Additionally, Nosko et al. (2010) found that the average Canadian user studied filled in only 25 percent of all the personal information boxes Facebook asks users to include in their profile when they sign up, although younger people and those looking for an intimate relationship were more likely to reveal more personal information in their profiles than older users and those already in intimate relationships. This suggests that the architecture of disclosure is a work in progress.

This is partly because users on Facebook are engaged in a sort of "identity play" in which individuals try out different "presentations of self" (Goffman 1959). Indeed, Facebook might be most attractive to young people because it allows them to play with identity during a phase of psycho-social development where a sense of self is still being defined (Matsuba 2006). But it allows for this process to take place in front of a hand-picked "audience." This sense of "self-in-progress" produces a mediated communication largely driven by trying on a "range of possible selves" (Kao 2000) more than "listening to other selves" (Ibrahim 2010, Krämer and Winter 2008).

As a site for a general expression of identity, Zhao et al. (2008) view SNS sites like Facebook as a nonymous third type of environment where rather than create new selves, actors seek to express their "hoped for possible selves" or "images of the self that are currently unknown to others" (1819). This aspirant self is an identity that one seeks to adopt in the world but cannot because of a variety of different limitations (height, physical attractiveness, shyness, lack of access to networks, and so on). A nonymous environment like Facebook provides opportunities for those excluded from offline opportunities to realize their hoped for identity.

This desire to engage in "identity play" to try out different presentations of self is, in some ways, easier on social networking sites. This may be the case because social networking sites provide fewer non-verbal cues (facial expressions, body language, and so on). As such, users may be less inhibited in deciding to post information and photos about themselves (Bargh et al. 2002, McKenna and Bargh 2000). However, as young people have become more savvy regarding the external threats, the degree to which they will disclose intimate details to their online networks has diminished. Still the overriding impulse for revealing personal information is the desire to "be seen" and to receive validation from others (Stern 2004). Raynes-Goldie (2010) suggests that young people do not disclose willy-nilly, but rather use devices like creating aliases and performing "weekly wall cleanings" to manage their social identity (for example, who sees the performance of the self Online). Viewed in this way, Facebook is more than the "high school cafeteria table" writ large; it is more like having the ability to choose who gets to enter the cafeteria in the first place.

Facebook and Political Identity

How does this "trying on of possible selves" connect to political identity formation? Research on this subject has emphasized the links between SNS sites and political activism. The ease of many-to-many communication brought about by SMS has reduced the transaction costs involved in joining social movements (Earl and Schussman 2003). The ease with which individuals can create content and connect with one another to share content is viewed by other scholars as a harbinger of a more democratic and egalitarian global order (Benkler 2006, Jenkins 2006, Shirky 2009.

Because Facebook is still a relatively recent phenomenon, the literature on individuals using the technology for political purposes is limited. However, there is little doubt that the Facebook application has had broad social effects. By facilitating the formation of social networks, Facebook provides movement entrepreneurs with accessible audiences. A recent Pew survey found that nearly one-third of young people aged 18–29 used SNSs for political purposes (Lenhart et al. 2010).

Facebook may have some positive effect upon political engagement. Park et al. (2009) found four primary motivations for participating in a Facebook group: socializing, entertainment, self-status seeking, and information. The authors found that students who used Facebook to engage in information seeking or socializing were more likely to participate in political group activity. However, those who used Facebook for entertainment were not any more likely to engage in political activity than those who didn't use Facebook at all. Similarly, Feezell et al. (2009) found that belonging to a political Facebook group was associated with higher levels of political engagement including voting and expressing interest in politics.

Earlier work on the discursive potential of Facebook groups provides a mixed picture of its democratic potential. While Kushin and Kitchener (2009) found generally civil discourse within politically oriented Facebook groups, Feezell et al. (2009) found the discourse on Facebook political groups were characterized by incivility and by false statements and half-truths about political affairs. As such, they found that user participation in Facebook groups was not associated with greater levels of knowledge about political information and policy issues than those not involved in Facebook groups. The upshot of this early scholarship is that Facebook might aid in mobilization, but not necessarily in the development of good citizens.

Jackson and Lilleker (2009) suggest Facebook group discourse, particularly when initiated by formal organizations like political parties, is characterized by "weak interactivity" in reaching out to members because of their desire to control their message. Their analysis of candidate websites in the British Parliamentary elections of 2009 led them to refer to political party Facebook groups as *Web 1.5*, which they define as the "extensive use of the architecture of participation, but much less use of the community's democratic structure" (2009: 248).

Social critics (Morozov 2011, White 2010, Gladwell 2010) suggest that despite the increase in participation, Facebook might do more harm than good in the political process. Morozov (2011) refers to the ease with which individuals can create and join communities of interest as *slacktivism*. He suggests that this ease of membership and identification detracts from more serious and coordinated efforts to effect social change. The positive feeling associated with affiliating with a movement might satisfy one's need for social connection without one engaging with formal political power. Additionally, small acts of political participation online have been seen by some as counterproductive. Zuckerman (2010) contends:

> There's a case to be made that the actions taken by US supporters of the Green Movement were counterproductive – they added credence to the regime's case that US and UK forces were attempting to topple the Iranian government and that the Green Movement was an external, not grassroots, domestic force. There's also a case to be made that there's nothing online activists could do in the face of a determined repressive government and that we shouldn't have expected any change to come from online activism. (Online)

White (2010) faults activist organizations themselves for this shortcoming. He decries an obsession with marketing techniques, what he calls *clicktivism*, for the decline in the power of left activism:

> The end result is the degradation of activism into a series of petition drives that capitalise on current events. Political engagement becomes a matter of clicking a few links. In promoting the illusion that surfing the web can change the world, clicktivism is to activism as McDonalds is to a slow-cooked meal. It may look like food, but the life-giving nutrients are long gone. (White 2010: Online)

Put another way, this critique contends that Facebook allows users to engage in social activism without resulting in a corresponding change in their political identities. A "one-click" approach to activism does little to create what García-Bedolla (2005) calls *mobilizing identities* where citizens incorporate activism into their core social and political identities.

A counter to this argument is that Facebook's value is less about mobilization and more about providing what Salter (2005) calls *radical public spheres* that provide additional spaces for marginalized groups to have a voice in public life. More importantly, information technologies help shift political discourse to more informal venues that are less subject to elite control (Dahlberg 2007). Within these decentralized, autonomous spaces, individuals can explore various aspects of their identity and develop a stronger sense of who they are and what issues are of primary concern to them.

Facebook and the Politics of the Personal

In this book, I propose a way forward in our understanding of how Facebook affects politics by linking it to the ways in which Facebook encourages us to disclose and connect with others. I suggest that Facebook facilitates a deep engagement with the *personal*, a world inhabited by individuals expressing (and receiving) thoughts and feelings to self-selected networks in the hopes of receiving validation for their identity performance. This emphasis on "the personal" or the performance of identity colors the way users see the political world.

Goffman (1959) differentiates between a "back stage" performance of a private self and a "front stage" performance or public self. Goffman defines a front stage as "that part of the individual's performance which ... functions in a general and fixed fashion to define the situation for those who observe the performance" (1959: 32). From this perspective, Facebook use is less about instrumental action and more about exchanging information to perform identity. Goffman points out that a *front* is part of a broader *performance*, or "all the activity of an individual which occurs during a period marked by his continuous presence before a particular set of observers." This performance consists of several elements or "expressive equipment" including:

> The setting – "items which supply the scenery and stage props for the spate of human action played out before, within or upon it."
>
> Appearance – "those stimuli which function at the time to tell us of the performer's social statuses."
>
> Manner – "those stimuli which function at the time to warn us of the interaction role the performer will expect to play in the upcoming situation." (Goffman 1959: 22)

This *expressive equipment* takes on a unique dimension on social networking sites. Absent are the signs and signifiers that characterize face to face interactions. In its stead are "digital signifiers" which include text, images, avatars, social networks, testimonials and so on (Boyd and Heer 2006). In this sense, a digital front stage represents the ways in which users perform public identities in the absence of traditional signifiers that characterize identity maintenance.

On Methodology: Exploring the Politics of the Personal Using Facebook Groups

One way to gain insight into how Facebook encourages a personal engagement with private life is by examining Facebook groups. Unlike Facebook *pages*, which were set up more as profile pages for companies, celebrities or other entities, the *groups* were built around interactivity. The *groups* feature was intended to allow users to connect with other users based on similar interests. As such, it is Facebook's effort to create what Granovetter (1973) called *weak-tie* networks based on shared interest. Groups, according to Facebook, "allow people to come together around a common cause, issue or activity to organize, express objectives, discuss issues, post photos and share related content" (Facebook.com: Online). Facebook allows any of its members to start a group. The content is restricted to that which is not offensive. Users then create a title and provide a description of the group. Groups can be open for all, by invitation only, or restricted. Open groups allow anyone to join and invite others to join. In addition, all group content is searchable and viewable by anyone on Facebook. Closed groups are searchable, but the content as well as membership, is restricted. Secret groups are not searchable, nor is the content accessible by other Facebook users. For the purposes of searching groups, Facebook lets users categorize the groups into types. Curiously, administrators cannot remove content from the groups, only individual users can do that.

Groups have been a popular feature on Facebook. According to Facebook, the average user is "connected to 80 community pages, groups and events" (blog. Facebook.com 2010). Facebook groups have grown exponentially in the past year. One way to analyze the political identity formation process on Facebook is to examine the formation of political Facebook groups. The social networking application provides citizens with powerful tools for expressing their political views and aggregating interests around issues of common concern. A Google query of Facebook groups I conducted in October 2011 yielded 519 million hits. The website AllFacebook.com, which tracks Google's indexing trends, reported that Google had indexed 620 million Facebook groups in February of 2010. The same website reported that Google had indexed 52 million groups in October of 2009, a 12-fold increase in a matter of months (AllFacebook.com). While it is next to impossible to determine the percentage of these sites that are political or activist in nature, it is not far-fetched to presume that they rank in the tens of millions. The ubiquity of Facebook, coupled with the ease with which a group can be formed, makes this tool a convenient form of political expression.

Throughout this book, I illustrate Facebook's impact on political identity by providing examples of political Facebook groups. Throughout 2011, I conducted a content analysis of 250 politically oriented Facebook groups. Using *Google Translate*, I examined Facebook groups from 32 different countries in 23 different languages. When individuals browse groups on Facebook, they are provided with a drop-down menu that provides users with different genres of groups from which they can browse. One group includes the category "general interest/politics." Facebook presents users with over 500 political groups from which to browse. An analysis of these groups highlights how Facebook's unique architecture shapes how individuals engage with political life.

Organization of the Book

In Chapter 1, I discuss some of the prevailing arguments challenging the social and political efficacy of the Internet. I examine arguments that suggest the SNS sites might have a deleterious impact on democracy by cutting into our attention spans, changing our core relationships and encouraging us to focus on banal and narcissistic content. I suggest these arguments miss the mark in explaining Facebook because they do not account for Facebook's key strength – it satisfies the utopian-communitarian impulse on the Web for community while serving a neoliberal, individualist market based view of the utopian Web. Without understanding this unique juxtaposition, it is difficult to understand Facebook's allure and its impact of public life.

In Chapter 2, I discuss what I call Facebook's *architecture of disclosure* in which they use a variety of tools to draw users into their personal networks. This architecture leverages users' desires to *disclose* and *connect*, things that have typically been thought of as public acts, for private market-based gains. The chapter discusses the various ways Facebook encourages this process.

In Chapter 3, I discuss how this could produce harmful consequences for democratic life. In particular, I discuss how the *architecture of disclosure* emphasizes what Arendt (1958) calls "small things" by connection us to our personal networks at the expense of the shared "world of things" between people; instead, Facebook draws users into what Baumeister (1987) calls the "problem of the self," or the quest to "present the self" through performance for legitimization and validation. This exacerbates what Sennett calls "the fall of the public man." In its stead is a self-preoccupied with his personal networks.

In Chapter 4, I discuss the effects of this on democratic life. In particular, I examine critical and post-structural approaches that critique neoliberal hegemony in modern democracy. I suggest that there are conditions under which Facebook encourages the development of *passive subjects* by encouraging users to see public life through the lens of the personal. By emphasizing personal identity performance within self-selected networks, users are less apt to make connections between their lives and impersonal structural forces.

In Chapter 5, I examine arguments that emphasize the importance of *the personal* in public life because it aids in the cultivation of *voice*, particularly for the marginalized, as central to vibrant democratic life. I argue that, while *voice* can be critical and important for democratic societies, its value as a tool for social change is limited if voice is not connected to larger, impersonal structural forces. I argue that Facebook builds on a society that emphasizes *voice* over *listening* and equally important democratic virtue.

In Chapter 6, I look at how Facebook emphasizes the performance of political identity over other forms of communication. I argue that the *architecture of disclosure* leads to the performance of political identity through symbols and stories. These symbols and stories can take a variety of forms, but they are often based on ethnic or nationalist impulses. I discuss the possibilities for *project* (Castells 200) or *mobilization* (García-Bedolla 2005) identities based on identity politics. In Chapter 7, I explore the critique that Facebook is not a vehicle for political activism. I review the literature on Facebook as a mobilizing tool. I argue that the politics of the personal can be highly successful in mobilization in contexts where "the self" is repressed through totalitarian action. Through the dissemination of stories and symbols, Facebook can serve as a focal point for galvanizing groups around collective myths. I also discuss the limits of this approach on Facebook. Because Facebook is a private company whose market model is based on creating a public sphere, it is often indifferent to how the medium is used.

In Chapter 8, I examine the importance of privacy as a political tool. I discuss Facebook's role in contributing to the development of what I call *the specified self.* This self uses the tools of technology to gain knowledge about the self. I argue that a self that is completely known to itself and others is a flawed political subject, particularly when those expectations are placed upon public life.

In Chapter 9, I discuss the nation state as a "friend." Highlighting efforts by public figures to be viewed as a "friend" creates the impression that the public can be part of the personal. This disempowers political subjects by narrowing the gulf between the *public transcript* and the *hidden transcript* (Scott 1992). In addition, it creates an expectation that the public should have the same characteristics as personal networks. I use Jay (2010) to make the case for *mendacity* in politics and show how Facebook cuts against this necessary temperament in political life.

I conclude the book by highlighting the importance of "listening on Facebook." Facebook does indeed promote what Salter (2005) calls *radical public spheres* that include marginalized voices; the medium also fragments discourse spaces in ways that inhibit cross-cutting deliberation (Mutz 2006). I make the case that the health of democratic societies is dependent upon cultivating habits of democratic attention (Bickford 1996) and in particular cultivating habits of *talking to strangers* (Allen 2004). I highlight ways in which this can occur. In addition, I discuss challenges to Facebook's viability going forward and highlight ways in which the company is responding to them. I caution that Facebook's *architecture of disclosure* is an unsustainable business model and suggest ways in which a social networking site could be built upon *cooperation* rather than *connection*.

Chapter 1

Facebook and the
Utopian/Dystopian Dialectic

It is easy to deride Facebook. The application seems to be constituted primarily of seemingly narcissistic and trivial "status updates" that distract from "real" issues in the world. The narrative that Facebook is "making us stupid" (Carr 2008 or indicative of a "cult of the amateur" (Keen 2007 resonates with a news media that relies on polemics. As a consequence, writing and theorizing about Facebook's perceived role in public life mirrors writing about the Web in general. Either a utopian narrative emerges that emphasizes the Internet's emancipatory potential or a dystopian narrative that posits the Internet as a colossal and historic time suck that threatens democratic health in a number of ways, by contributing to a dumbing down of society (Keen 2007), a shortening of our attention spans (Carr 2010), a trend towards a self-satisfied "slacktivism" (Morozov 2011), a growing digital divide (Hargittai 2008) and allowing us to retreat to insularhomogeneous networks based upon shared experiences or interests.(Boyd 2010 that encourage selectivity bias in collecting information (Prior 2008).

None of these arguments is entirely without merit when applied to the Web in general. But I argue that these conventional challenges to the Web's social efficacy do not apply directly to Facebook. If we are to accurately assess Facebook's impact on power and politics, we must situate the analysis within this broader conversation regarding the efficacy of SNS applications or lack thereof for political transformation. This chapter places Facebook's impact on politics within the larger conversation over the socio-political potential for the Web in general, with particular attention to the ways in which conventional challenges to the Web fail to account for Facebook's unique position. Instead, it is instructive to look at early *Web utopian* thought to understand Facebook's appeal and its potential impact on political life. Facebook presents a curious merging of market/individualist notions of the utopian Web and communitarian/collectivist notions of the Web. This is an important insight because Facebook as a business provides us with a *sense* of community for market-based, individualist ends. It is a *sense* and not a reality because it is a mediated public that we self-select, not the spontaneous, unfiltered public that exists in real life. Put another way, by giving us a "sense of the public," our relationship to and expectations of actual public life are changed. In subsequent chapters, I'll discuss how this reality of Facebook leads to more serious challenges to democratic governance. But before we can do this, we must explore conventional challenges to the Web and how they apply to Facebook.

The Power of Facebook

The advent of information communication technologies (ICTs) has brought about significant transformation in our civic lives. The emergence of ICTs has created a radical shift in the way we gather political information, the way we construct our daily habits and the quality and number of social interactions. As Benkler (2006) argues, increased server storage capacity, the proliferation of personal computers with fast microprocessor speeds, and the advent of broadband Internet access have combined to make it possible to store vast amounts of easily retrievable information in "the cloud." This trend will only strengthen in the coming years. A recent report by the Kaiser Family Foundation discovered that kids in 2009 spent 7.5 hours a day interacting with ICT devices compared to less than 6.5 hours a day in 2005 (Rideout et al. 2010). As the *New York Times* reported, this surprised the research team because they did not think the subjects of the study could possibly squeeze in any more time for engaging with these new media tools (Lewin 2010). Additionally, 70 percent of kids reported having no parental limits on the amount of digital media they consume (Rideout et al. 2010).

Perhaps no other application online has produced as much loyalty and has been as transformative to the individual habits as Facebook. Facebook's dramatic rise could be predicted by examining its use among college students. As early as 2005, 85 percent of college students had a Facebook account (Arrington 2007). Indeed, if Facebook were a country, it would be third largest in the world (Fletcher 2010). According to the Facebook monitoring site SocialBakers.com (Wauters 2011), Facebook gained close to 250 million new members in 2010, bringing its worldwide user rate to 585 million, an increase of about eight new users every second. The greatest concentration of Facebook users reside in the United States which accounted for about one-fourth of Facebook users in 2010 (174 million) (SocialBakers.com 2011). However, Facebook's reach extends beyond the West. Indonesia has the second-largest Facebook population in the world and India, Mexico and the Philippines are in the top 10 in terms of Facebook users (SocialBakers.com 2011). While 18–34-year-olds make up over 50percent of the worldwide Facebook population, those aged 65 and over are the fastest-growing population, an increase of 124 percent in 2010. It he popularity of the sites does not appear to be waning (SocialBakers.com 2011).

Despite the proliferation of Facebook, we know little about how this transformation of our daily lives impacts public life. The movement of numbers of people toward mass-scale online network engagement is in its infancy. In exchange for attention and small amounts of personal information, users in the cloud are given ubiquitous access to documents and tools that allow them to efficiently cultivate their network of relationships. But how are these relationships changed by our "life in the cloud"?

Much of the writing on how applications like Facebook impact politics and power are shaped by a dialectic between early Web utopian discourses that presume an inherent virtue to online communication and the predictable and important dystopian backlash. Later in the chapter, I sort Web utopianism along two dimensions, a liberal utopianism (private) and a communitarian (public) utopianism. I argue that Facebook's power comes from merging these two strands of Web utopianism by allowing people to attain the "public" benefits of communitarian utopianism while preserving the "private" individualism of liberal utopianism.

Both of these utopian discourses, however, have produced a counter-narrative which emphasize four key features: information overload, selectivity bias, digital divide and lack of empathy. In this chapter, I will briefly examine these challenges to the Web in general, and in particular how these challenges apply to Facebook. I argue these challenges do not resonate as critiques of Facebook because they miss the key benefit of Facebook to users: *merging individual choice with a perceived collective public benefit*. In later chapters, I lay out the potential harm to democratic societies from such a merging of individualist and communitarian visions of the Web. But first I discuss whether these challenges to a Web utopian narrative hold muster.

The Dystopian Web

The lived experience with ICTs motivated a set of challenges to these utopian ideas. Questions emerged about the transformative potential of ICTs. As a result, the pendulum seems to have lurched towards a dystopian view of the Web's effect on public life. Applied to Facebook, these would seem to foretell a negative net effect on social and political phenomena. The dystopian pushback to Web utopianism includes five strands: information overload, selectivity bias, slacktivism, digital divide and empathy/friendship decline. While each of these critiques point to important issues in the social and political impact of Facebook and other SNS applications, none of conventional views of how the Web might harm social and political life seems to quite fit Facebook. I address each in turn.

Information Overload

A central concern is that the amount of information thrown at us through the Internet is exceeding our capacity to discern its quality. Rather than expose us to the world of ideas and make us liberal, empowered global citizens, the Web mires us in the world of banality. Ironically, while the collective knowledge of the world is being digitized and placed within our grasp, we may fail to take in their wisdom because we cannot get out from under the deluge of Twitter posts, texts and Facebook status updates that occupy our attention. As Smith (2011) quipped "if the Internet is cocaine, then Facebook is crack." As I discussed in the last chapter, humans are hard-wired for social connection. An application like Facebook that facilitates these connections provides what looks like information but really amounts to meaningless dross.

Carr (2010) argues that this flood of information is affecting our ability to pay attention to longer, more involved arguments. In an effort to filter the mass of information, we take to skimming and summarizing rather than remembering and reflecting. Rather than make us more engaged, reflective and deliberative citizens, ICTs might encourage our more impatient, selfish, petulant selves. Carr suggests that "the cloud" serves as a disincentive for reflection by encouraging the processing of information in small, discrete, chunks. In a widely cited article in *The Atlantic*, Carr highlights how his ability to process information has changed as his use of ICTs has increased: "… my mind now expects to take in information the way the Net distributes it: in a swiftly moving stream of particles. Once I was a scuba diver in the sea of words. Now I zip along the surface like a guy on a Jet Ski" (2008: 58). Powers (2010) calls for a *technology sabbath* to reclaim time for thought and contemplation.

Thus a key critique would be that this instantaneous culture of information means that we may develop participatory habits, but without the cognitive capacity to process and reflect upon the information's meaning, a task vital to deliberative citizenship. Keen (2007) observes a tendency among Web users towards an "infantilized-self" that prioritizes "intellectual self-stimulation" (194) over "the impartiality of the authoritative, accountable, expert" (41). The result is a networked information economy that has "novices speaking to novices" (52). Keen observation begs the question of whether we are in danger of producing a generation of citizens incapable of engaging difficult ideas.

Political theorists decry the lack of civic literacy among voters and "the willingness and ability to engage in public discourse and to evaluate the performance of those in office" (Galston 1991: 227). While the amount of political information needed for a functioning democracy is debated, a dystopian view would suggest that what little attention was left for political information gathering and reflection has been irredeemably lost by Facebook.

Rather than usher in this era of "wise crowds" full of content creators, the Web has moved towards SNS sites that cultivate friendship networks. A recent Pew survey found that young people's use of ICTs is moving away from content-sharing sites like YouTube and Flickr and towards social networking sites. Additionally there has been a significant decline in blogging by teens over time. In 2007, 28 percent of teens reported blogging, by 2009 than number had been reduced to 14 percent (Lenhart et al. 2010).

There is reason to be cautious about fully embracing this critique. Blair (2010) notes that fear of "information overload" represents a theme that runs throughout history. She notes that as early as the third century BC, complaints about "the abundance of books" were prevalent. These concerns periodically emerge as new technology replaces old ways of gathering knowledge. The printing press in the mid fifteenth century significantly changed the way knowledge was received and reflected upon. The printing press increased information by an order of magnitude: it made books cheaper, but by making book-production more efficient, it invited the production of subpar manuscripts and took attention away from quality works.

In all these instances, however, the proliferation of information had pro-populist, pro-democratic consequences. Similar arguments can be made about Facebook. If the printing press made it easier to publish bad books at the expense of good ones, Facebook frees individuals from the need to say anything important. SNSs may constitute a new level of "information overload" where we engage in vast amounts of information dissemination and perusal that seemingly proceeds without any real motivation or intention. From this perspective, most Facebook status updates are mental dross free of anything that could be classified as "information" for public purposes (Hindman 2009). As Smith (2011) wryly observes about his own Facebook use:

> I've figured out how to block Farmville and MafiaWars and obscene stuff like that, but there's no way to similarly keep at bay the barrage of images of other people's babies (a sensitive issue at this stage of the life-cycle), nor the whooping and hollering of sports fans (no less tedious in its written than in its audible form), nor all the bickering about having to grade papers among my academic peers, nor the predictable self-affirmations of the mainline liberals who make up the greater part of my cohort. (Online)

But this "banal talk" acquires greater importance when it comes from those we know. The daily musings of our intimates has always been more important to us than treatises from the great philosophers or positional papers from government agencies. Indeed this everyday interaction with our intimate social networks might make us more aware of the world around us.

Rather than make us less empathic, Facebook seems to connect us more to others. Hampton et al. (2011) found that Facebook users exhibited a number of positive civic attributes. When the team looked at frequent Facebook users (for example, those who visited the site at least once a day), they found this group was *three* times as likely as non-Internet users to feel that people could be trusted. Additionally, Hampton et al. (2011) found that Facebook users had closer ties than non-users and received more social (companionship), emotional (receiving advice) and instrumental support (tangible assistance) than non-users.

Further, a lack of complete knowledge about the political process might not be a prerequisite for effective citizenship. A vast literature in political science over the last four decades has documented the lack of information of the part of American voters (Converse 1975, Kinder and Sears 1985, Delli Carpini and Keeter 1997). Bartels (1996) suggest that in the absence of accurate information about policy issues, voters effectively use cues and information shortcuts to make political decisions. Further, errors in decision-making at the individual level are randomly distributed among the general population and thus when aggregated have little impact on elite decision-making. Lau et al. (1997) argues that despite their lack of information, citizens vote in accordance with their stated preferences the vast majority of the time.

Selectivity Bias/Homogeneity

But perhaps this is the main problem with Facebook. It isn't that we are flooded with information, but rather, we are flooded with what Sunstein (2001) calls the *daily me* of content. Our flood of information is based on social networks comprised of individuals with whom we already agree politically. If Facebook exacerbates our already built in tendency to form social networks around shared characteristics, then our information gathering won't be neutrally misinformed, as Bartels (1996) suggests, but will be more skewed towards whichever ideological "tribe" is ascendant.

An analysis of the level of political polarization in the United States is instructive. In the United States, the electorate is the most divided in a generation. In 2010, 60 percent of whites voted for the Republican Party and 37 percent voted for the Democratic Party, the largest margin since the National Election Study began polling (Brownstein 2011). By contrast, 73 percent of all non-white voters – African-Americans, Hispanics, Asians, and others – backed Democratic United States House of Representatives' candidates in the mid-term election, according to the new analysis. A similar pattern was evident among perceptions of President Obama's job in office. While 22 percent of non-white voters disapproved of President Obama's performance in office 65 percent of white voters expressed disapproval and half of White voters expressed strong disapproval.

While important socio-economic shifts independent of the Internet are responsible for this polarization (increasing number of minority voters, realignment of conservatives into the Republican Party, and so on), one could argue that Facebook might serve to increase polarization. Lazarsfeld and Menzel (1963) found that political opinions flowed through friendship networks, particularly through *influentials* that shaped opinion on political issues and candidates. Mutz (2006) suggests a similar phenomenon is occurring in contemporary American politics.

Much of the recent scholarship on selectivity bias in online information-gathering suggests a mirroring of the broader political polarization literature. Lawrence et al. (2010) find that the political blogosphere mirrors Mutz's (2002, 2006) finding about homogeneous networks. In surveys of political blog readers, they found significant ideological distance between conservative and liberal blogs and little ideological cross-pollenation. Being a part of an active online community often leads to greater political participation (increased voting, campaign donating and persuading others) but also leads to increased ideological polarization. Similarly, Hargittai (2007) found that Website linking behavior on political blogs suggests strong ideological bias. Gilbert et al. (2009) found significant agreement in the comment section of political blogs: about four times as much "agreement" as "disagreement" (as opposed to twice as much agreement for tech or entertainment blogs).

But Facebook networks are not blogs. There is good reason to believe that online homogeneity is not as serious a problem on Facebook as it might be on other forms on online communication. Geographic proximity and shared interest may be more closely associated with network formation than individual homogeneity.

There is some reason to be cautious about the idea that Facebook promotes homogeneous network formation. Goel et al. (2010) found that Facebook friends were more homogeneous in their political views than random groups, but the difference (75 percent agreement for Facebook friends vs 63 percent for randomly assigned groups) was negligible and they underestimated the extent to which those in their networks agreed with them on policy issues.

On the plus side, social network members "are probably surrounded by a greater diversity of opinions than is sometimes claimed, (but they) generally fail to talk about politics, and that when they do, they simply do not learn much from their conversations about each other's views ... the extent to which peers influence each other's political attitudes may be less than is sometimes claimed (Goel et al. 2010: 10). The inference here is that, as it concerns politics on Facebook, most users either shy away from political discussion or simply assume more similarity within their online network than actually exists. Thus the polity might remain largely uninformed, but will not become subject to an "echo chamber" effect in the receipt of political information

Because Facebook is based on *social proximity* and not shared interest there is more of a likelihood of ideological heterogeneity. There is not a direct overlap between what your friends and family believe and what you believe. In addition, Williams and Gulati (2007) note that Facebook's architecture of profiles and status updates make it more likely that one could be inadvertently exposed to contrasting political messages.

Instead, people have broad-based impressions of those in their friend networks (general religious, political orientations, personality traits). Goel et al. (2010) find that people overestimate how similar their political views are to those in their online social network. People on Facebook assumed those in their network shared beliefs on policy issues like abortion, illegal immigration and health care to a greater extent than was actually the case. This mirrors trends within the US electorate where perceptions of friends' political attitudes are wildly different than their actual views (Baldassarri and Gelman 2008).

This makes sense, given that Facebook's purpose is *social connection* and as such, political conversation might inhibit maintaining relationships with family and friends. Eliasoph (1998) noted this as a reason why Americans fail to engage in everyday political discourse. This fear of offending those socially proximate to you has positive consequences, of course (ironically we may engage more in politics if we talk less about it Online), but it also has the effect of truncating political dialogue.

Slacktivism

A third core criticism is that the Web makes us *slacktivists* who substitute real activism for low-cost, low-benefit political behavior (Morozov 2011. Gladwell (2010) wrote an influential article in the *New Yorker* in which he criticized net activism for failing to foster the *strong ties* necessary to sustain activism. He cites

McAdam's (1986) work that suggests activists in the US civil rights movement weren't simply committed to the goals of the movement, but also had close friends that were directly impacted by civic rights. Gladwell argues that Facebook produces *weak tie* relationships that are good for diffusion of information, but not so great at developing the sustained bonding social capital necessary for activism.

Benkler (2006) observed that the Internet, and social networking in particular, *lowered transaction costs* and allowed for people to collaborate without the necessary trust bonds that sustained previous interactions. Benkler's notion is that one can collaborate without the sustained intensity of desire needed to overcome transaction costs. Because costs are so low, people can participate with little temporal, physical or physical cost to them. A prime example of this is the myriad of Facebook fan pages dedicated to social causes that have millions of members. You can extract *microactivism* (Marichal 2010) from casually interested persons (for example, small five cent domations or "like" denotations).

Both Morozov and Gladwell claim that activism requires temporal and physical cost to be effective. Morozov (2011) argues that these lowered transaction costs allow people to gain a "sense of activism" without having to actually engage in activism. Gladwell argues that movements require more hierarchical organizational structures to maintain sustained action. Applications like Facebook cultivate non-hierarchical networks structures and as such do not have the centralized authority necessary to sustain action and in the political process it is the sustained access that compels change.

The claim that online networks encourage thin ties while face-to-face interaction encourages strong ones is dubious. Research on friendship networks suggests that individual's offline networks closely approximate their online ones. Rather than simply promote weak ties, Facebook can amplify or attenuates the strong-tie bonds that we form offline. While research is in the early stages, Facebook users might be more civically engaged than non-users (Kahne and Middhaugh 2009, Feezell et al. 2009.

Kahne et al. (2010) found that the more people engage politically online, the more likely they will engage offline. Kahne et al. (2010) for example found that among US based youth, spending time in online communities seemed to promote more general civic engagement. They contend that social network activity spills over into offline engagement. Engagement with "online participatory communities" tied to youth interests exposed young people to a diverse set of viewpoints and made them more interested in politics. According to Hampton et al. (2011) Facebook users were 53 percent more likely to vote than non-members, 78 percent more likely to try and influence someone to vote, and over two and a half times more likely to attend a political meeting or rally.

The challenge for movement activists is not how to make Facebook networks strong-tie networks, but rather the challenge is to build strong-tie networks offline that can be leveraged through online tools. There is no reason to expect that the presence of Facebook would have lessened the urgency or import of the civil rights movement. Facebook does not operate in the absence of offline social networks, but rather are a compliment to them.

A prime example of this is the 2008 US presidential elections where the Obama campaign used social networking As Obama's online organizing coordinator Joe Rospars put it "There was never anything online that was there for online's sake" (Farrell 2008: Online). It is most effective as a vehicle to facilitate face to face mobilization activities. The Obama campaign used the Web as a means to facilitate pre-existing offline relationships. The Internet was not a mobilization vehicle in and of itself, but a means to accomplish traditional political tasks.

The point missed by the *slacktivist* thesis is that social networking sites like Facebook can accommodate a whole range of different types of network formations. Individual networks can be small, long lasting and dense with high levels of interchangability between nodes or they can be large, diffuse and with lowinterchangability. Individual networks can have aspect of both small, long-lasting, transitive, strong-tie networks and large, informal, weak-tie networks (Christakis and Fowler 2009. Facebook networks range from the college student who "friends" a stranger from halfway around the world or the husband who "updates" his wife to pick up a carton of milk from the supermarket. There is no one network formation, but a myriad of different ways that individuals connect.

If Facebook has a deleterious effect on politics, it is not because it provides too much information, devalues friendship, or leads to slacktivism. It is more important to examine how these networks interact. Christakis and Fowler's path-breaking work on social networks finds that they have a significant impact on behavior. They find that:

> Students with studious roommates become more studious. Diners sitting next
> to heavy eaters eat more food. Homeowners with neighbors who garden wind
> up with manicured lawns. And this simple tendency for one person to influence
> another has tremendous consequences when we look beyond our immediate
> connections. (2010: 8)

As far as it concerns politics, the possibility exists that political engagement can be contagious. However, we need to think of Facebook more as an *interaction effect* rather than as a direct causal mechanism for sustained engagement. Rather than argue whether or not Facebook is good for political mobilization, the question should be "when is Facebook good for political mobilization"?

Digital Divide

It is possible that Facebook as an interaction reproduces within-country and between-country structural inequalities. If both on-line and off-line social networks are largely homogeneous in nature and part of that homogeneity is tied to race and socio-economic status, then Facebook might foster greater social inequality. Internet scholarship has moved beyond binary classifications in explaining the digital divide.

A number of models have appeared to capture the differences in Internet uses between groups. These include: "use-diffusion model" (Shih and Venkatesh 2004), "usage gap" (van Dijk 2004), "second-level digital divide" (Hargittai 2002), and "emerging digital differentiation" (Valkenburg et al. 2006). Studies find vast differences in how users access the Internet. Relevant factors include the level of autonomy the user has, the number of access points a user has to get online (Hassani 2006), the amount of experience a user has (Eastin and LaRose 2000, Livingstone and Helsper: 2007, Valkenburg et al. 2006), and so on. (DiMaggio et al. 2004, Hargittai 2008). Hargittai and Hinnant (2008) found significant differences in how 18–26 year olds they studied used the Web. They found that those young adults with high educational attainment used the medium for "capital enhancing" activities (DiMaggio et al. 2004), including visiting job-related sites, acquiring financial information, health information or news (Howard et al. 2001).

This distinction between how the Internet is used has critical implications for citizenship formation. While a sizable portion of the US population still lacks broadband access (Zhang et al. 2008), the broader question for political scientists is how users interact with the medium. While social scientists have looked at how differential usage patterns affect social inequality (van Dijk 2005, DiMaggio et al. 2004, Hargittai 2008, Selwyn 2004, Warschauer 2002, Chen and Wellman 2005), they have not examined the ways in which variations of usage patterns affect opinion and attitude formation.

To what extent is the digital divide reproduced on Facebook? The lack of data on this question makes it difficult to know how much the digital divide applies to Facebook itself. One might presume that it enhances inequality. Facebook's ability to sift through friend requests to cultivate our own network gives us more control over the *homogeneity* of our networks. Boyd's (2010) preliminary work on "digital ghettos" suggests that youth tend to replicate homogeneous offline friendship networks on SNS sites. However, whether this applies to political attitudes is not as well explored.

If true, this tendency towards homogeneity might explain the positive benefits of connection. It is possible that much of the social contagion effect Christakis and Fowler encountered has more to do with "sameness" between network members than with social network formation. Aral et al. (2009) looked at 27.5 million user texts on the Yahoo Go mobile network and found that homogeneity accounted to more than half of the similarity in behavior, suggesting that online networks are simply reproducing offline homogeneous networks. Indeed if networks online reproduce offline "sameness" then SNS sites like Facebook do little more than reproduce structural inequality.

The Dystopian Web: Summary

These conventional arguments about the Web (information overload, homogeneity, slacktivism, digital divide) do not seem to get at the core way in which Facebook transforms social and political life. It may inundate us with information (Carr 2010, but so did the printing press (Blair 2010). It connects us closer to our personal networks, but these are probably politically heterogeneous (Goel et al. 2010. It might encourage slacktivism (Morozov 2011), but it also enhances civic engagement, at least in the United States (Hampton et al. 2011), there might be a digital divide on Facebook (Boyd 2010) but no more so than the rest of the Internet (Hargittai 2008).

So what are we to make of Facebook's role in social and political life? I argue that to understand its most consequential impact, we must recognize that there are really *two* Facebooks – a free-market-based *private* Facebook and a communitarian-based *public* Facebook, both tied to a strand of Web utopian thought. Facebook satisfies two strands of Web utopian thought and as such serves as a powerful and unpredictable mechanism for social change. By incorporating both libertarian and communitarian versions of Web utopia, Facebook creates a platform for connection that does not challenge underlying neoliberal assumptions and serves market-based ends.

The Private Facebook

Early Web theorists believed in the medium's power to devolve power to the individual and the market. These *hyper-empowered* early adopters were perceived to be beyond the control of the nation state. Thus early writing emphasized the autonomous nature of the cyberspace and the obligations to preserve the Web from hegemonic control. Barlow's (1996) "A Declaration of the Independence of Cyberspace" highlights the libertarian nature of early "cybercitizen" discourse:

> We have no elected government, nor are likely to have one, so I address you with
> no greater authority than that with which liberty itself always speaks. I declare the
> global social space we are building to be naturally independent of the tyrannies
> you seek to impose on us ... cyberspace does not live within your borders ... It is
> an act of nature and grows itself through our collective action." (18)

A great hope of "cybersociety" during this early period was a convergence of the world toward a rights-based, neoliberal/modernist conceptions of citizenship. Early cyber-utopianists envisioned a global community that was more secular, more tolerant, less nationalistic and more accepting of "free market" values. Katz (1997), who first coined the term "digital citizen" in a *Wired* magazine article, found that the generation of early adopters online in the mid-to-late nineties were: "profoundly optimistic about the future, they're convinced that technology is a force for good and that our free-market economy functions as a powerful engine of progress" (70).

Further, the Web would provide users with the ability to become *content creators*. Jenkins (2006) posited a convergence culture where individuals would share their own work and play an active role in creating and disseminating information. While

Jenkins celebrated the collective aspects of this future, the emphasis was on the individual's ability to be empowered through the opportunity to create and share his or her work. Rather than one-to-many forms of communication, the future of content would be "many to many." The ease with which individuals had access to content creation and sharing tools meant everyone would be a creator, an idea elaborated upon by Clay Shirky's (2009) book titled *Here Comes Everybody*.

Through Facebook's many applications, users have the ability to serve be the *content creator* of one's own life. Through likes, status updates, photos and other applications, users are crafting a pastiche of their daily life by *disclosing* elements of themselves. The emphasis on the site is on providing *the individuals* with a venue to explore and present themselves to others. More importantly Facebook preserves for users the freedom to select who is allowed to view this self-presentation. By allowing who can become one's friend, users appear to be in control of the process *of being* in the digital world. From this perspective, it is a form of the neoliberal Web utopian dream. This neoliberal ethic of the free market as a core engine for social good characterized most efforts to formulate a theory of "digital rights." From this perspective, the freedom to choose when and where you speak is the freedom to cultivate a "voice." Observers saw this ability to express voice as a right beyond the regulatory capacities of the nation state. As Post and Johnson (1996) opined: "the volume of electronic communications crossing territorial boundaries is just too great in relation to the resources available to government authorities" (Online). As such, the Internet would continue the march towards the promotion of liberal values. Revolutions in Moldova, Burma, and Iran motivated Web utopianists to usher in a new era of "Facebook democracy" where vast numbers of connected youth could coordinate protests through SNS applications and bring about the overthrow of totalitarian regimes.

Even if these movements weren't always entirely successful it forwarded a narrative that SNS sites allowed for a transparency that was beyond the control of the state and as such would bring about a globally connected world of "digital citizens." Because these sites could not be controlled by nation states, totalitarian regimes were on borrowed time when it came to their rule. Facebook's massive networking power would signal a true "end of history" whereby totalitarian states would be incapable of maintaining their grip on power.

The view of digital citizenship that underlies this *cyber utopianist* perspective is one in which the state has a limited role in governing the Web and free-market principles of individual choice are ascendant. Formal political institutions should thus interfere with the content of ICTs as little as possible. A "free Web" will allow *netizens* to pursue their utilitarian notions of "the good," which include unrestrained access to commerce, hence calls for nation states to not filter Internet content, place excessive taxes on Web-based transactions, or guarantee privacy rights online. This view of the utopian Web saw it as able to accelerate the development of the free-market and free-expression around the world.

The ease with which nation-states like China have been able to filter out content which elites find objectionable has challenged this early conception of a boundless, ungovernable Web. The fact that ICTs has turned out to be much more constrainable by states than previously believed (Goldsmith and Wu 2006) suggests that the state can play a role in restricting rights on the Web. However, the underlying belief of a neoliberal, market-based utopian Web remained an ideal.

The Public Facebook

But this rights-based approach to the early Web constitutes only one strand of how the Web would transform society for the good. Another strand of utopian thought posited the ability of the Web and SNS sites like Facebook to help usher in a more democratic and emancipatory future through greater *connection*. Sanguine pronouncements on the democratic and participatory possibilities of new technologies abound. Concepts like *free culture* (Lessig 2004), *participatory culture* (Jenkins 2006, the *networked information economy* (Benkler 2006), and the *peer to peer* (P2P) society (Bauwens 2005) all herald the power of the Web to encourage more active, participatory citizens through their ability to collaborate with others. These projects emphasized the power of networks to overcome collective action problems and organize themselves into networks that could produce value (Benkler 2006). This initiated a series of works on the "wisdom of crowds" (Surowiecki 2004) and "crowdsourcing" (Howe 2006) that emphasized the power of networks to add value. This view of the utopian Web emphasized the importance of *connection* to human empowerment.

This emphasis on connection has historically played out within the public sphere. If connection has value for individuals in society and is good for societies as a whole, the state has a vested interest in fostering them. Christakis and Fowler (2009) defines a network as "a group of people who are much more connected to one another than they are to other groups of connected people found in other parts of the network." They find a whole range of behaviors that are affected by individuals within network. Social network scholars have observed *social contagion* effects for a variety of behaviors including obesity, college academic achievement and having children. In each instance, connection to a social network was able to change individual outcomes for the better.

Marshall (1964) defines social citizenship as the right to "a modicum of economic welfare and security to the right to share to the full in the social heritage and to live the life of a civilized being" (69). Marshall cited the right to education as a genuine social right of citizenship, because the aim of education during childhood is to shape the future adult citizen. This view presumes that as social beings, we are engaged in a common project and without the maintenance of the commonweal, the individual "pursuit of happiness" cannot be realized. Individual "happiness" orientations are driven by the institutional arrangements in which one finds him/her self. This utopian project then presumes that ICTs can, through sharing, help individuals and societies access these *social rights* through connection and collaboration.

As such, in 2003, the World Summit on the Information Society (WSIS) met in Geneva and established 11 key principles for the creation of an "information society for all." Among these included positive rights including "the development of an accessible information and communication infrastructure," "access to information and knowledge," and "capacity building" (Leuprecht 2005). For all of these abstract principles to be realized required significant investment in both physical and human capital, but the investment in these resource would yield high returns for nation states that, in turn, would have "high capacity" citizens.

Inherent in this broadened role for the state is rooted in Marshall's (1964) view of the individual's inherent "political rights" which would be encouraged through participation in a "digital public sphere" and "social rights" which would be enhanced by the opportunities to connect to others through ICT tools. This expanded set of "rights" is echoed in Westen and Madras (2006) formulation of a "digital bill of rights" that basically echoes that United States' Bill of Rights, but with a few positive rights modifications including the right to "email access" and the right to conduct government business online. The underlying basis of this "bill of rights" was to provide citizens with the tools of participatory governance:

> Democratic systems of governance are about to undergo significant, even seismic, changes. These changes will not involve such comparatively simple questions as "Who will be our next President or Prime Minister?" or "Will current political parties retain their control of basic institutions?" The impending changes are more fundamental. They will involve deeper, more structural shifts that will move nations away from their traditional reliance on "representative democracy" toward newer, emerging forms of "direct democracy." The current revolution in communications technologies will play a catalytic role. (Westen and Madras 2006: Online)

This affirmative role for the state is rooted in the Web's ability to create a public sphere that can rival forms of power and inequality. This view suggests that ICTs, through the ability to collaborate, could inspire the collective action necessary for social change. This ability to form global social networks would result in a "democratization of the imaginary" (Appadurai 1996). In this view, citizens all over the world could join networks based on an ethos of global human dignity and work to have it carried out in the world. These hyper-empowered, networked digital citizens could transform society by the power of collection action. In other words, connection can change the world.

This set of ideas and images, so the utopian narrative goes, produces what Henry Jenkins (2006) calls a *participatory culture* where individuals create communities of interest around images, music, thoughts and other types of creative content. These *peer producers* develop habits of engagement that can be oriented towards social action. Barack Obama's victory in the 2008 presidential election is often held up as an exemplar of the latent political power of participatory culture. The Obama campaign's success in generating volunteers and donors through the facilitation of small-scale SNSs like locally based Facebook groups stands as a model of how to use the Web for electoral success (Bagui and Parker 2009).

Facebook provides an appealing platform for users to connect with one another. The allure of Facebook stems from our need to be part of a network. However, inherent in the ideal of a *public sphere* is that it is not *private*. The ability of a society to derive benefits from connecting with others is predicated on the notion of a "public enterprise" with which all members are concurrently engaged. Facebook appeals to both individualist/private views of the good life on the Web and collectivist/public views of the Web because it gives users the impression of a public sphere while allowing them the ability to present themselves to a pre-selected public, an inherently private sphere act.

Summary

Facebook seems to bridge the distinction between a *neoliberal* Web and a *communitarian* Web. By providing a space for social connection, Facebook would seem to enhance the public sphere by linking us to one another. But at the same time, Facebook serves *neoliberal, market* ends by giving us the ability to *choose* our social-networks (making our networks "mediated publics") in ways that enhances private, market-based activity. This bridging of public and private makes *Facebook* a formidable phenomenon. But does it give us a "sense" of the public sphere rather than the actual thing? I turn to this in the next chapter.

Chapter 2
Facebook and the Architecture of Disclosure

In 2008, Facebook engaged in a fateful set of meetings where the nascent company sought to crystalize a viable business strategy. They hired Sheryl Sandberg, a well-respected executive at Google to run the company, or to "scale their growth" in corporate speak. To chart out a long-term strategy for the company's expansion:

> She convened a series of regular after-work meetings at the company's downtown Palo Alto offices, ordering in food and scrawling potential revenue opportunities on white boards. The possibilities, she recalls, boiled down to two categories— making users pay or making advertisers pay. Employees quickly agreed with her that the latter was far more appealing. "It was stressful because this was about our entire business and all of our revenue," she says. (Stone 2011: Online)

Back in 2008, the company was in a significant growth phase, but was still struggling to adopt a sustainable business model. It was encountering challenges from its users on a number of fronts, the largest of which concerned *Beacon*, an application that divulged user-purchasing information without user permission. That same year Facebook had partnered with Microsoft to place *banner ads* on the site, but the revenue from this partnership was not large enough. Its core challenge was how to commodifiy the social-capital maintained and developed through user's social networks. Rather than charge the user for the service, it was going to sell the user as a member of a network as a commodity. The company settled upon the idea of "social ads" that usually specified which of a member's friends "liked" an advertisement or advertiser. This key idea of using social networks in the process of branding launched Facebook into what it is today, a company that generated close to two billion dollars in revenue in 2010 (Vascellaro 2010).

This large influx of capital is based on information that users voluntary submit. That's the genius of the Facebook enterprise. It is built on the fundamental human need to connect. More importantly, it depends on you forging deeper and more sustained contact with your "friends." The more you share about yourself, the better for Facebook and if Facebook's founder is to be believed, the better for you as well (even if you don't know it yet).

This fateful decision spawned Facebook as we know it today. If you wanted to design a perfect machine to get you to reveal intimate (if sometimes banal) details about yourself to others, it would look a great deal like Facebook. Every element of the site is designed to make us do what we are biologically wired to do: *share*. While sharing fosters the cooperation necessary for the development of vibrant, functioning democratic societies, it also is the key element of Facebook's monetization strategy.

The Philosophy of Publicness

But sharing is not simply Facebook's market model, for Mark Zuckerberg, Facebook's founder, it is a moral imperative. He is keenly aware of the irresistible push towards social connection. In an interview he gave to David Kirkpatrick as part of his book *The Facebook Effect*, Zuckerberg lays out a *philosophy of publicness* that constructs revelation as a moral/ethical imperative: "The days of you having a different image for your work friends or co-workers and for the other people you know are probably coming to an end pretty quickly ... Having two identities for yourself is an example of a lack of integrity" (199).

Zuckerberg couches his notion of *radical transparency* with a belief that it will lead to social good: "... the world will be better if you share more" but people have to be brought "to the point where there is more openness" (Kirkpatrick 2010: 200). He sees privacy as a niggling obstacle to a grand vision of an interconnected world. Facebook's core challenge to its business is reconciling the paradox between the users' concern for *their* privacy coupled with an interest in the private lives of those in their network. In other words, people want the social benefits of *revelation* while controlling how and when they reveal themselves. They may want to control the what, when and how of what they reveal, but the pleasures of revelation seem to be more powerful than the desire to "stay off" Facebook.

A value exists to "observing one another" online. For starters, it is a non-invasive, low-cost way to increase the frequency of interactions. Robin Dunbar (2010) notes that expanding one's social network has an evolutionary purpose. In the savanna, the size of kinship networks was a fundamental element to survival. As our neo-cortexes grew and developed, we were able to manage larger networks beyond our immediate kinship groups. Hence the now famous "Dunbar number" that suggests we are cognitively bound to 150 members in our social network because we do not have the ability to "socially groom" more than that number (Dunbar 2010: 24).

If user statistics are any guide, the social imperative to connect is strong. In the United States, SNS use has almost doubled since 2008 (Hampton et al. 2011). The average age of an SNS user in the United States has gone from 33 years of age in 2008 to 38 years of age in 2010. In 2010, over half of SNS users in the United States were over 35 years of age. A 2011 Pew Internet and American life project found that almost half of all adults surveyed in the United States reported using an SNS site and of those, 92 percent use Facebook (Hampton et al. 2011). Over half of users in the United States (52 percent) accessed the site on a daily basis (compared with 33 percent of Twitter users). In the United States, on any given day:

15 percent of Facebook users update their own status.
22 percent comment on another's post or status.
20 percent comment on another user's photos.
26 percent "Like" another user's content.
10 percent send another user a private message (Hampton et al. 2011).

Facebook's growth has not been limited to the United States. Of the roughly 476.3 million Internet users in Europe in 2010 (58 percent of the total population), 208.9 million of them, or 43 percent of all Internet users, had Facebook accounts (InternetWorldStats.com 2011). This constituted 24 percent of all Facebook accounts in 2010 (RoyalPingdom.com 2011).

Why is this medium so popular? Some may post on Facebook to keep up with far away friends, some use it to work out internal issues or some simply use it as a way to supplement their offline networks. Baker and Moore (2010) created a typology of bloggers that might be useful for explaining Facebook users. Bloggers, they argued, blogged for therapeutic reasons, to connect with others, as a substitution for offline relationships, or to emphasizes an idealized self rather than an uncensored self.

Ledbetter et al. (2011) argue that Facebook's popularity comes from its basic site structure that satisfies both the need to both *self-disclose* (Acquisti and Gross 2006, Mazer et al. 2007) and to *connect* with others (Donath 2007, Ellison et al. 2007). Because Facebook communication is, more often than not, supplementing offline interactions, it can serve as critical support for maintaining friendships over both short and long distances (Quan-Haase 2007).

A recent study by the Pew Center for Internet and American Life found that the average Facebook user had 229 friends (Hampton et al. 2011). Of those 229 friends, the overwhelming majority replicated offline networks. The typical friend list contained:

- 22 percent were people from high school.
- 12 percent were extended family.
- 10 percent were co-workers.
- 9 percent were college friends.
- 8 percent were immediate family.
- 7 percent were people from voluntary groups.
- 2 percent were neighbors (Hampton et al. 2011: Online).

In addition, the Pew study found that only 7 percent of Facebook friends had never met offline and roughly 20 percent could be classified as "friends-of-friends" or "dormant" social ties that are not currently active relationships (Hampton et al. 2011). While Facebook users directly interact with only a small percentage of their friends on a regular basis, (Golder et al. 2007) the upshot of the findings in the Pew survey is that Facebook networks are made up mostly of existing offline relationships. The majority of those whom a user interacts with on Facebook are part of ongoing social relationships and all the emotional investment that entails (Wellman and Hampton 1999).

Indeed a number of recent studies trumpet the positive attributes associated with frequent Facebook use. For example, a 2011 Pew study found that Facebook users in the United States who used the site several times a day were:

- 43 percent more likely than other Internet users and more than three times as likely as non-Internet users to feel that most people can be trusted;
- had 9 percent more close, core ties in their overall social network compared with other Internet users;
- scored an additional 5 points higher in total support, 5 points higher in emotional support, and 5 points higher in companionship, than Internet users of similar demographic characteristics. (Hampton et al. 2011: Online)

Facebook and Social Capital

The Pew studies reconfirm work done by a number of scholars showing a link between social-network use and social capital (Ellison et al. 2007, Steinfield et al. 2008, Valenzuela et al. 2009). Bourdieu (1986) defines social capital as "the aggregate of the actual or potential resources which are linked to possession of a durable network of more or less institutionalized relationships of mutual acquaintance and recognition" (248). Putnam (2000) broke down social capital into *bonding social capital* based on strong in-group ties and *bridging social capital* based on informal, intra-group weak ties. Granovetter (1973) emphasized the importance of weak-tie capital in providing critical information like job prospects or health information.

While seemingly banal, status updates serve important social purpose. Selg (2010) found that Facebook networks provide the same social benefits as offline networks: job tips, housing prospects or business technical assistance. While the nature of the network matters, these friendship networks can also be seen as valuable assets that can be effectively mobilized. Social networking provides a venue for more information exchange (Fogg and Eckles 2007). As such it facilitates the information sharing needed for forming trust bonds (Frohlich and Oppenheimer 1998).

Ellison et al. (2007) found that among college students, Facebook enhanced both bonding (strong tie) and bridging (weak tie) social capital. They also found that those who had lower reported levels of self-esteem were more likely to see increases in social capital from Facebook use.

However, social capital benefits only accrued to users if they employed the site for information seeking about "actual friends" rather employing the site to find new friends (Steinfield et al. 2009). In addition, frequency of use was significantly associated with amassing social capital from Facebook. Baker (2010) finds that the highest levels of social capital went to high intensity users, characterized by the level of intimacy, reciprocity and emotional disclosure present in Facebook interactions (Ellison et al. 2007).

The Architecture of Disclosure

While disclosure and connection might be good things for society, what happens if we think of them as information? What matters then is not the where and when disclosure happens, but the amount of information that is shared. At the 2008 Web 2.0 Summit in Silicon Valley, California, Mark Zuckerberg posited a new theory of revelation for the twenty-first century:

> I would expect that next year, people will share twice as much information as they share this year, and next year, they will be sharing twice as much as they did the year before ... That means that people are using Facebook, and the applications and the ecosystem, more and more. (Hansell: Online)

Hansell (2008) dubbed this proclamation *Zuckerberg's law*. Zuckerberg's law, as it were, is more than a philosophical musing, but a market necessity for Facebook. It signals a continued shift in the production of information from paid professional (and public) content to unpaid amateur (private) content (Keen 2007). Information on Facebook is *hyper-personalized*, a magazine populated by writers you have self-selected and know personally (and to which you contribute yourself). Carr (2010) likens it to a refrigerator that manufactures its own food. But all this disclosure/information is also data. Companies are in an all-out battle to figure out how to use this information to encourage more consumption. As a CEO of Redfin, a real estate site, noted in a 2011 Business Week article:

> The most coveted employee in Silicon Valley today is not a software engineer. It is a mathematician ... The mathematicians are trying to tickle your fancy long enough to see one more ad. (Kelman in Vance 2011: Online)

But to get to this point where you want to see one more advertisement, companies need to know more about you. The problem is that people are reticent to reveal personal information to strangers. But the very nature of personal information makes it appealing to *disclose* to friends. Psychologists suggest that self-disclosure leads to greater intimacy in interactions (Laurenceau et al. 1998). But before we disclose certain elements of ourselves, we seek to know that we are disclosing in a safe space. Disclosing can open us up to ridicule, embarrassment or even physical danger. So for disclosure to occur, we need a level of comfort that we have some control over the setting in which we are disclosing. And Facebook is keenly aware of this.

How does Facebook encourage individual disclosure when the very nature of disclosure is that it be private? One way I argue Facebook does this is by creating a *choice architecture* (Thaler and Sunstein 2008) that encourages disclosure, or an *architecture of disclosure*. The idea of a *choice architecture* challenges notions of individuals as rational decision-makers that seek to enhance their self-interest by gaining information about an action and weighing costs and benefits before engaging in said action (Friedman 1953). A rational approach to decision-making posits a "rational decision-maker who lays out goals and uses logical processes to explore the best way to reach those goals" (Stokey and Zeckhauser 1978: 3). As such, a rational decision-making approach to Facebook would suggest individuals acquire information about and weigh the costs and benefits before disclosing on the site. Facebook would seem to subscribe to this view of human behavior. As an example, Facebook regards signing up for the site as tacit acceptance of their policies. According to Facebook's vice president for public policy:

> Everything is opt-in on Facebook. Participating in the service is a choice. We want people to continue to choose Facebook every day. Adding information — uploading photos or posting status updates or "like" a Page — are also all opt-in. Please don't share if you're not comfortable. (Schrage 2010: Online)

The presumption is that Facebook is simply a neutral platform that allows individuals to make rational decisions about posting. By contrast, a *choice architecture* approach is rooted in *institutionalist* and *behavioral economic* approaches to decision-making that posit institutions can influence decision-making by *structuring choice* so that the costs associated with an institution's desired behavior is significantly lower than the behavior desired by the individual *ceteris paribus* (all other things being equal). These *nudges* (Thaler and Sunstein 2009) work to produce desired behavior in actors without their conscious knowledge that the institution has structured their choice.

As an example, Goldhaber-Fiebert et al. (2010) found that when users were shown, as a default, longer term "commitment contracts" for maintaining a fitness program, they were more likely to choose longer-term contracts for themselves. Hence, they concluded, individuals could be *nudged* into accepting longer-term fitness commitments by structuring the default choice. Similarly, in the United States, *the Pension Protection Act* of 2006 incentivizes employers to opt employees into a retirement plan (Beshears and Weller: 2010) and elements of the 2008 Affordable Care Act in the United States created an opt-out provision for the purchase of health insurance (Detmer 2010).

A number of scholars have found that small changes in a utility calculus impacts outcomes, even in instances where the benefits significantly outweigh the costs. In 1997, the Mexican government instituted a "conditional cash transfer" program entitled *Opportunidades*, which paid families a modest sum of money to keep their children in school and get them annual medical check-ups. The result was that a small-scale *nudge* was enough to significantly increase school and annual check-up attendance rates, not only in Mexico but in most other countries where similar programs were tried (Rawlings and Rubio 2005) found that Kenyans would only walk to get water from a clean spring if it was less than a 3.5-minute walk (Glennerster and Kremer 2011). In effect a small *nudge* in the distance to a clean well worked wonders. The authors found similar effects with malaria nets (Duflo and Banerjee 2011).

Part of the reason behavioral economics is effective is because we are *satisficers* (Simon 1972) rather than utility maximizers. Our rationality is "bounded" by choice structures because it cuts down on information retrieval costs. We might care about privacy on Facebook, but not enough to engage in an involved process of information search to figure out how to change the settings. *Choice architectures* are useful for institutions because they can legitimate their desired outcomes. Facebook's choice to make information *radically transparent* can thus be interpreted by as a *ceteris paribus* user "choice," and not structured by Facebook itself. This observation by a former Facebook employee highlights the way Facebook can legitimate this own preferences for information:

> My observation of Facebook as a company (its people, including its executives) is that it cares a lot about privacy. It spends a lot of time thinking about it, it spends a lot of time thinking about how to protect its users' privacy, and then (ironically) it is continually surprised at how the vast majority of its users don't end up really caring at all to make use of various privacy-protection mechanisms built into the products. (Wong 2010: Online)

While this is the perception of one former employee, it serves as an example of how structured choice can be taken as a *ceterus paribus* choice. The truth is that users care about privacy, but the choice architecture has been set up to structure their choices towards disclosure. When applied online, choice is motivated by default settings written into code (Shah and Kesan 2003). Default settings are seldom changed because either users are unaware that the changes are possible or lack the technological sophistication/self-confidence to change the setting themselves (Shah and Kesan 2003). But default settings are only one of the mechanisms available for getting users to reveal more information. These range from the obvious to the subtle. An example of a subtle change in choice architecture is in 2008 when Facebook changed the *status update* bar from the more general and ambiguous "how are you feeling today" to the more specific "what's on your mind"?

This phenomenon of a user-base that is not technologically proficient and thus not as comfortable changing default settings becomes more prevalent as SNS sites become adopted by a wider public. In the last two years, the demographic profile of Facebook users has skewed older. This is the inevitable result of Facebook's growth strategy. But as more and more people have signed up, the number of people who are technologically savvy declines. As an example, when Facebook changed its privacy settings in 2009, 10 percent of users complained, when they did so in 2010, fewer than 1 percent did (Boyd and Hargittai 2010).

The Newsfeed

One way in which a simple change in code changed the individual behavior on Facebook is the *newsfeed* feature. Prior to the *newsfeed*, Facebook's architecture tended towards the private because you had to actively seek out information about your friends. As Clive Thompson points out in a 2008 *New York Times Magazine* article about Facebook:

> Browsing Facebook was like constantly poking your head into someone's room
> to see how she was doing. It took work and forethought. In a sense, this gave
> Facebook an inherent, built-in level of privacy, simply because if you had 200
> friends on the site — a fairly typical number — there weren't enough hours in
> the day to keep tabs on every friend all the time. (Thompson: Online)

But the *newsfeed*, through a simple change in code, provided a steady stream of content about users' friends without their prompting. The users can now, by default, learn about their friends' status rather than having to exert the effort to seek it out. A mode of being that Reichelt (2007) refers to as *ambient intimacy* or "being able to keep in touch with people with a level of regularity and intimacy that you wouldn't usually have access to, because time and space conspire to make it impossible" (Online).

This ability to forge deeper social connections as a default with practically no transaction costs radically alters how we relate to Facebook and to each other. Benkler (2006) notes that the proliferation of high-speed computers networked to servers significantly lowers transaction costs for all forms of exchange. If we think of maintaining friendships as a problem of *lumpiness* (for example we don't have the time and resources to maintain deep relationships with all of our friends), then Facebook provides the opportunity for converting these previously *lumpy* relationships into *granular* ones. Benkler suggests that *granularity* that allows users to break down a project's component parts into small-scale tasks that can be done with little expenditure of time or money (2006: 113). A response to a status update costs less than a physical visit and takes much less time than a phone call. Thus friendship maintenance can occur without significant production or transaction costs for any one contributor.

And as Benkler (2006) notes breaking work down to the granular level can create new ways of collaborating. Just like a Wikipedia entry, one contribution out of context can seem trivial, but seen in full it provides a rich picture of an individual or a group of friends. As Thompson notes:

> Each little update — each individual bit of social information — is insignificant
> on its own, even supremely mundane. But taken together, over time, the little
> snippets coalesce into a surprisingly sophisticated portrait of your friends' and
> family members' lives, like thousands of dots making a pointillist painting. This
> was never before possible, because in the real world, no friend would *bother* to

call you up and detail the sandwiches she was eating. The ambient information becomes like "a type of E.S.P.," as Haley described it to me, an invisible dimension floating over everyday life. (2008: Online)

Rather than make us more disposed to transparency, status updates are intimate because we are part of a self-selected network of people to which we have been "let-in." We aren't interested in a stranger's vacation photos, but having access to a friend's vacation photos gives us a sense that we know more of them. And this sense that we know more about our friends and our friends know more about us is powerful.

Facebook and its Evolving Privacy Policy

Another way in which Facebook uses behavioral economics to encourage disclosure is through changes to its privacy policy. During the early years of Facebook the company wrestled with the issue of privacy as it attempted to build a sustainable business model. In 2005, users had a high level of control over their personal information on Facebook. Only members of the groups specified in a user's privacy settings could had access to their personal information. By 2006, the default privacy setting had changed to allow information to be shared with "your school, your specified local area, and other reasonable community limitations that we tell you about" (Opsahl 2010: Online). One year later, Facebook added a search feature that allowed the users' name, the users' school name and their photo to be searchable by anyone on Facebook (Opsahl 2010).

In early 2009, Facebook changed its privacy policy to read:

Information may be accessed by everyone on the Internet (including people not logged into Facebook) may be associated with you outside of Facebook (such as when you visit other sites on the Internet), and may be imported and exported by us and others without privacy limitations, ... and may be imported and exported by us and others without privacy limitations ... ." (Opsahl 2010: Online)

One month later, default settings allowed for information such as: "name, profile photo, list of friends and pages you are a fan of, gender, geographic region, and networks you belong to" (Opsahl 2010: Online) to be accessible throughout Facebook and to "Facebook-enhanced applications" without the ability to modify the privacy settings (users, however, could restrict the ability of others to find them through search). The uproar over this policy change resulted in a scaling down of how much information was shared to third parties (Opsahl 2010).

In February of 2010, Facebook introduced an instant personalization feature that allows websites to "personalize" their sites with the data included in your Facebook account. Data that is set to "default" via opt-out, like a user's birthday, would now be used by the third party site to "personalize" your individual user experience. To turn it off was not a simple exercise. It requires a user to log into the site, find privacy setting, look for the heading "apps and websites," select "edit settings," find "instant personalization," select "edit settings," close a popup entitled "understanding instant personalization," scroll to the bottom of the page, uncheck a box labeled "enable instant personalization on partner websites" (Rogers 2011: Online). The rationale from the company was that without the *instant personalization* of its users, the usefulness of the Facebook experience would be diminished:

> Joining Facebook is a conscious choice by vast numbers of people who have stepped forward deliberately and intentionally to connect and share. We study user activity. We've found that a few fields of information need to be shared to facilitate the kind of experience people come to Facebook to have. That's why we require the following fields to be public: name, profile photo (if people choose to have one), gender, connections (again, if people choose to make them), and user ID number. Facebook provides a less satisfying experience for people who choose not to post a photo or make connections with friends or interests. But, other than name and gender, nothing requires them to complete these fields or share information they do not want to share. If you're not comfortable sharing, don't. (Schrage 2010: Online)

Facebook must effect a subtle balance between notions of individual choice and privacy and an inherently social "need to share" information. Facebook's architecture of disclosure posits individual choice as tantamount to the user's *choice* to use Facebook. For the company, signing up for Facebook served as tacit acceptance of its privacy policies. In April 2010, Facebook announced its new "connections" policy. For Facebook, the new policy meant that if you "liked" a link or post, Facebook treated it as public information. In addition, a vast array of personal information (education, hometown, current city, work history, hobbies and so on) became public:

> When you connect with an application or website it will have access to General Information about you. The term General Information includes your and your friends' names, profile pictures, gender, user IDs, connections, and any content shared using the *Everyone* privacy setting. ... The default privacy setting for certain types of information you post on Facebook is set to "everyone" ... Because it takes two to connect, your privacy settings only control who can see the connection on your profile page. If you are uncomfortable with the connection being publicly available, you should consider removing (or not making) the connection. (Opsahl 2010: Online)

The last part of Facebook's updated policy statement was telling. It put the onus on the users not to make a connection if they were uncomfortable with it being private. A core problem with connections is that you cannot list a hobby and not have it shared through connections even if you signed up to Facebook under a different policy (for example, there are no *grandfather clauses* on Facebook). If you "liked" an article on hiking, for instance, that information became public record accessible to a whole range of people. Facebook justified the change by noting that grouping people who "like" similar things might allow them to connect with each other. The result of *Connections* is a greater opportunity for more network formation based on shared interest, but at what cost? Facebook's Vice President of Public Policy noted that it was simply responding to customer use patterns:

> It turns out that less than 20 percent of users had filled out the text fields of this information. By contrast, more than 70 percent of users have 'liked' Pages to be connected to these kinds of ideas, experiences and organizations. That is the primary reason we offered the transition — because it reflects the way people are using our service already. (Schrage 2010: Online).

Again the assumption is that Facebook users are rational actors and if the costs of sharing information became too onerous, they would simply stop making connections. In December of 2010, Facebook again enacted a change to its profile page along these lines. The company removed the *tabs* section of the profile page and replaced it with a smaller menu. That space was taken up by a listing of basic information: relationships, education, work, birthdate, and location. The new profile also added a sampling of photos in which the user has been tagged.

While the looks of the profile page was changeable through the settings, it presents prospective users more information, particularly more visual information, about potential contacts. The explicitly purpose of the profile change was to increase the amount of activity on its site. The hope was that by providing more information about users, more opportunities for connection (and data dissemination) would occur. As Mark Zuckerberg explained to the US television show *60 Minutes*:

> You can see all the things that you have in common with that person ... It gives you this amazing connection with that person in a way that the current version of the profile that we have today just doesn't do. (Zuckerberg 2010: Online)

The change was subtle. Rather than place personal information under the profile photo, Facebook moved the information up to the top of the page. In addition, rather than a single profile photo, the new Facebook profile provided visitors to a user's main page with five recent photos in which the user has been tagged. The new profile also included a history of relationships with Facebook friends and recent comments between two friends. It provided visitors with a sampling of what being a particular user's friend would be like. By making individual pages more appealing, the hope was more connections would be formed and more "information" would be generated.

In June of 2011, Facebook modified its privacy settings once again. The company put in place a "tag suggestions" feature that used facial recognition technology to help users identify people in photos. Under a "tag your friends" section, users could see multiple photos, identified by facial recognition software, of a user in one screen. The result is an application that facilitates the work of tagging for the user by "suggesting" a tag. Viewed in another way, this feature lowers the transaction costs for tagging. This of course was touted by Facebook as a time saving feature. But in addition to saving time, it places another brick on the extensive scaffolding Facebook has been building for the past few years. Again, Facebook rolled out the new feature by forcing users to "opt out" of the application rather than allowing them to "opt in."

Facebook and the Privacy Paradox

This constant need for Facebook to turn disclosure and connection into information that can be commodified means it must perform a sleight of hand with users' notions of public and private. To achieve a private market-based end, it must compel us to engage in *connection*, something that has historically been considered an integral part of public life, and as such, has been an important element of resisting both market based and governmental power. In essence, it must give us the impression of social citizenship while continually changing the terms of that citizenship to produce more disclosure and connection to serve its own market-based ends.

What are the consequences for individual users of this blurring of private and public? Eric Schmidt, the CEO of Google is reported as saying that he think believes Web users want Google to "tell them what they should be doing next" (Gibson 2010: Online). This belief is consistent with a market-based, neoliberal view of the Web that suggests companies should strive to give consumers what they want. In keeping with these methods, Google announced in December of 2009 its *customized search* feature which used a range of user-data to intuit what users are looking for when they conduct a search. While Facebook does not share its algorithms, making it impossible to know if Facebook does the same, Pariser (2011) anecdotally noted that he found Facebook seemed to track which of his friends' links he clicked on and which friends updates he "liked." Over time, he noticed those he "liked" had a higher probability of appearing at the top of his feed.

But a sizeable number of users are keenly aware of the precarious position they are put in by Facebook. Largely dependent upon a private business to groom personal connections, many users see Facebook as more than a business and become upset when changes to the site are made. Facebook users might be the commodity being sold, but they are a commodity that can get unruly. As an example, in my examination of political Facebook groups, I found several instances of Facebook groups created for the express purpose of challenging the company's practices.

One group, created by a user in Ireland called "*Facebook SHOULD NOT allow anti-homosexuality groups and discussion boards*,"[1] was created for the purpose

---

1   Facebook SHOULD NOT allow anti-homosexuality groups and discussion boards. (n.d.). In *Facebook* [Group]. Available at: http://www.facebook.com/group.

of taking Facebook to task for not enforcing its hate speech policy. The group's main page described its purpose as designed to:

> encourage Facebook to stop violating its own terms and conditions. Recently there have been a small core of hateful and murderous people discussing the killing and hating of gay people through the medium of Facebook. Thanks to pressure this group exerted these groups have been removed entirely and so have many of their creators profiles.

Throughout the site's main page, the administrator posts an exchange with Facebook regarding their policy toward "hateful language." The fervor and dedication with which the administrator pursues a satisfactory response regarding Facebook's policies is akin to that of citizens seeking redress from their government. As an example, the administrator posts an email from Facebook asking the users to send specific links but reiterating that they believe in an open exchange of ideas. The administrator's response is that he/she has repeatedly asked Facebook to uphold their TOS regarding homophobic language, but has refused to do so:

> Facebook have absolutely failed at upholding their own terms and conditions and have fobbed me off time and time again, even when asked blatantly for their feedback regarding my claims ... Please don't fob me off or patronise me - I have never asked you to remove a group that centres around discussion regarding nature/nurture/religion. My group deals with discussion over these issues. We only report the groups that CLEARLY contravene your own terms and conditions ... and Facebook continually fails to respond.

The page highlights the extent to which this user takes seriously the discourse space Facebook has created. In many ways, this plays to Facebook's advantage. It wants to create an *architecture of disclosure* where users feel they "own" the space. That the ownership means users will on occasion challenge the company makes the architecture of disclosure all the more authentic and legitimate.

Another example from the groups I examined was a site from a user in the United States entitled "Demand that Facebook General Counsel Ullyot Resign" challenges Facebook's hiring of Tell Ullyot, a former attorney in the George W. Bush administration, as their general counsel.[2] The user's rationale for the creation of the site was that hiring of a former Bush administration Justice Department official. The site administrator's rationale for creating the group highlights the highly personal and sensitive nature of user content on Facebook as well as the commodification of that information:

---

php?gid=19233901206. [accessed: 9 August 2010].

2   Demand that Facebook General Counsel Ullyot Resign. (n.d.). In *Facebook* [Group]. Available at: http://www.facebook.com/group.php?gid=27834866771&v=photos [accessed: 6 August 2010].

> Ullyot is now the go-to guy for questions about deals that involve the data you trust Facebook with. Given the power of Facebook as a political organizing tool, is that something you're comfortable with? ... Facebook's newest employee – someone you are making money for every time you log in – is deeply involved in some of the most unsavory and inhumane policies that our country has been embarrassed by in decades ... Send Facebook a message by joining this group – Ullyot's extremist agenda is not compatible with the vast amounts of personal information stored at Facebook.

Whereas another company's response to these challenges might be to remove the group, Facebook's response to groups of this nature is to leave them alone. Facebook must place a veneer of democratic accountability in its decision-making. As an example, in response to customer dissatisfaction with a change in its privacy policy in 2009, the company created a "user rights and responsibilities" document along with a "virtual town hall" in which to discuss the comments. As Sifry (2009) noted, the company put in a byzantine, two-step, electoral system for changing "the user rights and responsibilities" document that would affect privacy settings:

> If more than 7,000 users comment ... we will also give you the opportunity to participate in a vote in which you will be provided alternatives ... The vote shall be binding on us if more than 30 percent of all active registered users vote. (Online)

The company knew full well that 30 percent of over 150 million registered users were not going to vote on company policy, particularly since the company did very little in the way of advertising to let users know about the "town hall" (Sifry 2009: Online). But by creating a seemingly public democratic forum for the operating policies for what essentially constitute a private company, users are reassured that the venue in which they are disclosing and connecting is open and transparent. In reality, Facebook currently enjoys a "worldwide license" on content posted to the site (Hendry and Goodall 2010).

For Facebook to succeed, it must appear as a public good, not a private company. As such it must carefully construct an image of a responsiveness and attentiveness primarily concerned with responding to its user community, much like politicians must do with their constituents. For example, Facebook has a track record of introducing controversial changes to its site and responding to criticism by assuring users that they are "listening" and will "make improvements." For example in 2011, Facebook announced plans to share phone numbers and addresses of users to developers. The rationale was greater efficiency in shopping transactions online:

> With this change, you could, for example, easily share your address and mobile phone with a shopping site to streamline the checkout process, or sign up for up-to-the-minute alerts on special deals directly to your mobile phone. (Purdy 2011: Online)

Facebook temporarily halted the decision in response to "useful feedback" from its customers. But Facebook noted that this was only a "temporary halt" of the policy until they found a way to make it clear to users when they were about to provide this sensitive information:

> "Over the weekend, we got some useful feedback that we could make people more clearly aware of when they are granting access to this data," Facebook wrote. "We agree, and we are making changes to help ensure you only share this information when you intend to do so." (Purdy 2011: Online)

Facebook's *pull back* strategy is what Kingdon (1984) calls a *softening up* process in the promotion of controversial public policy ideas. Legislators might introduce a policy change anticipating it will meet resistance, but by sending up the "trial balloon," citizens become accustomed to the possibility of the policy being enacted. Facebook, much like a government, could "soften up" its users by getting them used to the idea of making more data publicly available while at the same time seeming to appear accountable to its users.

Another example of Facebook's *softening up* strategy emerged in June 2011. As a result of the company's decision to use facial recognition software to help users tag friends, a feature called *tag suggestions*, the company received significant criticism from both the United States Congress and the European Union. In a response to a Los Angeles Times reporter's question about the feature, a company spokesperson issues this response:

> We launched Tag Suggestions to help people add tags of their friends in photos; something that's currently done more than 100 million times a day. Tag Suggestions are only made to people when they add new photos to the site, and only friends are suggested. If for any reason someone doesn't want their name to be suggested, they can disable the feature in their Privacy Settings. When we announced this feature last December, we explained that we would test it, listen to feedback and iterate before rolling it out more broadly. We should have been more clear with people during the roll-out process when this became available to them. Tag Suggestions are now available in most countries and we'll post further updates to our blog over time. (Mitchell 2011: Online)

This response characterizes Facebook's painstaking strategy for dealing with unpopular (but necessary for the business model) changes: tout the benefits of the application (help people add tags of their friends in photos), detail the steps taken to ensure privacy and user responsiveness (user can disable the feature ... we listened to feedback), admit responsibility for not communicating the changes effectively (we should have been more clear), and make no further commitments (we'll post further updates to our blog). This need to appear unusually responsive and accountable highlights the extent to which Facebook must act like a public institution to serve its private ends.

The Commodification of Disclosure

But the main purpose of all of this connecting and disclosing is not for public ends, but is rather for the ultimate purpose of commodifying information. While the insight that Facebook is a profit-making enterprise is not new, it is important to recognize that the ways in which it seeks to make a profit are distinct and have a powerful impact on social and political life.

Every *disclosure* or *connection* on Facebook is an additional data point that can be compiled into a larger marketing profile where you are the commodity sold to advertisers. There are lots of commodities on Facebook. In 2010, Facebook surpassed Google by constituting just over 7 percent of all web traffic (Smith 2010). Facebook generated 1.86 billion dollars in advertising revenue 2010, almost three times as much as in the previous year (and expected to double to 4 billion in 2011) (Horn 2011). Facebook garnered 12.2 percent of the online *banner ad* market in the United States in 2010, second only to Yahoo.com, and expected to increase to 17 percent of all US banner ad revenue (Oreskovic 2011).

The user base is its main source of revenue, luring prestigious advertisers to the site like Adidas, JPMorgan Chase and Coca-Cola. In April 2011, a number of news agencies reported that Facebook was preparing to launch in initial public offering that could value the company at 100 billion dollars (Fowler and Das 2011). In January of 2011, Facebook received a cash infusion of close to two billion dollars, 450 million of which reportedly came from Goldman Sachs (Womack and MacMillen 2011). Although investor interest in the Facebook remains strong, by September, Mark Zuckerberg had decided to postpone an IPO launch until May 2012 to focus the company on product development (Ghosh 2011).

While Facebook has a bright future, its sustainability rests on the relentless pursuit of "clicks." As a former Facebook employee lamented "the best minds of my generation are thinking about how to make people click ads" (Hammerbacher in Vance 2011: Online). But the trick for Facebook is how to get people to "click" while not seeming as if that is their intention. It took time for Facebook and the Web in general to figure out that solicitations had to be unobtrusive and seemingly unsolicited to work. Facebook's failed "gifts" application is a prime example.

Through Facebook "gifts" users could send virtual gifts that cost users one dollar. Companies would use these "gifts" to promote products. As an example, Warner Brothers Pictures used the gifts application to promote the movie *Speed Racer* by allowing members to give each other *Speed Racer* cars as gifts (Todi 2008). In 2008, over 270,000 Facebook gifts were given per week and they were estimated to bring in approximately $15 million of revenue for the social network (Todi 2008: 20).

Facebook discontinued the "gifts" application on December 2010. Why did it fail? The reason for its failure highlights the challenges inherent in expanding the architecture of disclosure. In many ways, this highlights the distinction between the "two Facebooks" detailed in Chapter 2, one that promotes market-based private consumption and one that promotes public networking and connection. When the Facebook based on using the medium to build a "personal brand" (Shih 2009) comes across the Facebook that is more disposed to use Facebook to cultivate a "public," the result is increased suspicion on the part of users. There are spaces on Facebook where corporate "personal branding" can take place on Facebook (for example, pages are more useful for branding while newsfeeds are better for "social grooming"). However, blending these social and market-based aspects of Facebook requires more seamless, organic and unobtrusive interventions.

McConnell and Huba (2003) found that businesses that were most effective at marketing were those that created "customer evangels" or customers so thrilled by their experience with a company or product that they become "converts" and "spread the gospel" of a product within their own Facebook networks. The company could then use the trust built within the evangel's social networks to carry the company's message rather than attempt to directly appear as a "friend." As Shih (2009) notes, social networking is advantageous to marketers because it provides the opportunity for "customer contextuality":

> Instead of diving into the hard sales pitch (which simply doesn't work these days) ... users can start with small talk over favorite sports teams and music, and friends in common, to build trust. Especially in this age of fraud and spam, trust is more important than ever (3).

This "small talk" on Facebook is thus serving dual purposes: to connect those in a network through disclosure while at the same time creating intimacy and attachment to products for the purposes of market-based consumption. This seamless melding of the two facilitates the user disclosure and connection Facebook needs to remain a viable business.

APIs, the Social Graph and the Architecture of Disclosure

While the outlook for Facebook looks bright, for Facebook to grow as a business, it has to figure out how to continually get you to disclose more of yourself. To do that, Facebook cannot remain limited to its own site but must expand to the rest of the Web. To do this, Facebook is relying on *application programming interfaces* (APIs) that allow for two or more sites to exchange data and for third parties to get or give data. This allows users to carry their Facebook identity across platforms. Through the company's API platform, *Facebook Connect*, users can "like" a blog entry on another page, have it appear in their status update, while a third party has access to the information. In 2010, Facebook launched a redesign of its *Facebook Platform* an API allowed for enhanced *interoperability* between applications. As Zuckerberg (2010) explained on the Facebook blog:

> We are making it so all websites can work together to build a more comprehensive map of connections and create better, more social experiences for everyone. We have redesigned Facebook Platform to offer a simple set of tools that sites

around the web can use to personalize experiences and build out the graph of connections people are making. (Online)

This is essential for Facebook's future growth. Without an API, Facebook cannot grow beyond the activity on its site. This is part of what Zuckerberg calls the *social graph*. The social graph is a concept in network theory that constitutes "the global mapping of everyone and how they are related" in the digital world (Fitzpatrick 2007 Online). Applied to Facebook's business model, the concept of the social graph posits to an online digital world where users have a distinct identity they carry with them throughout the Web. If we could have this identity, it would simplify our travels around digital space, much like a "passport" simplifies our travel around the world. This is precisely how it is envisioned by Zuckerberg (2010):

> This next version of Facebook Platform puts people at the center of the web. It lets you shape your experiences online and make them more social. For example, if you like a band on Pandora, that information can become part of the graph so that later if you visit a concert site, the site can tell you when the band you like is coming to your area. The power of the open graph is that it helps to create a smarter, personalized web that gets better with every action taken … We think that the future of the web will be filled with personalized experiences … For example, now if you're logged into Facebook and go to Pandora for the first time, it can immediately start playing songs from bands you've liked across the web. And as you're playing music, it can show you friends who also like the same songs as you, and then you can click to see other music they like. (Online)

It is curious that this example Zuckerberg uses of a digital identity that we take from site to site is oriented around consumption. From this perspective our "digital citizenship" based on our "unique identity" within the Web is employed to enhance our consumption habits. However, the idea of a social graph facilitated by APIs was not originally conceived of as a means to enhance marked-based consumption.

Bodle (2011) argues that the interoperability of APIs is a staple of the open Web that allows for the development of a digital social graph providing users with new ways of sharing and participating. APIs originally had an anti-monopolistic intent, to prevent dependency on a single company to provide a product or service. However, while APIs originally were intended to drive innovation and competition, Bodle (2011) argues Facebook is using APIs to achieve market dominance (320). As an example of the importance of APIs to Facebook's business model, Facebook provides a universal "like" button that can be placed on other websites. The like button differs from the "share" button in that it allows the storing of information for future use that would allow more targeted presentation of information. For example, a blog could include "posts your friends liked" on its page. By taking the ability to *disclose* and *connect* off the Facebook site itself, it expands the impulse to share to more sectors of one's digital life.

In addition, Facebook invites developers to create third-party applications that encourage more user revelation. Perhaps the most popular use of third-party applications is social network gaming. Parks Associates (2011) estimates that upwards of 250 million people play social-networking games each month. Zynga, the maker of online games accessed through Facebook, has two of the most popular social-networking games *CityVille* and *FarmVille*. In April of 2011, Zynga was valued at 8 billion dollars, an increase of 81 percent in the first quarter of 2011 (Levi 2011). FarmVille, Zynga's most popular game, allows users to adopt a virtual farm where they can plant and harvest crops, adorn their farms with all sorts of decorations, and engage in collaborative behavior by harvesting each other's crops or giving each other gifts. Social games make money for Facebook as well. Anything purchased by players within social games must be done so using proprietary *Facebook credits*, of which Facebook gets 30 percent profit.

But as anyone who has played the game can attest, FarmVille isn't much of a game at all. The entire purpose of the game is built on mutual obligation you have with your "friends" who are also playing the game. As Liszkiewicz (2010) notes:

> If you plant a field of pumpkins at noon, for example, you must return to harvest at eight o'clock that evening or risk losing the crop. Each pumpkin costs thirty coins and occupies one square of your farm, so if you own a fourteen by fourteen farm a field of pumpkins costs nearly six thousand coins to plant. Planting requires the user to click on each square three times: once to harvest the previous crop, once to re-plow the square of land, and once to plant the new seeds. This means that a fourteen by fourteen plot of land—which is relatively small for *FarmVille*—takes almost six hundred mouse-clicks to farm, and obligates you to return in a few hours to do it again. (Online)

Liszkiewicz (2010) points out that the game is so boring and repetitive that as you advance through different levels, you are given bonuses that allow you to play the game *less*. The only connection to playing this game is *reciprocity*. We don't want to harm our relationships by refusing a request, so the game:

> ... entangles users in a web of social obligations ... when users log into Facebook, they are reminded that their neighbors have sent them gifts, posted bonuses on their walls, and helped with each others' farms. In turn, they are obligated to return the courtesies (Liszkiewicz 2010: Online).

Liszkiewicz notes that games are usually characterized by their sense of play, spontaneity and freedom. Instead, Zynga games are dictated by routine, obligation and the sense we as human beings have to not offend those within our social networks. From personal experience, a refusal to accept a *FarmVille* gift from a loving aunt might be met with an icy glare over Christmas dinner.

All of this forced reciprocity produces a vast amount of "data" for Zynga Vance (2011) reports that Zynga collects 60 billion data points per day (for example, the length of time a user plays, the time of day during which they game is played, the objects purchased in the game, and so on).

The reciprocity also matters for Facebook because it keeps you on the site for longer periods of time. There is good, growing evidence to suggest that the more you connect with others on Facebook, the more you share on the site. Zhang and Zhu (2011) argue that group size on social networks dictates the level of individual participation on the Web, particularly for "sociable" members. They refer to this as the "warm glow" phenomenon whereby the more people see a contribution, the greater the psychic benefits to the contributor. Hofstetter et al. (2010) found that a greater number of online social ties were linked to increases in content which then had a reciprocal effect on expanding social ties. They attribute this to a "network effect," a reciprocal relationship whereby adding more friends leads to the creation of more content, which in turn leads to expansion of one's social network.

Further, while most of us aren't serial revealers on Facebook, the most frequent posters are more narcissistic and revelatory than infrequent posters. Buffardi and Campbell (2008) examined personality self-reports of Facebook users and found that narcissistic personality profile were significantly more likely to be more frequent posters and were more self-promoting in their posting activity. Mehdizadeh (2010) examined personality self-reports form 100 Facebook users and found that individuals with higher narcissism scores posted more often and had more self-promotional content in their posts. Since these studies were not longitudinal, there is no way of knowing whether the causal arrow also runs in the opposite direction (for example, does frequent Facebook use make you more narcissistic?) A market incentive does exist for encouraging users to cultivate their narcissistic side, whether true or not.

Convenience or Coercion

The commodification of Facebook activity raises an important question. Are users being coerced or *convenienced*? Do users not have a right to engage in self-commodification if they so choose? To modify the title of Web scholar Jared Lanier's (2011) book *You Are Not a Gadget*, how do we reconcile the fact that many of us might not mind becoming gadgets if it means we are exposed to consumer products we are already predisposed to like? Does a model in which the user can "opt-out" of becoming entirely commodified by either changing their privacy settings or personally managing what they share on Facebook serve as enough ethical protection against the charge of coercion, particularly when compared to Google's model of data accumulation which has no such protections? Mark Zuckerberg makes this point as he describes how Facebook differs from Google:

> Let me paint the two scenarios for you. They correspond to two companies in the Valley ... On the one hand you have Google, which primarily gets information by tracking stuff that's going on. They call it crawling. They crawl the web and

get information and bring it into their systems. They want to build maps, so they send around vans which literally go and take pictures of your home for their Street View system. And the way they collect and build profiles on people to do advertising is by tracking where you go on the Web, through cookies with DoubleClick and AdSense. That's how they build a profile about what you're interested in. Google is a great company, but you can see that taken to a logical extreme that's a little scary. On the other hand, we started the company saying there should be another way. If you allow people to share what they want and give them good tools to control what they're sharing, you can get even more information shared. But think of all the things you share on Facebook that you wouldn't want to share with everyone, right? You wouldn't want these things to be crawled or indexed-like pictures from family vacations, your phone number, anything that happens on an intranet inside a company, or any kind of private message or email. So a lot of stuff is getting more and more open, but there's a lot of stuff that's not open to everyone. (in Kirkpatrick 2010: 323)

From an individualist, market-based view, Facebook is based on the notion of individual choice. In Hobbesian terms, the user is "free from restraint" on Facebook and as such can dictate what to share and when. But even given this restricted view of a "free choice," there are many reasons to be skeptical about Zuckerberg's comparison to Google. First, inherent in a freely made choice is the ability to change one's mind. A user can assess the pros and cons of sharing information on Facebook and make the calculation that the benefits of participating in a revelation regime is worth the cost. However, if that decision cannot be reversed (for example, the users reassess their participation and would like to opt-out) then it is not a freely made choice.

Indeed "opting-out" once you have been a part of Facebook's *architecture of disclosure* is difficult. As of late 2011, Facebook has a remarkably byzantine process for deleting accounts. For the few who choose to leave Facebook, the company makes it incredibly difficult to find a delete button. Once you navigate through the several screens it takes to delete your account, you are required to endure a two-week waiting period. In addition, you are given a less definitive "deactivate" option that renders your account dormant. Upon deactivating, a gentle reminder appears that your "(friend) will miss you" along with a set of pictures the user has been tagged in. Again, the company is skillfully employing "thick bond" social capital to keep you engaged with the architecture of disclosure.

Even if you are able to exit, the issue of your past Facebook life remains. An entire industry has emerged around the desire former users have of erasing their digital past. A Silicon Valley-based company called *DeleteMe* helps erase your online past. They charge $10 for every deleted account and $50 for a deleted search result. They do this, not through sophisticated code, but by calling companies on their own privacy policies and following up with legal action if the data is not removed (Carr 2010). The implication is that without legal threat, companies are likely to sell your information.

Perhaps a more pressing concern vis-à-vis paternalism is that it meets the condition of full information. To meet the conditions for making a non-coerced decision, an agent must approximate full information. This is an abstract concept not possible in reality. However, approximating perfect information or being as transparent as possible with information is paramount to making a claim that a decision has been entered into without coercion. Here Facebook's *architecture of disclosure* is troubling. Since 2005, the company has systematically revised its policies towards an "opt-out" approach to allowing Facebook to disseminate user information. In addition, the company has changed the basic layout of its page in ways that allow non-friends to gain more information about users. In other words Facebook has changed the terms of membership after the member has joined in and accrued benefits from the site.

But all of this presumes that we are rational agents when we are sharing Facebook data. In reality, the pull of connection is a powerful force. Each of us wants to belong. When others whom we consider close friends and family are posting intimate details about their lives, we are compelled to reciprocate or be excluded from the bonding process that is taking place. We can find alternative ways to connect to be sure, but Facebook creates a medium that places this interaction in front of us on a constant basis. While it might be far-fetched to say that Facebook coerces users into providing this information, it has figured out a way to facilitate the basic human need to disclose and connect in a way that makes it difficult to resist. Turning your engagement in your social network off by "opting out" is an option, but it is one that comes at a significant emotional cost for many.

But as I have discussed in this chapter, pushing users to disclose more of their selves to their community is central to Facebook's business model. The big problem is that we are seldom allowed "under the hood" of this massive *disclosure turned information*, data collection process. Facebook is putting together granules of our digital life to create a composite of who we are for the purposes of marketing. But who is that person? Is it a public-self? Is it a private self? Is it a third self? How do we get to talk back to this composite of us? Do we have any say in how this person is created?

Contrary to Mark Zuckerberg's view, Facebook users are concerned with privacy. The persistent myth that young people are less concerned about revealing their personal information to strangers is not supported by the evidence. Metzger and Pure (2009) found that college students on Facebook were indeed concerned about privacy but were not sure how to configure the settings to restrict the dissemination of their user data. A recent survey done by the Pew Center for the Internet and American Life found that young, 18–29-year-old SNS users in the United States were significantly more likely than older users to manage their reputations online. When compared with users over 30 years of age, users aged 18–29 years old in the United States were more likely to change their privacy setting, delete comments from others about their profile, remove their name from pictures they were tagged in, and *defriend* or refuse friend requests (Madden and Smith 2010).

What people want, particularly young people, is the ability to control the disclosure process. Hundreds of millions of users are relying on Facebook to provide a context where they can do so. But it is hard to manage that process when Facebook also needs to make a profit. Stewart Brand (1987: 202) is famous for saying "information wants to be free," but in practice Facebook has changed the slogan to "information wants to be commodified." This *architecture of disclosure* is not simply designed to help us connect with one another, it a means to an end of personal data collection and aggregation with the goal of increasing advertising revenue. But how many of us have really thought through the implications of using a platform provided by a private company as a forum for disclosure? At the very least, the monetization of the intimate might, at the very least, seem ethically problematic.

An illustrative example of how poignant and intimate disclosure and connection can become on Facebook was chronicled in December of 2010. In *A Facebook Story*, Ian Shapira writes about Shana Greatman Swers, a 35-year-old consultant as she updated her Facebook network on the birth of her child, through post-partum complications and her ultimate death. What was so striking about the posts was the love and encouragement of her and her family and friends' posts, even in the face of her impending death. After her passing, one of her friends posted this on her page:

> Shana, the kids prayed for you tonight, for Isaac, and for Jeff. I know how much you love children - one of the last things I remember you saying to me, "I love the Annex Staff" - they have been praying for you for weeks. Tonight they prayed for Miss Shana in Heaven, and as children do, they took your passing with consideration, but without understanding. I think they are too alive to understand it. Isaac – one who laughs - Sarah's only son – what a beautiful name for a beautiful child. With your great gifts and Jeff's, he will be an amazing man. You have left so many things to all of us, and you have left a great legacy in him, too. (Online)

The stream of updates and responses published in the *Washington Post* article reveals a tight-knit community of people who care deeply for each other. The ability to notify others of your joys and sorrows and have them affirmed by a community of loving friends and family (and to be able to in real time and to affirm the joys and sorrows of others) is a core human value. But this intimate disclosure of deep pain and sorrow seems out of place somehow, particularly when there are banner ads in the corner of the page.

Nevertheless, monetization might be the cost we pay for a powerful vehicle for connection. Facebook could be sending us kicking and screaming into something that is good for us. Perhaps we in the West have a myopic bias towards the private and the individual. Tufekci (2008) argues that this might simply be a return to past eras in history where relationships were fixed and information about private life was widely known. Zuckerberg's effort in this light could be a radical transformation of Western society back toward interconnectedness in a way that answers they key criticism of modernity as too focused on individualism and rationality. Indeed,

Zuckerberg unwittingly gets at this core critique of modernity when he describes the power of Facebook:

> You can integrate a person's friends into almost anything and make [it] instantly more engaging and viral ... You care so much more about your friends. It's not an intellectual thing. It's hard-wired into humans that you need to focus on what the people around you are doing. It's this very visceral, deep thing. (Gelles 2010: Online)

On its surface, it appears to harken back to antiquity, to Aristotelian notions of politics. Aristotle first brought up the idea of a public life based on friendship as rewarding and beneficial for society. Indeed the private life was seen as mundane and common. The *good life* was a life shared in public. Without this common engagement, we would be diminished, unable to adopt the virtues necessary for the full expression of humanity. As such, Facebook theoretically enhances *the good life* by making it easier for us to live a life in common. These bonds are supposed to lead us to be wiser, more humane people. This would appear to be supported by the aforementioned scholarship that links frequent Facebook use to greater levels of trust, social capital and political engagement. As mentioned in the last chapter, Hampton et al. (2011) found that Facebook users were twice as likely as non-users to feel that "people could be trusted."

But a curious paradox exists in our Facebook age. Why, in an age where we are so much more connected through vehicles like Facebook that supposedly enhance our connectedness, are we becoming less empathic in general? Konrath et al. (2011) found that college students in the United States were 40 percent less empathic when compared to their peers in the late 1970s and that decline has accelerated in recent years. The researchers used a university of Michigan survey that asked questions regarding whether students felt "soft-hearted" or had "tender feeling for others" and whether "other people's misfortunes disturbed them."

In addition, the Konrath et al. (2011) found that US college students scored much lower on two key indices of empathy: *perspective-taking* or the ability to think about how another might feel measured by the *General Social Survey* question: "I sometimes try to understand my friends better by imagining how things look from their perspective" and *empathic concern* which measured the extent to which a subject had an emotional response to other's suffering measured by the question "I often have tender, concerned feelings for people less fortunate than me," an often-used measure of altruistic behavior. A key reason for this decline in empathy might be a sense of "empathy overload" attached to having access to too much information about global affairs.

How do we make sense of this puzzle? One answer might be that as Facebook pulls us closer to our intimate networks, it distances us from the world "out there" outside the purview of our network. Indeed Facebook derives its utility from its intimacy. We are uninterested in the minute details of people with whom we have no relationship. There is a *privacy* that underlies the seemingly public enterprise of Facebook. As such, those who seek to use Facebook to "make friends" find it difficult. Bessière et al. (2010) found that using SNS to meet new people was correlated with depression.

Mark Zuckerberg often talks about the idea that privacy norms have evolved over time (Arrington 2007). But one thing that has always been in tension is the desire to disclose to our intimates and the desire to branch out and present ourselves to those outside our immediate world. These dual impulses, to feel "at home" and to "lose oneself", are strewn throughout art and literature.

The biggest challenge Facebook poses for social and political life is how it affects this tension between the familiar and the strange. Rather than move in the direction of greater transparency, I'd argue Facebook allows us to expand and deepen our personal networks, not at the expense of public life, but in a way that encourages us to see the public through the lens of the private. Facebook creates a reasonably safe setting to disclose, but to do so, it must appear as if the revelation is under our control. We are interested in revealing, but as a form of mutual disclosure, not as voyeurism. As such, *Facebook revelation*, or revelation in private, facilitates disclosure in a way that is mutually beneficial (for example, we affirm and become affirmed by others). However, Facebook does not encourage the impulse to break away from our networks and put ourselves in situations where we are not affirmed, where we are strange. How does our engagement with the world change when we can be "at home" at all times? We do not yet understand is how this pull towards our personal networks affects the ways in which we engage with those outside of our networks. I turn to this question in the next chapter.

Chapter 3
Facebook and the Decline of the Public

College professors around the world struggle with Facebook for their students' attention. One strategy is to forbid laptops from the classroom. But doing that removes an essential tool for note-taking or learning further about the topic. The Web is a useful supplement for classroom learning, opening students up to the world of ideas and concepts with which they are unfamiliar or, more to the point, with which they are uncomfortable or challenged. However, the competition between university faculty and Facebook is a metaphor for the way in which Facebook challenges public life.

Facebook is the biggest social networking application in the world. The site is still in its toddler phase, but has achieved an impressive global reach, with 800 million active users worldwide, half of which access the site daily (Facebook. com: 2011). But this global spread happened in a matter of months. A mere three years ago, MySpace had a larger user base than Facebook. To Internet scholars, that seems like a million years ago. Because of Facebook's rapid rise, we know little about the impact the application has on our experience of the social world. In this chapter, I make the case that Facebook produces a preference for personal disclosure and connection in ways that structure users' expectations of public life. I argue that viewing public life through the lens of *the personal* creates challenges for citizenship and democratic political institutions.

To return to the classroom example, the power of *disclosure* and *connection* to a network of intimates is difficult to compete with. I am a stranger to most of my students. They don't know me. They have no way of knowing whether what I'm saying in the classroom will be useful. More to the point, they might have little patience with concepts or ideas about major issues in the world they have little control over. By contrast, on Facebook, they do have control. They can build deeper connections with people they have already vetted, people to which they are socially proximate. They can share intimate, subjective, feelings and observations about the world around them. They can talk about people they like, what professors are wearing, or how much fun they had the night before. Each update from a friend is a small jolt to the brain's pleasure center that makes the Facebook the bane of college professors everywhere.

But what if I'm talking about impersonal systems and structures that do not have Facebook accounts or provide status updates? What if a discussion about the eurozone debt crisis isn't based on intersubjective assessments, but requires the development of seeing beyond the personal and recognizing the impersonal world of institutions and processes that do not have a Facebook account? What if global warming is actually *a thing out there* and isn't subject to how someone's friends "feel" about it. A tsunami caused by radical shifts in temperature that is about to crash over you isn't interested in whether you "like" it or not.

The only way for the professor to compete with Facebook is to make the subject personal. Rather than expect that students will listen to an hour-long lecture on transnational finance, the academy (particularly in the United States) has moved towards "engaged learning" and "participatory learning" that connects students more deeply to the subject matter. To "break through" to our students, we need to articulate how the subject matters to them. In the main, this is a good thing. Forcing college professors to reflect upon the *why* of a particular subject is important. But there is a part of me that wonders whether in our haste to make things relevant, we've failed to stress the importance of embracing things that are seemingly irrelevant, *strange* or difficult to crystallize into the personal.

Sharing in a Pre-Selected Public

Boyd and Ellison (2007) point out that technology challenges our conventional understandings of public and private, by creating *mediated publics* that have characteristics of publicness but are not quite public in that they are filtered, be it through shared interest in a subject or by kinship or some other factor. Boyd (2007) notes that mediated publics like Facebook have four defining characteristics: persistence of content, searchability, replicability of digital material and invisibility of audiences. Facebook is a distinct subset of a mediated public. It exhibits the first three characteristics but Facebook's audience is not invisible; instead *lurkers* are known. Facebook is a nonymous space (Zhou et al. 2008) for users where audiences are known (with caveats) to the user. This is an important distinction. Unlike a blog whose audience is only limited by who can find it, Facebook allows the user to limit who sees the content. While friends-of-friends can see your responses to a friend's post, your status updates are restricted to your pre-selected network. In that sense, a Facebook social network is a pre-selected *public*.

Users on Facebook post all sorts of material. But the extent to which people self-disclose online is driven by the personal orientations, predispositions they bring to Facebook. Tufekci (2008b) notes that a user's attitudes towards online self-disclosure and online social connection affect their orientations towards online interactions. However, there are some trends in posting behavior on Facebook. In general, people forward or share materials that produce strong emotional responses. Berger and Milkman (2010) found that people were more likely to share content that made them anxious or awed them over material that made them sad or content. This makes sense on Facebook. Status updates scroll past our screens at a rapid rate. For an update to be captured and responded to by the rest of the network requires something extraordinary, more outrageous than the ordinary. Anxiety or amusement is more likely to keep us reading than contentment or sadness. A funny or alarming bit of content helps break through the clutter of status updates on Facebook.

As I discussed in previous chapters, this form of communication has a myriad social benefits: increased social capital, increased feelings of trust and efficacy, access to information and resources through weak ties, and enhanced interest in politics. However, for all the good that this architecture of disclosure produces, there are reasons to be skeptical that an enhancement of satisfaction from one's personal network necessarily translates directly into an enhancement of public life. To explore this question, we should look into the distinction between private and public.

The Public and the Private

In *The Human Condition,* Hannah Arendt (2003) argues that *the public sphere* plays a critical role in human life. Without a public space to discuss collective concerns, citizens have no sense of "how to be" in the world. Arendt argued that without an explicitly *political* public life (for example, discussions of collective concerns), we have no real sense of who we are as people. A clearly *political* public life, in other words, was reserved for developing our sense of self:

> it was the only place where men could show who they really and inexchangeably
> were. It was for the sake of this chance, and out of love for a body politic that made
> it possible to them all, that each was more or less willing to share in the burden
> of jurisdiction, defense, and administration of public affairs. (Arendt: 2003: 193)

The emergence of ancient city-states gave "men" a "second life", a *bios politikos* whereby they could disclose and connect with others. In the classical world, there was a clear divide between one's private life *(idion)* and one's communal life *(koinon).* Arendt argues that ancient Greeks and Romans saw the *res publica* as a counter to the futility of private life. Private life was merely an avenue for mundane self-preservation. The private was the realm of labor, of slaves and women who toiled only to sustain life. Household matters were seen as necessary evils to be carried out in the service of public excellence.

But Arendt argues our conceptions of the public and the private have changed. In modern times, the private world of *work* has been elevated to the primary means of seeking "excellence." *The public* in the modern world has becomes a means of using scientific rationality to "improve society." As such, the individual matters less in the public realm. Public debate and deliberation matter less than "engineering" society and "managing" society. As such, rather than seek "excellence" through public life, "distinction and difference have become private matters of the individual" (Arendt 2003: 193).

This substitution of the social for the political as the key element of public life is lamentable for Arendt. Arendt, like her mentor Heidegger, suggests that language, or *talk* is what makes things real. Without a venue for sharing ones experience, a public sphere, events exist in a limited reality:

Each time we talk about things that can be experienced only in privacy or
intimacy, we bring them out into a sphere where they will assume a kind of reality
which, their intensity notwithstanding, they never could have had before. (199)

It is one thing to have an opinion, it is another to voice that opinion. A private
feeling needs venues for its actualization. Indeed not only should these venues for
actualization exist, they are essential for excellence. For Arendt (2003):

no activity can become excellent if the world does not provide a proper space
for its exercise. Neither education nor ingenuity nor talent can replace the
constituent elements of the public realm, which make it the proper place for
human excellence. (199)

For things to "exist," there must be a public in which to discuss them. This public
thus becomes a "world of things" between those who have it in common. Further,
this public realm provides the diversity of viewpoints necessary to vet ideas and
cultivate wisdom in individuals. Without a diverse space for discussion of ideas,
we are limited in our thoughts and capacities. We revert to becoming *private
people*, "imprisoned in the subjectivity of (one's) own singular experience"
(Arendt 2003: 205).

In *The Filter Bubble*, Pariser (2011) picks up on this strand in Arendt's thinking
to criticize Web 2.0 applications like Google and Facebook. He notes that these
applications' practice of tailoring content to individual preferences pulls us away
from engaging with the diverse views. But the reality of Facebook is that we are
exposed to different ideas on a regular basis. As I discussed in Chapter 1, our
networks on Facebook are not homogeneous. Because our networks are based
on social-proximity, we come into regular contact with people whom with we
disagree. The idea that we are in filter-bubbles on Facebook is not supported by
the evidence. But another element of Arendt's argument is more telling of what
Facebook may do to our politics.

Arendt notes that the type of content discussed in public determines the
greatness of a culture. She notes that focusing on "small things" means a receding
of the public realm, a trade-off of charm for "greatness." Arendt points out that
some emotions, like pain, are so subjective that they are "removed from the world
of things" and thus *irrelevant* to the public sphere:

there are a great many things which cannot withstand the implacable, bright
light of the constant presence of others on the public scene; there, only what is
considered to be relevant, worthy of being seen or heard, can be tolerated, so
that the irrelevant becomes automatically a private matter. (Arendt: 2003: 200)

By this she does not mean they are unimportant, but rather they are deeply
personal. She goes on in that passage to speak of emotions like "love" that become
irrelevant, or seem to lose a sense of authenticity, in the public sphere because of

their deeply personal nature. Once they are employed for political purposes, they lose an essential quality. Because these emotions are so powerful, there is a draw towards a retreat to the private. She suggests that the complexity of an impersonal modern society encourages a retreat into "small things" or an expansion of the private sphere where these deep emotions can be felt. As an example, Arendt uses the French romanticization of everyday things:

> within the space of their own four walls, between chest and bed, table and chair,
> dog and cat and flowerpot, extending to these things a care and tenderness
> which, in a world where rapid industrialization constantly kills off the things
> of yesterday to produce today's objects, may even appear to be the world's last,
> purely humane corner. (Arendt 2003: 200–201)

Arendt notes that what is lost when we expand the private sphere of the personal and abandon the impersonal sphere of the public is a world of "the human artifact, the fabrication of human hands, as well as to affairs which go on among those who inhabit the man-made world together" (2003: 202). This collective, tangible, world "out there" is what binds us together, what is truly public. We are all impacted by a system of transnational finance, but without a public sphere to "bring us all to the table" we do not engage in discussion about these tangible things. Arendt draws the analogy to a seance where the "table that brings us all together" is removed to describe the loss of the public sphere:

> What makes mass society so difficult to bear ... the fact that the world between
> them has lost its power to gather them together, to relate and to separate them.
> The weirdness of this situation resembles a spiritualistic seance where a number
> of people gathered around a table might suddenly, through some magic trick, see
> the table vanish from their midst, so that two persons sitting opposite each other
> were no longer separated but also would be entirely unrelated to each other by
> anything tangible. (203)

In large part, Facebook shrinks the table. Not because individuals cannot talk about "the world of things." Indeed they often do on Facebook. But Facebook takes the table away because its architecture of revelation is designed to turn your disclosure into a commodity. It is primarily concerned with increasing the daily stream of emotions, anecdotes and insights that populate the majority of Facebook content because those can be more easily be commodified. Facebook is more concerned with discussing the subjective, personal "small" elements of everyday life rather than the objective, impersonal "big" of public life that takes more time to digest and articulate, requires deliberation and is more difficult to commodify.

This manifests in the groups I studied in two ways. Few of the Facebook groups I studied, focused on specific policy issues. When they did they either emphasized local politics or emotion-laden political issues. Examples of these local-level "small things" groups were a Colombia-based group called "Transmilenio"[1] created to advocate for reduced transit rates for students, or a Norway-based group called "Keep Odderøya open" challenging the move of the Vest-Adger Museum to the Odderøya region of Norway.[2] Another group was created to prevent the use of the Vattenfall nuclear reactors in Krümmel and Brunsbüttel.[3]

When Facebook encourages "small-thing" group mobilization, it serves an important function in democratic societies. Local issues are important and need to be addressed and challenged when those affected might be harmed by a policy. More troublesome, however, is when Facebook groups form around "bigger" issues of public life. When Facebook users talk about "big issues" as we all are wont to do from time to time, the pleasures of disclosure and connection become a frame through which we see the public sphere. Even when we engage in "big" issues, we do so through the lens of subjective personal experience. While the personal has a role in public life, there are dangers when the personal becomes the way in which we relate to public life. When we see public life strictly through the lens of the personal, we fail to see the "table that brings us all together."

When users created groups to talk about national issues, they often chose emotion-laden elements, particularly those with high *negative valence*, or those objects that can elicit strong negative emotions in users (Heider 1946). One group, created in the United States, was entitled "PEOPLE AGAINST OBAMA NOT ATTENDING THE MEMORIAL DAY SERVICE."[4] The title of the site, all in capital letters, suggests the intent of the group is to convey anger and urgency. The group's description (also all in capital letters) highlights the strong negative-valence of the subject:

PRESIDENT OBAMA WILL NOT BE LAYING THE WREATH DOWN ON THE TOMB OF THE UNKNOWN SOLDIER THIS YEAR, A PRESIDENTIAL TRADITION. I BELIEVE THIS IS A SLAP IN THE FACE TO ALL VETERANS AND TO ALL PEOPLE WHO KNOW A VETERAN OR WHOM HAS LOST A LOVED ONE. HE IS THE COMMANDER-IN-CHIEF

---

1 Nosotros Los Estudiantes Exigimos Que Le Vajen al Transmilenio (*We the students demand a reduction in Transmilenio*). (n.d.). In *Facebook* [Group]. Available at: http://facebook.com/pages/NOSOTROS-LOS-ESTUDIANTES-EXIGIMOS-QUE-LE-VAJEN-AL-TRANSMILENIO/236378712422?sk=info [accessed: 11 August 2010].

2 Hold Odderøya åpen - Stopp Setesdalstunet (Keep Odderøya open). (n.d.). In *Facebook* [Group]. Available at: http://facebook.com/group.php?gid=19241993896&v=info [accessed: 12 August 2010].

3 Aus bleibt Aus! (From left off). (n.d.). In *Facebook* [Group]. Available at: http://www.facebook.com/group.php?gid=49306932747 [accessed: 5 August 2010].

4 PEOPLE AGAINST OBAMA NOT ATTENDING THE MEMORIAL DAY SERVICE. (n.d.). In *Facebook* [Group]. Available at: http://facebook.com/group.php?gid=126484550704019 [accessed: 15 August 2010].

AND ITS (sic) HIS DUTY TO BE THERE BUT INSTEAD HE IS GOING TO CHICAGO FOR MEMORIAL DAY.

While this issue is obviously of concern to the user, it represents the emotional and symbolic elements of politics. Whether or not the President of the United States laid a wreath on the Tomb of the Unknown Soldier does not directly impact troop levels of military spending. But the issue is accessible to the group creator because it can easily be translated into a synecdoche for the president's more broadly perceived disrespect for the military.

Similarly, most policy-specific groups were formed around high negative-valence issues. Two other examples include a South African-based group called "Restore the Death penalty to South Africa,"[5] and a group based in Norway called "Stricter penalties for abuse and murder of children!"[6] In each instance, the description of the group lists a litany of murders used to legitimate the policy perspective of the group's creator. While these are important national social policy issues, they are also among the easiest to personalize since they directly involve harm to the self. Similarly, they are the easiest to express anger over because they are high negative-valence issues.

Facebook and Problematizing the Self

And this is where Facebook poses a challenge for democratic systems. It provides us with a public forum to express our views, but it also facilitates a deeper connection with a satisfying, personalized world of subjective feelings and emotions. This reveling in our personal spheres exacerbates a preoccupation with the self, or to use Baumeister's (1987) language, the problematization of the self. The need to "find oneself" or "self actualize" a hallmark of Western modernity. Introspection is not something that people did throughout the Middle Ages. The self during this period was more associated with social roles than with individual feelings and personality.

But a casual glance and Facebook shows that it largely comprises *presentations of the self* – one's feelings and subjective reflections about the world. In antiquity, the self was defined by actions rather than feelings, hence the call to "know thyself" was probably more about understanding one's usefulness to the whole rather than being "in touch" with true feelings. Baumeister (1987) argues that there is little evidence of an introspective, inner-life before the sixteenth century. But from the sixteenth century on, a move was afoot to define the self through the self, whether it be the Romantics' call for self-fulfillment through the expression

---

5   Bring Back the Death penalty to South Africa. (n.d.). In *Facebook* [Group]. Available at: http://facebook.com/group.php?gid=9125638371 [accessed: 6 August 2010].

6   Strengere straffer for mishandling og drap av barn! (Stricter penalties for abuse and murder of children!) (n.d.). In *Facebook* [Group]. Available at: http://facebook.com/group. php?gid=281228184356 [accessed: 7 August 2010].

of passion, love and creativity or the Puritans' reflection of self-expression through work (Baumeister 1987).

The culmination of a *search for the self* through emotion and personality culminates in a therapeutic culture in which feelings define the core-self. A political manifestation of the search for the self is the effort to make society conform to what one finds in this self-discovery. In many ways, Facebook is the therapeutic-self writ large. Through a status update, users announce themselves primarily to their intimate peer-networks. It is a massive marketplace of feelings, quips, observations and commentaries, all seeking legitimation and legitimating at the same time. Harris and Kamvar (2009) produced a series of visualizations of this vast amalgam of thoughts, feelings and recorded experience throughout the web in a 2009 piece entitled *We Feel Fine*. By culling the vast range of feelings in the blogosphere through content analysis, they are able to make curious, but scientifically invalid, statements like "the world is feeling anxious at three times the normal level" (Online).

We are always presenting who we would like others to think we are on Facebook. This presentation means that, at the very least, we think deeply about how others see us. But if perceptions of self-worth come in part from our social networks assessments of us, do we are predisposed to conceal elements of our "actual selves" in our self-presentation. In reality, we don't want to present our "actual selves" to the world if that process leaves us vulnerable to being rejected. We want to be seen as an individual, while at the same time being accepted. Facebook gives us an opportunity to present ourselves to the world in ways that lessen the possibility of rejection because our networks are self-selected.

Facebook is primarily a world fueled by which feelings and emotions. The Facebook team (Facebook.com 2010) conducted a content analysis of status updates. Using 68 word-categories from the LWIC dictionary that capture "meaningful psychological and linguistic constructs, along with a list of words belonging to each category" (Online), the team broke status updates into "parts of speech," emotional content and topic. They calculated the percentage of words that belonged in each word category. Looking at 1 million updates from US English speakers they found a negative correlation between age and "negative emotions," "swear words" and "anger." For example, younger posters tended to be more revealing of socially unacceptable emotions on Facebook. The older that people were, the more likely that they would share "positive emotions" (Online).

More importantly, updates containing positive emotions were much more likely to be "liked" than comments containing negative emotions. To the extent that we seek affirmation and legitimation of our self-presentations online, this produces strong incentives to be positive on Facebook. However, the Facebook team also found that negative comments were more likely to elicit comments from others in the network, suggesting that even if no "hate" button exists on Facebook, negative affective emotions do initiate discussions of some sort on Facebook.

But what types of discussions take place on Facebook? Seemingly, they fall squarely into Arendt's discussion of "small things":

Generally, people tend to talk about what they are (or should be) doing at a particular time of day. For example, words about sleep increase at night and peak in the early mornings, when people should actually be sleeping. Words about occupation and school are increased in the mornings (perhaps while we're on our way to work/school). Words about social processes and leisure are low during the mornings (when people are either in school or working), but they increase as the day goes on. (Facebook.com: Online)

There is nothing inherently wrong with chatting about what is, to use Arendt's language, the *charm* of private life. Facebook didn't invent this desire. However, Facebook does "colonize" more of our daily discourse space by facilitating interactions with our personal social networks. And we are more disposed to talk about "shared things" with this group. Whereas "chats" between personal friends about everyday things might have taken place around the dinner table, at a coffee klatch or around the water cooler, these chats are now ambient and mediated. Whether they are negative or positive assessments, they are about "everyday things" and they are mediated in such a way that they are less likely to be connected to "the world of things" out there that link our private, personal life to public, collective life.

This viewing of public life through the lens of the personal is particularly pernicious because the personal is more secure and within our control. Turkle (2011) argues that our increasing reliance on technology draws us into "risk free" relationships that produce "companionship without demands" (66). The problem with mediated communication that takes the risk out of relationships is that actual human interaction becomes more problematic. If we can satisfy our needs to disclose and connect within forums where we can invent ways of being with people that turn them into something close to things," we are more likely to do so (224).

Rather than draw us into more authentic relationships, the ambient awareness of Facebook emphasizes the convenience and control of other relationships while reducing what we expect from others and ourselves as friends. Facebook and other SNS sites allow for an "alternative to processing emotions in real time" (Turkle 2011: 206).

As an example, in interviews with teens in the US, Turkle found that they resisted talking on the phone because it was "too stressful" (for example, it did not provide the distance to manage their performance). She found that teens were more comfortable with technologies like texting and Facebook that allowed them to craft their emotional responses to produce "a deliberate performance that can be made to seem spontaneous" (Turkle 2011: 200).

But in all this crafted talk, we lose something very valuable to public life – spontaneity. As Turkle (2011) suggests:

> Once we remove ourselves form the flow of physical, messy, untidy life — and both robotics and networked life do that — we become less willing to get out there and take a chance" (154).

From this view, it is worth asking whether Facebook drives us towards a type of self, or is it possible that our own sources of self-worth dictate how we use Facebook? Stefanone et al. (2011) found that Facebook users who based their self-worth on the approval of others, physical appearance, and winning in competitions use Facebook for longer periods of time and were more apt to share photos than users who derived their self-worth from academic competence, family love and support, and being a virtuous or moral person. In other words, the "search for the self" on Facebook was contingent upon one's self-orientation to the world "out there."

This poses a chicken-or-egg question: If our "search for the self" draws us further into the world of our presenting our own subjective experience, can it also change how we derive our self-worth? We are multiple parts at multiple times, full of contradictions and idiosyncrasies. If there is an authentic self, it's not easy to present to others fully, even via frequent status updates. If Facebook accelerates the impression management process so we are always managing who we think we should be rather than simply becoming who we are, what does that mean for our role as public citizens?

A study by a research team at Edinburgh Napier University (forthcoming) finds that college-age Facebook users in the UK with a higher number of friends feel more stress over having to maintain status updates. As Kathy Charles, head researcher, explains in a BBC Interview about the unpublished research:

> It's like being a mini news channel about yourself. The more people you have the more you feel there is an audience there. You are almost a mini celebrity and the bigger the audience the more pressure you feel to produce something about yourself. Many also told us they were anxious about withdrawing from the site for fear of missing important social information or offending contacts ...
> Like gambling, Facebook keeps users in a neurotic limbo, not knowing whether they should hang on in there just in case they miss out on something good."
> (Edinburgh Napier University 2011: Online)

What is the source of this anxiety? If we are presenting ourselves to those we already know, why would there be pressure to "produce something about yourself"? Perhaps the anxiety is over whether we are presenting our *authentic self* online. Heppner and Kernis (2007) define an authentic self as "the unimpeded operation of one's true or core self in one's daily enterprise" (248). Central to this idea is an awareness of one's true preferences. But where does a "true self" come from. Pre-modern notions of the "true self" situate it within Platonic "ideal forms," Aristotelian notions of "higher good," or Christian notions of "the eternal soul" (Wright 2008). But what if, as Heidegger (1978) notes, the self is an emerging phenomenon that we create from a range of possible selves? From this view, there are many selves we could become.

Making human connection granular makes it easier to connect and Facebook is developing and architecture of disclosure that encourages us to disclose and connect even more. But is there a point ot all of this connection? What if we're sharing simply for the sake of sharing? Connecting for the sake of connecting? We are reflexive beings; not only do we want to be fulfilled but we want to signal to others that we are fulfilled. We're not only interested in our own self-actualization but in whether or not society perceives us as self-actualized.

Too much of a preoccupation with our subjective emotional life at the expense of objective, impersonal, collective public life runs the risk of leading us down a rabbit hole, partly because Facebook can never help us know our *true self* "prior to and apart from all roles" (MacIntyre: 1981: 56). The impulse to "problematize the self" pulls us deeper into the world of subjective feelings and emotions and away from the impersonal world of "things" out there. This gets reflected in a politics of the personal that emphasizes feelings and emotions in public life. In later chapters, I will illustrate that this manifests itself in a process of political discourse as identity management where much of the political presentations in Facebook groups deal with the individual's reaction to the political world (in-groups, out-groups, political candidates, political parties, and so on).

Of course, this may not be such a bad thing. It is possible that a politics of the personal is the way we enter the world of the public. Facebook is enveloping us in the process of searching out our subjective feelings to present the self to others. But this is the basis of mobilization. One's subjective anger at a political condition might resonate with the political anger of others similarly situated. In Chapter 6, I highlight how a politics of the personal can enhance mobilization around subjective emotions. But I want to offer that there is a value in political life to "just experiencing" the self rather than constantly searching the self to recording and updating one's personal experience.

This is not to say that foregrounding feelings and emotions can have positive effects as well. In many ways, feeling and emotion is how we connect with the outside world. The emphasis on the self and self-reflection is an important hallmark of liberal, democratic cultures. Viewed from this perspective, individual selves on Facebook are discrete independent entities worth knowing. Rather than be reduced to your station, problematizing the self means that the self matters. By extension, other selves matter as well. Because of this, Facebook is both a celebration of community and a celebration of the centrality of the liberal self.

Viewed in this way, Facebook is an emancipatory tool. We can explore ourselves publicly with the support of our social networks. If the Romantics believed that our duty was to "find our purpose" we now have the tools to do this in a public forum. If the self can be understood through Heidegger's (1978) notion of *Daisen*, or that the self exists as a number of possibilities for future being, perhaps Facebook gives us the possibility to "try out" these different selves as part of an ongoing, interactional, intersectional process of becoming?

Facebook serves to ratify the worth of our presentations of the self. We are all in competition to be legitimated, but legitimation of Facebook is based on cleverness, humor, shock, empathy, and so on. With our network of friends, we can all have a tacit agreement to reaffirm each other in our self-worth without having to seek that validation from outside of the network. We can differentiate ourselves through our social networks without the messiness of differentiation in public life which exposes us to uncertainty and *strangeness*.

Making human connection granular makes it easier to *present the self* through "likes" and "status updates" and to receive others' presentation of their selves. Before, catching up with a friend required a lengthy phone call, a letter or a time-consuming and costly visit. Showing friends your slides from the family vacation once required pulling out the carousel and projecting slides onto a wall. But these activities, as mundane and time-consuming as they might be, required a physical expense of effort to consummate. They also presented us with real-time interaction that introduced elements of uncertainty and spontaneity. As such those activities created no gaps between the times we "experience the self" and the time were spent "proclaiming the self" for presentation to the network entire network.

An example of this is the face that only 5 of the 250 Facebook political groups I studied asked fellow Facebook users to discuss a range of alternative views on political issues. Seldom was the term "all view are welcome" found on a Facebook political group. Examples of the few deliberation-based groups was a Morocco-based groups called "The national strategy for integrated youth" (translated from Arabic)[7] which was designed as a "forum as a space for dialogue and debate and put forward ideas and the difficulties associated with the issue of young people" and a Sweden-based site that invited "consumers food producers, retailers and restaurants to open dialogue on better food. However, these sites were few and far between.

But truly "knowing the self" requires dialogue and deliberation. It requires doing the hard work of placing oneself in difficult situations and engagement with diverse others. In *Nicomachean Ethics*, Aristotle lays out five distinct forms of knowledge, or what he called *intellectual virtues*: epistemic (*episteme*), intuitive (*nous*), philosophic (*sophia*), technical (*techne*), and a less discussed virtue he called phronesis, or "increased experience with and knowledge of particulars, interactions, and contexts."

From this perspective, engagement with the world "out there" is about acquiring civic wisdom. Flyvbjerg (2001) suggests we think of phronesis as an ability to be multi-perspectival in approaching public problems. He uses the Dreyfus model of skill acquisition to highlight how social science might contribute to civic learning. In this model, people go through five stages of knowledge. New learners start at a "novice" stage where they must strictly adhere to a set of rules to complete tasks, then to an "advanced beginner" stage where they can compare rules with limited experience. Some move to the "competent performer" stage where they are able to adapt the rules to distinct contexts. Fewer move to the stage of "proficient performer" that is able to make instinctive choices about the rules based on their aggregated experiences. A select few move to the final *expert* stage where the performer is intuitive, holistic and synchronous (Dreyfus and Dreyfus 1980).

---

7   حملة وطنية من أجل أن حضف لجأ الشباح (The national strategy for integrated youth). (n.d.). In *Facebook* [Group]. Available at: http://facebook.com/group.php?gid=112848732063869 [accessed: 12 August 2010].

In this context, engagement with the public world can add to phronesis by increased experience with and knowledge of particulars, interactions and contexts. We only really get to this "civic wisdom" through hard personal work, but if Facebook encourages us to prioritize our personal presentations of the self at the expense of the strange, uncomfortable world "out there" our chances of doing this work get minimized. To do much of this work requires us to be periodically untethered from our private, personal networks to examine ourselves in different contexts, to engage with fear, uncertainly, discomfort, loneliness, disconnection, and so on. But these are these subjective emotions that help us stand outside of our preconceived narratives about how the world should be and help us gain the wisdom to be public people engaged with the impersonal world as it is.

Facebook and the Decline of Publicness

What effect does this ability to *proclaim our public self* on social networks have on our attitudes towards public life? To answer this question, it is useful to return to ask a question the sociologist Richard Sennett asked almost 40 years ago: "Is there a difference ... in the expression appropriate for public relations and that appropriate for intimate relations?" (1974: 6).

For Sennett, the answer was a definitive yes. He viewed the city as a public forum where *communicative* interactions would take place. This is different from *intimate* interactions that should take place in private. The city provided a "safe zone" for discussion and dialogue because it excluded personal, emotional, subjective expression. This safety was assured because theirs was a tacit agreement among all involved that the "roles" being played in everyday interactions were tantamount to masks. For Sennett (1974) revealing one's "inner self" in public was anathema to the necessary conventions of city/public life (for example, wearing drab clothing in the Victorian era so as not to be offensively expressive).

This, for Sennett, was the "public world," which has been lost in modernity. It was lost to a drive for self-actualization through the cultivating of an *authentic-self*. More importantly, the search for our inner self has left us as citizens with the inability to "play," or to try on different identities as do actors. This deprivation of our "inner actor," according to Sennett, leaves us wary of public life. The drive to "find ourselves" has left us with impoverished public spaces that are "strange" and "unknown" and hence devoid of interaction with the other.[8]

Early writing on the Web saw it as potentially complementary to Sennett's ideal public sphere. The Internet and, particularly computer-mediated communication (CMC) could ideally be seen as a prevalent means for negotiating identity in a

---

8   Henry Farrell referenced Sennett's work as part of a challenge to Mark Zuckerberg's view of radical transparency in 2010 in a post called "An Internet Where Everyone Knows You're a Dog" at the blog *Crooked Timber* [Online, 14 May].

freewheeling, anonymous space where "wearing masks" was a means of engaging in a form of identity play (Turkle 1995, Chandler 1998, Robinson 2007).

While not quite the physical space of the city that Sennett talked about, the early world of CMC provided the potential for creating a different kind of playful, contingent self. The reality, however, was that these spaces were far from Sennett's "public world." Instead, they were permeated with the same type of race, class and gendered bias that its offline counterpart inhabited (Nakamura 2002). But at the very least, it would de-emphasize the "search for the self" at the expense of the creative public "identity play" that Sennett described in *The Fall of the Public Man*.

The public search for a core identity would be unrecognizable to someone in eighteenth century England. In this society, man was an "actor" that presented emotions rather than revealed them. The display was an "artifice" whereby the "actor" self was removed "at a distance" for the performance of emotion. Public life was a *theatrum mundi* – where everyone was an actor. Genuine expression was regarded as unseemly. In this way, the "public space" of the early web provided much of the same flexibility and creativity afforded Sennett's eighteenth-century "inner actor."

But by the nineteenth century, according to Sennett, artifice was seen as disingenuous. Particularly in the United States where authenticity and integrity were core virtues. Public life was intended to express the virtues of authenticity and politicians were to "represent" genuine emotion rather than to "present" emotion as artifice. Public action became oriented around how one "represented" emotion rather than how it was "presented" (Sennett 1974: 26).

Sennett argues that the expectation of authenticity structures of expectations of public life in unrealistic and ultimately damaging ways. Our assessment of our broken political system is a reflection of this expectation of authenticity. *Playfulness*, or an air of disingenuousness, in public life is seen as a character flaw. We in the United States and Europe constantly decry the low character of our politicians and are disposed to "throw the bums out" at every turn.

In the United States, citizens often ask politicians: "Do politicians genuinely express remorse?" "Are they warm?" "Can they connect with the public?" What matters then is how the politician comes across (for example, is he one of us?). Our "anger," Sennett would argue, comes because we have lost our understanding of play and our ability to don appropriate "masks" in public life. The individual has become an "actor deprived of an art" (1974: 267).

Much of this can be seen in public life. On the right, admonishments that a politician is engaging in "political correctness" is an signal to a specific population that the politician is being inauthentic, or disingenuous, disguising the truth to gain material benefits for their, usually minority, constituency. On the left, politicians are seen as "selling out" to the dictates of corporate capital. What matters thus is perceived authenticity rather than the actual behavior of the elected official. The result, Sennett would argue, is a decay of the public world and a retreat into community to which we are already familiar. The result of all this is the development of a "world without politics" (Schmitt 2007: 116) where social and political forces are completely ignored by the "search for the self."

This critique emerges in popular discourse as a lack of civility. Sennett's "mask" can sound pejorative to some, but it is essential for a functioning democratic society. A modicum of politeness, inauthenticity perhaps, is central to making people feel comfortable with others. Without the norms afforded by a "mask of civility," the desire for people to engage with the other is diminished. The result is an unhealthy, unwelcome polarization in public life. As such, people retreat to those social networks in which they can find comfort. When they do engage politics, they do it with no "mask" or no sense in which there exists another "side." As such, they seek out those communities of interests that reinforce their preexisting views of public life.

Facebook groups encourage this form of political communication. Because there are no non-verbal cues to allow people to self-monitor their behavior, the Facebook group serves as more of a bullhorn to express one's feelings about politics rather than a forum to discover what one thinks about politics. One prime example of the tendency off users to use Facebook groups in this way was a US based group called "I Support the Students sent home for wearing the American Flag."[9] The description of the page was as follows:

> For those of you who support the students in California for getting sent home
> from high school for wearing Red, White, and Blue on Cinco De Mayo, Please
> join this group and help us get the word out about this disgrace to America!

One could envision the Facebook user reading about this story, feeling a sense of outrage and searching for a means through which they could express that outrage to others. The Facebook group serves as the perfect vehicle from which to announce one's dissatisfaction. In this case, as in many of the groups studied, there was no sense in which dissenting views were wanted or even welcome. The site was for expressing collective outrage.

Facebook did not create political polarization or incivility in politics. However, it does provide a cost-effective venue in which to spend time with one's comfortable network of intimates and semi-intimates. This engagement with our hand-picked social networks reinforces a set of expectations about how the world works and how one should behave with others. It frames the world for us as one characterized by *disclosure* and *connection*. And while *connecting* and *disclosing* can be noble pursuits, they lead us to a preoccupation with a mutual exercise in legitimating identity. The users who created the "I Support the Students sent home for wearing the American Flag" are seeking to connect with like-minded others. They are non-engaged in a process of trying to understand why the school did what it did. A

---

9   I Support the Students sent home for wearing the American Flag. (n.d.). In *Facebook* [Group]. Available at: http://facebook.com/group.php?gid=117439354953714 [accessed: 9 August 2010].

preoccupation with *connection* has serious implications for political life, particularly if we disclose and connect as an end in and of itself. As Sennett suggests: "Each person's self has become his principal burden; to know one's self has become an end, instead of a means through which one knows the world" (Sennett 1974: 4).

For Sennett, an obsession with the self, with the personal, leads to a non-recognition of the effect of larger social-structure on the individual life world. Much like Arendt's critique of the "expansion of the private sphere" a retreat to our personal networks on Facebook distracts us from the fact that impersonal, unemotional power dynamics take place independent of whether or not citizens are paying attention. But rather than engage these broader complex forces frankly, we engage them through the lens of *disclosure* and *connection*, we become "angry" at their inauthenticity or develop a "shameful dependency" to authority figures we don't believe are legitimate (Sennett 2003). But our emotion-laden responses to civil society and public institutions do not eliminate them. As such Sennett sees a "vacated" civil society as captured by "internalized domination and legitimation of an over-imposed, undifferentiated, normalizing identity" (Castells 2009: 9).

Facebook serves as an extension of Sennett's observation of the public man in modernity and his preoccupation with the self. However, it isn't correct to say that Facebook users are engaged solely in a narcissistic pursuit. In many ways, Sennett is writing in his time where that language of "self actualization" was more prominent. Indeed, it is not narcissistic to care about family and friends and be interested in their thoughts and feelings. But Facebook does envelop us in a personal world of feelings and observations where the object of the self's attention is familiar and comfortable.

Facebook allows us to create a pre-selected venue where we can comfortably present ourselves to others, and to receive others' presentations of themselves. Undoubtedly, the impulse to have our self-presentations validated by others is essential to our human nature. However, I argue that the more we seek to disclose and connect on Facebook, the more we instill habits of relating to the public, world "out there" through the personal world of disclosure and connection. But we've done little theorizing about what these habits of personalization, these norms of disclosure and connection, do to our shared public life. How does this emphasis on *the personal* change the ways in which we seek to engage in politics? This conflation of the market and the polis or political system has an effect upon us as political subjects. I will turn to that discussion in Chapter 4.

Chapter 4
The Personal Citizen

What does it mean to engage public life through the norms of *disclosure* and *connection*? Expecting the state to be a "friend" we can disclose and connect with conjures up frightening notions of centralized control, like in Orwell's *1984* or *Animal Farm*. Indeed a number of theorists have conceived of the Internet in general as an *electronic panopticon* (Lyon 1994) or *superpanopticon* (Poster 1996) where ubiquitous data capture and dissemination technologies can be uploaded and stored on servers in perpetuity and recalled at will for a whole range of purposes.

The term *panopticon* comes from Jeremy Bentham's design for a circular prison that allowed the guards to view each inmate. In a panopticon, one can be seen without ever being seen. Foucault used the panopticon as a metaphor for power. Rather than be top-down and hegemonic, Foucault contended that power was subtly present throughout social relations. As such, our behavior is controlled, but most of us do not see the sources of that control (Foucault 1977: 201). The result for most is docility about how their information is used by those in power (Foucault 1980: 155–156).

What makes the panopticon so effective is its subtlety. Foucault suggested that the panopticon has the effect whereby prisoners "interiorize" the norms of the overseer (1980: 155). The panopticon inculcates a specific psychic orientation towards "conscious and permanent visibility" (Foucault 1977: 201). As such, power in modern society is driven less by overt power and more by the construction of "self-policing subjects" (Foucault: 1982). As an example, feminist scholars posit gender relations as dominated by a male gaze whereby "a panoptical male connoisseur resides within the consciousness of most women" (Bartky 1998: 72). From this perspective, power results not from a centralized source, but from a social and ontological state that affects the individual's conception of the self.

Is Facebook a modern panopticon? The early Web was conceived of as the exact opposite of a panopticon. It emphasized anonymity and the ability to create identity willy-nilly. The debate centered more on whether this was a largely empowering phenomenon (Turkle 1995), allowing you to side-step hegemonic social norms and allowing for distinct discourse spaces where people can try on alternative selves or a place that allowed *anti-publics* (Cammaerts 2008) to engage in noxious discourse.

At first glance, the panopticon metaphor as applied to Facebook has some appeal. Through Facebook's *architecture of disclosure*, users become comfortable "being watched" by their pre-selected network and indeed seek the attention and recognition of those in their network. While they get to present what is watched, users of Facebook recognize their part of a *revelation regime* where sharing and disclosure are a central part of what takes place on the site. The compulsion to disclose and connect means that the individual takes upon himself the job of regularly "checking-in" to his online Facebook community.

The advent of mobile devices adds even more opportunities to "check in." The size of video cameras makes surveillance ubiquitous, but it is having places where video can be shared with a mediated public that makes it relevant. An important element of the architecture of publicness is the ubiquity of cameras. A combination of increased camera phone quality and the advent of 3 g and 4 g networks has lowered costs for disseminating large volumes of data. The ability to instantaneously share images has radically transformed our experience. Rather than take vacation photos to share with our family and friends later, we can now take the photo, post it to Facebook and wait for our network to respond to our experience.

The social media company *Popcorn* estimates that almost 300,000 status updates are posted to Facebook every minute and nearly 140,000 photos are uploaded to the site each minute (Flacy 2011: Online). Popcorn estimates that at that rate, it would take 15 minutes of photo uploading to equal the number of photographs stored in the New York public photo archive (Flacy 2011: Online).

In addition, by providing us with technologies whereby we can "watch ourselves" (for example, apps that can monitor your daily behavior and automatically post it to Facebook), people can automatically reveal elements of themselves (more on this in Chapter 8). A good example are run-tracking apps that allow for instantaneous posting of your morning run to Facebook or apps that allow you to share weight-loss goals to your network automatically.

But in each of these cases, these are things we want to share with our network. Cascio (2005) calls this voluntary and ubiquitous opportunity for capturing, storing and sharing personal data the *participatory panopticon*. This highlights a paradox regarding Facebook and surveillance. We want to be watched, but we want to be able to control what is watched and who is watching. Facebook is not a webcam. It allows users to construct presentations of themselves to a mostly hand-picked audience. As such, Albrechtslund (2008) challenges using the *panopticon* as a metaphor for social networking. He instead advocates for thinking of SNS as horizontal, mutual, and ultimately beneficial *participatory surveillance*. Rather than posit a hierarchical model of surveillance where subjectivity is removed from the watched, he proposes a model where we actively engage a mutually beneficial process of surveillance. This *participatory surveillance* helps build rather than eliminate subjectivity by allowing users to have power over what is being watched. The *gaze* goes from an external process transmitted to "self policing subjects" to an autonomous and empowering process where users control the gaze.

From this perspective, Facebook is a tool of liberation. Most of us are not on Facebook to spy on one another, but to disclose and connect with one another. Facebook gives us a self-selected "audience of watchers" from which we can craft ourselves. Through social networks, we get to control the watching process and hence have more leverage in power dynamics. Barry (2001) notes that the Internet allows for interactivity (you may) rather than discipline (you must). Rather than have content pushed upon them, Facebook users can control when and how they engage with the medium. Further, they are not constrained with respect to creative expression. Facebook isn't concerned with how and what you share as long as you do so. Jarrett (2008) argues that social interactions on SNS sites are determined by the affective logic of the user and not the machine logic of the site's information architecture. As Jarrett (2008) notes:

> The individual texture, content and style of any individual's contribution to their blog, wiki, Flickr image or podcast, although enabled by the interactive functions of the technology, are not entirely structured by those affordances. This leaves space for creative expression (Online).

This applies to Facebook as well. Because Facebook relies on the cultivation of pre-existing relationships, users already bring in external norms to the Facebook medium. As such, Facebook can be used to foster goals outside Facebook's purview, such as organizing protests for instance. In this way, Facebook places users in control of their presentation of self within their networks.

In addition, one can argue that Facebook's encouragement to disclose and connect lessens our acceptance of more pernicious forms of surveillance from the state. Nock (1993) sees surveillance as necessary in modernity because the social isolation of modern life creates a "society of strangers" (1) that must be controlled through surveillance because social norms are less capable of regulating behavior. Or, as Lyon (2001) put it, "surveillance is the paradoxical product of the quest for privacy" (21). Modernity sets up a dialectic between those advocating for security from "the stranger" in the form of surveillance and those who advocate individual privacy (Lyon 2001).

As such, Facebook may lessen the desire for state-based surveillance by making us more trusting of one another. Herein lies a potential core benefit of social capital for a democratic society (Putnam 2000). The more we are strangers to one another, the less we trust one another and seek and external agent (for example, the state) to maintain order by keeping tabs on us. Conversely, if we are *connected* we would be more resistant to surveillance strategies on the part of the state because we are no longer a "society of strangers."

But if we think of Facebook's popularity as a response to, not a replacement of, the alienation and anonymity of modernity that facilitates surveillance, then our assessment of its impact on society changes. Despite increased connection, we still live in an age of skepticism. Even on Facebook, we are not entirely able to know if someone online is being their authentic-self. The loss of "local information" inherent in online interaction devolves into a "growing savviness of the constructed character of online identity" (Andrejevic 2009: 222). In our own "search for the self," our inability to distinguish the authentic from the inauthentic (even in ourselves) leads us towards a hyper-skepticism that invites us to engage in active surveillance of those with which we engage online, a phenomenon Andrejevic (2009) calls *lateral surveillance*.

Even Facebook, a nonymous space (Zhao et al. 2008) where the identities of people in our network are known to us, is riddled with anecdotes about people who have "said too much." As a response, users have become more savvy about what they reveal to their networks. Indeed, Facebook users now know that employers or ex-boyfriends/girlfriends can surreptitiously pose as "friends" to gain access to their account. This sense that one can't be completely authentic on Facebook because there could be malevolent *lurkers* out there, motivates users to, at the very least, regulate their presentations of self.

Power and Permissible Control

This speaks to a broader level of cynicism in Western society in general. How do you forge authentic connection with others in an age characterized by a freewheeling flow of information? In a globalized world where we come in closer contact with one another but are still a "society of strangers," we are drawn to sources of connection that appear to be in "our control." Jarrett (2008) suggests that power on Facebook can be thought of as "permissible control" (Barry: 2001: 48), or the more seductive power that comes from not appearing to be powerful (Bourdieu 1991). From this critical approach, the power of Facebook comes through what Bauman (1992) calls *affective pleasure* (97).

From this perspective, we do not choose to be on Facebook so much as we are *lured* to Facebook by our innate need to control our lifeworld through controlling the process of *connecting* and *disclosing*. Because no one is directly forcing us into the interaction, we do not see Facebook's pull as coercive; instead we see it as highly gratifying. Hindess (1996) contends that this type of self-policing power is dependent upon the presumed freedom of the subject. Facebook's power is the presumed freedom is provides the user to present his/her identity. As Bauman (2000) puts it:

> Given the intrinsic volatility and unfixity of all or most identities, it is the
> ability to "shop around" in the supermarket of identities, the degree of genuine
> or putative consumer freedom to select one's identity and to hold it as long
> as desired, that becomes the royal road to the fulfilment of identity fantasies.
> Having that ability, one is free to make and unmake identities at will. Or so it
> seems. (83)

Turkle (2011) suggests we are "tethered" to our technology by its allure, its seeming ability to control the messiness of real-time, face-to-face interaction. Power is thus not about what Facebook makes you do, but in the potential exclusion from the future affect you might generate from your engagement with your Facebook group. In this way, it acts much like a highly desired product in a consumer market.

A common refrain among critical theorists is the lament that true individuality is unachievable in modern society (Adorno 1978, Habermas 1973, 1975).

The lure consumer culture, the increased sophistication of advertising, and the professionalization of political communication, has rendered individuals subject to developing "conformist identities" that promote consumption and compliance rather than identities based on values that transcend these institutions (Riesman et al. 2001).

As such, Carpentier (2007: 88) refers to most expression on blogs as "semi-participation" because it fails to engage the hegemonic power of corporate capital. Dahlgren (2005) speaks ruefully about Web 2.0 constituting a market-based "re-feudalization" of the public sphere characterized by the "vertical ownership" of code, content and bandwidth by a few corporations. Rather than provide marginalized voices with a discourse space, Web 2.0 creates a:

> a blurring of the distinction between public and private in political and economic affairs, a rationalization and shrinking of the private intimate sphere (family life) and the gradual shift from an (albeit limited) public of political and cultural debaters to a public of mass consumers. (Dahlgren 1991: 4)

From this perspective, Facebook could serve as a staging ground for the development of "conformist identities" based on legitimation of neoliberal, capital accumulation. The more people present themselves and watch others present themselves on social media sites, the more that information becomes captured and included in personal profiles that can be sold to marketers. Sheehan (2002) finds that while people are generally concerned about privacy, they are much less concerned about it vis-à-vis commercial online applications. As such, they are *disciplined* to accept the legitimacy of privacy violations for the purpose of market capitalism.

Evidence of this is the scant few political Facebook groups of the 250 studied that challenged neoliberal market principles. A few group pages sought to recruit members to Socialist parties, but very few sites addressed larger issues of global capital. When groups were organized for mobilization they tended to address nation states as with this one from the United States called "1,000,000 Strong Against The Stimulus Scam!"[1] that called on users to contact their elected officials to reject President Barack Obama's 2009 Stimulus Bill or this group or a UK-based site called "Boycott Beijing 2008 Olympics"[2] on the ground that the nation was a violator of human rights. Indeed, at least in these two cases, groups sought to support neoliberal positions on policy issues.

The terms "corporation" or "company" rarely appear within the title or description of Facebook groups. I could only find a handful of appearances of these terms. Only one "non-neutral" appearance of the term "company" appeared in the 550 instances, and that instance was part of a challenge to a state-run company. A group based in Chile called "President Piñera: You must make an International

---

1   1,000,000 Strong Against The Stimulus Scam! (n.d.). In *Facebook* [Group]. Available at: http://facebook.com/posted.php?id=139725785416. [accessed: 13 August 2010].

2   Boycott Beijing 2008 Olympics. (n.d.). In *Facebook* [Group]. Available at: http://facebook.com/group.php?gid=10654392885 [accessed: 4 August 2010].

Audit of CODELCO."[3] The group was created to pressure the country's president to investigate corruption and inefficiency within the state run copper company.

Why is this the case? In *Discipline and Punish*, Foucault (1977) defines *discipline* as "the correct training of the individual," which reproduces subjects oriented towards the dictates of the powerful. But how does Facebook "train the individual" to orient themselves towards the dictates of the powerful? I argue this happens because Facebook orients us towards the personal.

Rose (1990) claims that, since World War I, "psychologically inspired techniques of self-inspection and self-examination" have come to be utilized throughout social and political institutions, with the effect of shifting "the problems of defining and living a good life ... transposed *from an ethical to a psychological register*" (p. viii, his emphasis). For Rose, this distinction is critical because it produces an increased emphasis on the "care of the self" as central to personal and professional success. Rose suggests that because the tools for structuring a meaningful life, what Foucault et al. (1988) call "technologies of the self," have dictated an emphasis on self-esteem and personal satisfaction at the expense of "technologies of the self" geared towards living a virtuous and ethical life.

For Rose, this process of "self-inspection, self-problematization, self-monitoring, and confession" whereby we evaluate ourselves according to public norms, renders us passive subjects. These public norms we draw from have been subtly co-opted by political power and consumer society, or in his terms "the regulatory apparatus of the modern state" (Rose 1996: 26). By being socially driven to externally imposed norms of 'self-improvement" and "self-understanding" we have subjectified ourselves in a way that renders us docile political subjects:

> Incorporating, shaping, channeling, and enhancing subjectivity have been intrinsic to the operations of government ... not ... through the growth of an omnipotent and omniscient central state whose agents institute a perpetual surveillance and control ... Rather, government of subjectivity has taken shape through the proliferation of a complex and heterogeneous assemblage of technologies ... bringing the varied ambitions of political, scientific, philanthropic, and professional authorities into alignment with ... the selves each of us want to be. (Rose 1990: 213)

This last piece of this quote is important. The "technologies of the self" like Facebook allow us have our aspirations aligned with the dictates of political power and consumer society. The regulatory apparatus of the modern state is not something imposed from above, but it is something ingrained from within.

---

3   Presidente Piñera: Se debe hacer una Auditoría Internacional a CODELCO (President Piñera: You must make an International Audit of CODELCO). (n.d.). In *Facebook* [Group]. Available at: http://facebook.com/group.php?gid=281194070190&v=wall&ref=share [accessed: 2 August 2010].

For Rose (1996), a citizen preoccupied with the "self as a problem" is an ideal citizen in a neoliberal society. The elements of the self – freedom, choice and activity – are the hallmarks of an actualized neoliberal citizen (Palmer 2003). As such, citizens that pursue their own personal self-actualization, self-satisfaction project seldom question the efficacy of a neoliberal, capitalist system. This is the case because consumer society posits the citizen as an in-control, "active agent" that gets to choose between different types of consumption (Rose 1990).

Building on Foucault et al. (1988) one could see Facebook, at least in part, as a "technology of the self." As discussed in the last chapter, the part of Facebook that pulls us to disclose, pulls us further into the *personal*, a process of *presenting a self* to others and receiving self-presentations from others. This pre-occupation with self-presentation and self-disclosure, at the expense of larger structural forces that shape society, could be thought of as instilling a *discipline* towards ideal neoliberal citizens. Paradoxically, our engagement in a community becomes individualized. We choose the terms of our presentation of self. Who sees it? What is presented? The what, how and when of a status update are in our control, much more so than in everyday interaction where engagement with others is subject to more spontaneity and uncertainty (for example, factors that are beyond our control). As such, Facebook upholds the neoliberal idea of freedom, while providing users a forum for connection. But "choosing" to *perform the self* to a self-selected audience on a *setting* (Facebook) that encourages this performance in order to create a consumer profile of users is a pyrrhic choice. As Palmer (2003) highlights, one element of the tools of discipline is providing subjects with the illusion of choice:

> The paradox of user control, in fact, becomes that of the illusion of choice within which the user is offered up for a form of soft domination. Thus not only are discourses of consumer empowerment embedded in a neoliberal political agenda – embodied by its pillars of individualism, freedom and self-expression – the "performative subject" produced by most existing forms of participatory real time media is arguably the ideal flexible subject position enabled by contemporary capitalism (161).

From this perspective, more attention needs to be paid to Facebook as a *setting*. What forms of engagement and network formation does Facebook encourage. The user on Facebook is encouraged to engage with his/her network in ways that support a neoliberal impulse to see the *political subject* as a consumer. It is more than a little ironic that the private expressions of a user's intimate thoughts are accompanied by a banner advertisement.

One example of this is the *like* button, a central feature of Facebook's architecture of revelation. Franzen (2011) provides an interesting example of this phenomenon occurring on Facebook. He suggests that "liking" on Facebook becomes an assertion of consumer choice:

The striking thing about all consumer products — and none more so than electronic devices and applications — is that they're designed to be immensely likable. This is, in fact, the definition of a consumer product, in contrast to the product that is simply itself and whose makers aren't fixated on your liking it. (Online)

The emphasis on "liking" structures social interactions on Facebook. On one level, an emphasis on "likes" suits a market-based economy where consumption is a priority. The idea of a "like" button suggests a mediated space that encourages positive presentations of self at the expense of negative or *critical* presentations. Nowhere is this more apparent than in Facebook presentations of parenting. Few parents want to construct their identities as neglectful or abusive. As such, parents' presentations of children on Facebook consist of cute anecdotes or pictures of them smiling and enjoying themselves, with the occasional wry comment about the difficulty of parenting thrown in for good measure.

A positive presentation of self might be important in the private realm. But democratic societies are both *market* and *polis* and, as such, a discourse space needs to accommodate different types of discourse. But this would not be arrived at simply through Facebook's adoption of a "hate" button, although this would provide more data to convert into more sophisticated use profiles. Facebook as a public discourse space is better understood as a medium where people can collectively "hate" those things they find alien to group norms. However, Facebook groups are not a space that seems to accommodate a discussion of things by which citizens are confused or made uncomfortable – things where the individual's *presentation of the self* is not the primary motivation for engaging in communication, where "citizen-users" are trying to collectively figure out why a phenomenon is happening. An inability to move outside the personal world of "feelings" and to the public world of "shared things" legitimates those already made powerful in neoliberal societies.

As an example, Gerodimos (2010) finds that youth see civic engagement online from a consumerist paradigm (market-oriented) rather than from a civic-polis based view of citizen engagement. The result is a citizen as "consumer with caveats," who engages in politics subject to a series of "terms and conditions" (2010) for participating online that include:

> the benefits of civic action must be highlighted and they must be tangible; the reasons for engaging in such action should be transparent and relevant; the act of participation itself should not stress the individual's resources; the user-citizen-consumer should be able to choose why, when and how they will engage with a public affair or cause. (135)

Absent from this list is any consideration of civic duty or obligation. Curiously, Gerodimos (2010) did find other communitarian values became prevalent in youth narratives including "emotional engagement, empathy and willingness to engage with public issues and to make a difference, as well as the need to see that others care" (126).

But this need for politics to "emotionally connect" with users doesn't lead to a more vibrant democratic society. Marlin-Bennett (2011) makes a provocative argument that information technology does not so much make us positive, but has the effect of "flattening emotion" (137). For her, applications like Facebook mediate emotion by providing temporal distance that removes the contingency and element of surprise from emotional presentation. She quotes the poet Walt Whitman's view that "sensation is inexorably imbricated with passionate care" (136). As such, emotional presentation devoid of "meat" sensation is "flattened" or "exaggerated" either in the direction of being negative and aggressive or positive or ebullient (137).

A good example of Marlin-Bennett's points from the groups I studied was an England-based group called "ITS NOT RACIST TO WANT THE BEST FOR OUR COUNTRY."[4] The site's description, all in capital letters, encourages like-minded Britons to resist what the user perceives to be unwanted changes in their country:

> YOU SHOULDNT BE MADE TO FEEL LIKE A RACIST COS YOU WANT WHATS BEST FOR OUR COUNTRY ... OUR SOCIETY, OUR COUNTRY AND OUR EVERYDAY WAY OF LIFE IS BEEN THREATENED BY THESE PEOPLE WHO FLOCK TO OUR BORDERS IN THEIR THOUSANDS AND SEEK TO CHANGE US BY RADICAL AND EXTREMIST MEANS. THIS IS ONLY A FACEBOOK GROUP BUT ITS A PLATFORM FOR BRITISH PEOPLE WHO ALL FEEL THE SAME TO BE IN ONE PLACE AND SHOW THEIR SUPPORT FOR THE CAUSE. SOMETHING NEEDS TO BE DONE ABOUT THIS CRISIS AND THIS IS ONLY THE BEGINNING!!

The anger and frustration revealed in this user's narrative is palpable. But it is a discourse that one would have difficulty envisioning taking place at a dinner party. This is because communication on Facebook Groups is an asynchronous communication environments that where the parties are not simultaneous "co-utterers" (Galimberti and Riva 2001: 7). Online communication like instant chat can be synchronous, but on Facebook, communication was more like email where one person was the sender and the audience received the message. This is what Kock (2004: 177) called an environment with "low social presence" because they lack the non-verbal cues of face-to-face interaction, leaving users to "encode" what is missing from the communication.

The ability to control interactions might be more convenient, but it makes public life less free-wheeling and spontaneous. A *deeply personal* world is a secure world. But it is an increasingly predictable and routinized world. Does the

---

4   ITS NOT RACIST TO WANT THE BEST FOR OUR COUNTRY. (n.d.). In *Facebook* [Group]. Available at: http://facebook.com/group.php?gid=332774227635 [accessed: 12 August 2010].

architecture of disclosure connect you so closely to your pre-existing networks that it takes some of the "magic" out of everyday life? To think about this question, envision this quote from DeLong (2010) about Facebook's social graph:

> If you imagine a television designed around the social graph, you turn it on and it says, 'Thirteen of your friends like Entourage. Press play. Your dad recorded 60 Minutes. Press play.'" In other words, the world will be experienced through the filter of one's Facebook friends. (Online)

This more routinized and more predictable daily life matters on two levels. Interacting with friends spontaneous in "meat space" is different than engaging them online. Engaging with friends in a controlled mediated space makes us less comfortable with spontaneity and contingency. As such, we demand a public life that is free of these things. Second, interacting spontaneously with strangers, strangely in "strange places," is important for the development of essential elements of civic wisdom: humility, a sense of contingency, a desire to listen, an ability to ask the question "what if I'm wrong?" In a brilliant essay, Smith (2010) crystalizes her concern about Facebook in this passage:

> I am dreaming of a Web that caters to a kind of person who no longer exists. A private person, a person who is a mystery, to the world and—which is more important—to herself. Person as mystery: this idea of personhood is certainly changing, perhaps has already changed. (2010)

Smith (2010) highlights a core truth about democratic life. To be truly public, we need to be private. For true democracy to be realized online, "people must be able to imagine the embodiment, the reality of those they only meet in the sensory poor setting of cyberspace" (Marlin-Bennett 2011: 129). This lack of empathic connection to the other means we can't see that we are linked to a "world of things." If the Facebook political groups I studied are any indication, there is little empathic connection to strangers occurring on the site. Two ways in which in which we lose this embodiment and empathic connection to strangers is through how Facebook changes our sense of *escape*.

Facebook and Escape

The impulse to want to escape is a common condition of modern society. Cohen and Taylor (1992) characterize escapes as: "interruptions in the flow of life, interludes, temporary breaks, skirmishes, glimpses of other realities" (45). These instances of "breaking out of the routine" (48) can be as innocuous as watching TV or as potentially harmful as taking drugs. Breaks from routine are useful as escapes as long as they remain novel. Once things become normalized and routinized, they lose its ability to "resist" the routine of the everyday.

But Cohen and Taylor (1992) pose a paradox about escape. While we want breaks to be novel and exciting, at the same time we don't want our escapes to be too unfamiliar. We seek autonomy and self-determination through breaking with routine. But these attempts at escape are ultimately destined to fail us because we are a product of the routines our society produces. So when we escape, we do so with all of our societal expectations. So our escapes themselves are routinized (familiar TV programs, pre-packaged Disney tourism).

Facebook is a routinized escape into one's social network, particularly because the ability to participate in a system comprised of members of your personal network producing ambient updates can serve as an escape from the drudgery of everyday life without being too unfamiliar. When compared to MySpace, Facebook's main SNS competitor up until very recently, Facebook produces a pleasant medium for escape. Using McCluhan's (1969) famous distinction, Facebook is a *cool medium* where fewer of the senses are engaged and in which more active sensory participation is needed from the audience member. Facebook has a clean, linear, unobtrusive background. By contrast, MySpace was McLuhan's (1969) example of a *hot medium* – noisy, nonlinear and customizable. It is partly because MySpace allowed members more freedom to access the HTML and CSS programming codes to alter and personalize their pages. As such, the look of MySpace was more chaotic, informal and improvisational. By contrast, Facebook's clean, blocky, controlled layout means every profile is basically the same. MySpace was open and allowed for distinctiveness, but it meant that poor programmers could also create clunky scripts that took a long time to load thereby slowing up the process.

Why has Facebook nearly decimated its rival, particularly since in the West, the individual is the central paradigm? Although we are expected to be individual, authentic and autonomous in neoliberal Western Democracies, the more controlled environment of Facebook won. It has done so because the individualism we seek must take place within a prescribed set of rules (Lyon 1994). The core contradiction of modern Western life is that we are supposed to "find our authentic selves" within a rigid social structure. Hence the Starbucks barista is supposed to seem authentic but adhere to corporate strictures at the same time, a phenomenon Ritzer (1993) calls *false fraternization* (134).

In many ways, Facebook is a form of *false fraternization* not because the relationships we are engaged in on Facebook are false, but because they occur within a routinized setting, one that allows us to "safely escape" from the difficulty *private work* of friendship into a setting that is familiar while allowing us to engage in the nonymous identity play that appeals to our sense of the "specialness of inner life." Our sense of our own distinctiveness, reinforced by neoliberal culture, makes us want to impose ourselves on the world. As Cohen and Taylor (1992) put it we:

> attempt transformations of reality by bringing our fantasies into the real world. In other words, instead of allowing fantasies to be mere adjuncts to existing scripts, we actually set out to script our fantasies, to give some concrete expression to our imaginings. (109)

But to do this, we must engage in risk. While we love our routines because they provide us with a sense of "ontological security," we seek to distance ourselves from them for the very same reason. Facebook provides perfect vehicle for escape, it is familiar but provides the sense of structured novelty and spontaneity that a proper escape necessitates.

However, these aren't escapes at all in the true sense. Sharing photos of the family vacation or a pithy "motivational saying" from the day or playing FarmVille isn't really an escape … it is part of our friendship obligations. To truly be an escape we must break from what is familiar, we must:

> transcend the limitations of ordinary landscaping, to construct a realm so far
> away from home that literally and metaphorically you are *beyond reach* … For
> such trips, you must take risks. (Cohen and Taylor 1992: 196)

This is what Facebook denies us. The advent of smart phones and ubiquitous wireless networks make it difficult for us to truly retreat to "foreign spaces." Even when we are "beyond reach," we are a status update away from our social network. Cohen and Taylor (1992) suggest that we may do this as a way to make "foreign spaces," full of crime, pollution and diversity more predictable. Our desire to escape is mitigated by our craving for security and familiarity. We want novelty and excitement, but we want the comfort and security of familiarity. Cohen and Taylor (1992) presaged our modern condition:

> This it seems is how we are destined to live, as split personalities in which the
> private life is disturbed by the promise of escape routes to another reality – (and
> curiously) private life is held out as an escape. (155)

We escape the drudgery of "the private" by retreating into the personal on Facebook. But the private lifeworld gets constantly intruded upon by the larger social world "out there." Rather than have the mass media provide this unfiltered intrusion, the "world out there" is filtered by our online friendship networks. This makes the world "out there" seem understandable:

> For most of us … reality appears relatively friendly. Most of the time the world
> looks and feels like our own. We pass our time in it with the help of a set of
> established constructions which allows us to see it as stable, orderly, even
> "normal." (39)

What does this increased ability to retreat into a structured network of the personal? How does it affect the way we engage with others? I suggest that the *architecture of disclosure* changes our interaction with our networks by enveloping us in a system of permissible control, changing the nature of our relationships from "private work" to performance, and providing a convenient means of escaping the drudgery of routine by engaging with a network that is, unto itself, both routine and structured.

We all want to escape at times. If we can create a mechanism that allows us more sustained contact with a self-selected set of intimates (and quasi-intimates) most of us would take it, particularly because the familiar increases our ability to assess risk. Hsu et al. (2005) found that, when subjects were asked to guess the color of a card and knew how many red cards and black cards remained in the deck, subjects experienced more brain activity in the striatum, a part of the brain known for calculating rewards. When subjects were not told how many of each card remained in the deck but were asked to guess, subjects produced more activity in the amygdala, the brain's "fear center."

This manifests in political talk on Facebook by giving us an increased sense that we "know the world" because we "know others" in our networks. This calcifying of our lifeworld leads to the creation of Facebook political groups that are more focused on finding sympathetic others that "know the world" and can spot transgressions on what is true and correct or can help users uphold what is known. An example from the groups I studied was a France based group called "Proud to be French!"[5] that sought to organize meetings, presumably around things French.

But this "known world" is familiar and comfortable. It is also a world that lacks mystery and intrigue. Illusion is an important part of our intimate relationships. Part of what draws us to other people is what we do not know about them. Whitchurch et al. (2011) conducted an experiment on 47 University of Virginia undergraduates and asked them to rate their level of attractiveness to 4 male students based on their Facebook profiles. While the female subjects were drawn to men who the rated them as "appealing," they were even more drawn to the men for whom they had no information regarding their attractiveness rating.

In some ways, mystery about political belief is an important social glue. This is because for most people our within-network communication is about forming bonds and discussions of politics are things that can inhibit bonding. This is why we have a paucity of "political talk" in our public life (Eliasoph 1998). Hence the old adage, "never talk about religion or politics." Facebook users must walk a fine line between using political performance to connect with others who "know the world" the way they do and not alienating networks that are based on things other than political identity. Facebook groups allow for a channeling of political views that might inhibit bonding with others in the network towards a platform that is tailor made for the performance of political identity. But performing can be problematic. Feeling comfortable enough to engage in honest "political talk" reveals a self that is perhaps too certain of the response they will receive and too fixed in their sense of a political self. These selves can receive contradictorily political information, but the mediated nature of Facebook allows them to ignore it, or even eliminate the object of the political information from their purview.

---

5 Fier d'être Français (Proud to be French!) (n.d.). In *Facebook* [Group]. Available at: http://facebook.com/group.php?gid=8206789197&v=app_2373072738 [accessed: 12 August 2010].

Chapter 5
Engagement as Personal Citizens

Instead of asking whether Facebook leads us to participate in politics more, a more appropriate question might be whether Facebook changes how we think of politics. Up until now, Facebook scholarship has looked at whether Facebook enhances "civic engagement" (Ellison et al.2007, Kahne et al. 2010), but perhaps a more salient question is how and whether our engagement with Facebook affects what it actually "feels like" to be a citizen (Leblanc 1999). Perhaps Facebook's pull towards *the personal* is a net positive for civic life by bringing more aspects of everyday life into the realm of the political. If everyday identity construction is constitutive of the political, then Facebook's emphasis on disclosure and connection brings this aspect of social life to the fore.

One possibility is that Facebook further opens up a space for individuals to present themselves to a public. This very act is in itself political, particularly for marginalized voices that otherwise might remain silent and hence unseen. Feminist scholars (Benhabib 1996, Pateman 1970) have noted that women's everyday experience has been relegated to the "charm" of the private sphere. Elevating the "politics of the everyday" is a way to challenge against a normalizing hegemonic discourse based around a uniform public sphere. Theorists like Iris Marion Young (1990) and Chantal Mouffe (1992) critique a universal idea of "the public" because it disembodies beings from their particular experience. This emphasis on individual distinctiveness situates people within their unique contexts by seeking to affirm group rights. As Coleman (2005) suggests:

> The increasingly accepted notion that the personal is political challenges the belief that experience is only politically significant if it can be represented as a collective interest. As people have adopted more personalised conceptions of political life, greater significance has been attached to narrative testimony, dramatic enactment and public conversation as forms of political self-representation. (275)

This would suggest a heightened role for Facebook and other Internet tools in making the personal political by enabling a "differentiated citizenship" (Young 1990: 119) in which the "common good" is brought about by recognizing individual and group differences rather than by some search for a shared public consensus. Facebook allows users to engage politics from their "situated positions" (Young 1990: 56) rather than have to make an appeal from a dispassionate, rational "common good" position which Young (1990) considers artificial:

the ideal of impartiality in moral theory [that] expresses a logic of identity that
seeks to reduce differences to unity ... the stances of detachment and dispassion
that supposedly produce impartiality are attained only by abstracting from the
particularities of situation, feeling, affiliation, and point of view. (97)

My examination of political Facebook groups reveals that few groups develop
from "stands of detachment and dispassion." Rather than provide a forum for
discourse, Facebook groups facilitate a "plurality of voices." From Young's (1990)
perspective, this is normative for democratic life as it renders conflict, rather than
consensus, as constitutive of the political. From this perspective, the idea that
Facebook users should create groups that encourage deliberation and dialogue
emerges from naive notions of a monolithic public sphere where the conceptions of
the "public good" are neutral and not shaped by the powerful at the expense of the
marginalized. For Young, and other feminist theorists (Nussbaum 2001), politics
needs to be intimately private and emotional to be effective. A *personalization* of
politics brought about by Facebook is thus a welcome change from the rationality
and abstraction of the traditional "public sphere."

Personal stories are how we relate to the political. As Dewey (1991) noted,
notions of the public begin with private interactions:

> When the consequences of action are confined, or are thought to be confined,
> mainly to the persons directly engaged in it, the transaction is a private one
> ... Yet if it is found that the consequences ... extend beyond the two directly
> concerned, that they affect the welfare of many others, the act acquires a public
> capacity. (13)

Plummer (2003) makes the case that the personal can serve as a bridge between
the public and the private by emphasizing an *intimate citizenship*. Challenging
Arendt's views of public and private, Plummer argues that what binds us together
is personal life, the "erotic, intimate desires, pleasures, relationships and 'gender
experiences'" we all have (Plummer 2003: 151). The *good society* in Plummer's
view allows the public sphere to include a broad range of personal stories:

> Intimate citizenship does not imply one model, one pattern, one way. On the
> contrary, it is a loose term which comes to designate a field of stories, an array
> of tellings, out of which new lives, new communities and new politics may
> emerge. (152)

For Plummer, even if it were preferable to construct a more formal, impersonal
public sphere, it would be impossible to do now. For Plummer, there is no return
to Sennett's (1974) world of *masks* or Arendt's (1958) shared table:

> The changing intimacies of the late modern world, along with the ceaseless
> quest for more and more choices in one's personal life, have meant that many

lives are now engulfed in moral wars around family politics, identity politics, gender politics, religious politics, technological politics, and of course, sexual politics. (Plummer 2003: 34)

He advocates reconceiving citizenship to account for the individual's personal, inner life. In this *intimate citizenship*, we build common interest around stories of the personal. Online discourse would appear to be well suited for Plummer's *intimate citizenship*. Rather than one shared public sphere, the "virtual sphere" (Papacharissi 2002) has "several culturally fragmented cyberspheres that occupy a common virtual space" (22).

At its best, computer mediated communication (CMC) has provided a pathway for granting voice to these different stories of the personal. Blogs, for instance, allows users to construct a page and populate it with any personal story they choose. A comments section gives them the ability to track and gauge recognition and legitimacy from a diverse set of others. It allows people to break from the sense of alienation they might feel in a culture they think does not regard their views as legitimate. As Thompson (1995) noted about early blogs:

> From this maximalist perspective of the political, blogs do – in many cases – politicise the private, fuelled by the politics of visibility or 'the struggles for visibility', which characterise the 'non-localized space of mediated publicness. (247)

Cammaerts (2008) claims the blogosphere engages in "radical plurality" by turning the audience into "micro publics" with an emphasis on the intimate and the authentic. Facebook groups provide opportunities to create these micro-publics around shared issues. A number of sites were created to simply express support for or opposition to a specific group or event. As an example, a US-based group called "*If/When Proposition 8 Passes we will do Something about it!*"[1] that linked to a website to express opposition to a measure making gay marriage unconstitutional in California.

Groups like this one constitute what Mouffe (1992) calls an *agonistic public space* that serves as an "expression of dissensus" (in Carpentier and Cammaerts 2008: 11). As such, Facebook groups may help create the more pluralistic public sphere theorists like Young (1990) and Plummer (2003) regard as indicative of the *good society* where the Web encourages this assertion and cultivation of individual voice. *Groups* allowed for a diverse range of expression. Castells (2007) refers to this infrastructure as *mass self-communication*, a transmission to a potentially global audience through high speed, peer to peer networks that "is self-generated in content, self-directed in emission, and self-selected in reception by many that communicate with many (Castells 2007: 248).

---

1   If/When Proposition 8 Passes we will do Something about it! (n.d.). In *Facebook* [Group]. Available at: http://facebook.com/group.php?gid=92225500437 [accessed: 13 August 2010].

From this perspective, Facebook provides an *empowering exhibitionism* or a "refusal to be humble" or keep things private (Koskela 2004) that allows individuals to *exhibit* their identities in ways heretofore impossible. Many of the groups studied were created as personal proclamations rather than deliberative forums. Groups like *"Wherever I stand, I Stand with Israel!"*[2] (UK) or *"Stop special treatment of indigenous"*[3] (Norway) are more like revelations, things users needed to "get off of their chest," rather than exercises in consensus building.

This forum for public proclamation allows individuals "claim copyright to their own lives" (9). We have been socialized by a generation of reality television shows to embrace "looking into" the lives of others as a norm. Without shows like Big Brother and American Idol, it might not have been possible for people to become comfortable peering into each other's lives without apprehension. In these cases, users are looking to make these political statements in the hopes that others will "hear" them.

Facebook can thus be seen as "bringing the subject back in" to political discussion. Facebook provides an open venue for representations. Rather than have their views filtered through public officials, the Facebook group allows a proclamation of one's public political self. Koskela (2004) suggested within the context of webcams, that "it is a radical act to install a camera that shows your private life to an unknown audience" (206). A similar thing could be said about presenting a public self on Facebook, particularly if a user is presenting a marginalized identity or taking an unpopular position.

For example, a Venezuelan group entitled "DOWN WITH THE DICTATORSHIP IN VENEZUELA"[4] (translated from Spanish) that was created by the user for: "everyone who is against the Socialism of the 21th century, which is the same as the new dictatorship of the living ... all opposed to the disguise of the New Communism" (translated from Spanish). Facebook allowed this user a venue to express political dissent in ways that they may be reluctant to do in an off-line public forum.

Viewed in this light, Facebook's architecture of disclosure may encourage this intimate citizenship. To the extent that Facebook follows the model of the blogosphere, Facebook can be seen as participatory, interactive and emancipatory: it allows people spaces in which to express themselves politically. It allows the

---

2   Wherever I stand, I Stand with Israel! (n.d.). In *Facebook* [Group]. Available at: http://facebook.com/pages/Wherever-I-Stand-I-Stand-with-Israel/133611893319833 [accessed: 17 August 2010].

3   Stopp særbehandlingen av urfolk (*Stop special treatment of indigenous*). (n.d.). In *Facebook* [Group]. Available at: http://facebook.com/group.php?gid=53576620956 [accessed: 9 August 2010].

4   ABAJO A LA DICTADURA EN VENEZUELA. NO AL MIEDO.!!! (Down with the Venezuelan Dictatorship... no to fear) (n.d.). In *Facebook* [Group]. Available at: http://facebook.com/group.php?gid=75060492560 [accessed: 10 August 2010].

marginalized to tell stories previously relegated to private life, and this can equate to gains in a form of power.

Facebook and Political Listening

While the critique of a uniform public sphere is important, the expression of "voice" is insufficient in a vibrant democratic society. Hindman (2009) argues that in general, few people use Internet for politics (one tenth of 1 percent of all Internet traffic) and those who do they are greeted with a cacophony of elite voices. To the extent that the Internet has affected politics, Hindman argues, it is through "back end" functions (fundraising, volunteer coordinating, and so on) rather than "retail" ones. As such, Hindman (2009) argues that "speaking" online is of little consequence since no one is listening because "… only a few dozen political bloggers get as many readers as a typical college newspaper" (103).

Schlozman, Verba and Brady (2010) take Hindman's critique of the role of the Internet in politics one step further. They found that the proportion of donations under 50 dollars in the 2008 US Presidential election was the same offline as online (roughly 38 percent). The authors found that those who make small donations online are well off financially, leading them to conclude that while there were more contributors, the Web did not enhance the ability to bring in less-affluent donors. They extend this analysis into dissemination of information and find that the Web does not affect socio-economic stratification. They conclude there is "a strong positive relationship between [socio-economic status] and — with the possible exception of political social networking — every measure of Internet-based political engagement we reviewed" (506).

Davis (2010) echoes Schlozman et al.'s findings in the UK context. In his study of 100 interviews with political actors operating within the UK Parliament he finds that the Web enhances the public sphere within a narrow confined set of actors, what he calls a "fatter" public sphere, but that is creating a gap between the already engaged or interested and the already disengaged and disinterested. This gap reinforces what Couldry (2010) eloquently calls a "crisis of voice":

> Human beings can give an account of themselves and of their place in the world
> … Treating people as if they lack that capacity is to treat them as if they were not
> human; the past century provides many shameful examples of just this. Voice is
> one word for that capacity, but *having a voice is never enough. I need to know*
> *that my voice matters in various ways* (my emphasis). Yet we have grown used to
> ways of organizing things that ignore voice, that assume voice does not matter.
> We are experiencing a contemporary crisis of voice, across political, economic
> and cultural domains, that has been growing for at least three decades. (1)

Without understanding "that my voice matters," voice is wanting as a political tool. Bickford (1996: 13) refers to this as a failure of *democratic attention* in making assessments about others. Effective democratic deliberation requires the cultivation of this *attention* to make effective assertions about the motives of others. The expression of voice requires someone be listening to that voice.

It is very possible that Plummer (2003) is right that a return to a citizenship characterized by and objective and impartial public sphere is long gone. But effective democratic systems need at least some degree of deliberation. The view of democracy as deliberation is concomitant with Aristotelian ideas of democratic politics and Habermasian ideas of reason in political discourse (Dryzek 1990). A deliberative approach presumes an element of social learning about public affairs. Deliberative citizens in democratic systems acquire a set of skills include listening to the other, being openness to changing one's mind and being willing to live with difference (Roberts 1997, Ryfe 2002).

Early Web utopianists viewed the Internet as a *digital public sphere* where "people can deliberate about their common affairs, and as an arena, or space, in which this can happen naturally" (London 1995: Online). Like the English coffee houses and French salons of the seventeenth and eighteenth centuries, this idea of a *digital public sphere* was intended to be a space where citizens would come together in the spirit of egalitarian discussion about reasoned solutions to public issues. The public sphere, by definition, is independent from state and market. It is ideally "a discursive arena that is home to citizen debate, deliberation, agreement and action" (Villa 1992: 712).

A purely deliberative polity has always been a normative idea, not a practical reality. This is because either the powerful simply do not seek to include citizens in the power-laden process of decision-making (King et al.: 1998), it is impossible to eliminate the various dimensions inequality and marginalization from deliberative discourse (Young 1990); or because only a select few people want to be bothered with the mundane details of political life (Hibbing and Theiss-Morse: 2002).

Despite the promise of the early Web many of these challenges remain online. Himelboim (2010) found that in online news groups, 2 percent of people who start discussion threads attracted 50 percent of the replies. And of those who start discussion threads, more often than not, they are linking to other media sources rather than offering comments and opinion. Sixty percent of the time, the links were from traditional media sources. Similarly, Schradie (2011) found that the voices online were dominated by those with higher incomes and education levels, just as in offline life. She found that college graduates were one and a half times more likely to blog, two times more likely to post photos and videos and three times more likely to comment in online forums.

Perhaps Facebook might be a remedy to the problem of not listening to the other. As a path to more deliberate conversation, Facebook's *newsfeed* format provides an interesting counterpoint to the rest of the Web. As Kushin and Kitchener (2009) points out the "newsfeed" feature in Facebook changes the way information is received by users in ways that might allow for exposure to a plurality of perspectives. Because notifications of a group being liked comes across in an unfiltered stream of content, Facebook acts differently than the rest of the Web where users explicitly seek out political news. The newsfeed lets people come across a group with a hyperlink to the page without having to actively seek it out. Brundidge (2006) found that while individuals did seek out likeminded partners for political discussion, they were not averse to engaging with non-likeminded partners "when they are inadvertently exposed to them" (7). Conceivably, this leads to an engagement with information one might not have necessarily sought out.

Of course, people might choose to ignore a newsfeed item about a group whose views they vehemently disagree? But on issues where the lines are not as clearly drawn, Facebook could initiate a conversation among one's social network that can travel across weak ties. One interesting feature of Facebook's newsfeed is the ability to gain a glimpse of other people's social networks. When someone provides a status update and a user comments on it, they can see everyone else who has commented on that same update, whether they are friends or not, meaning the status update serves as a key node for interaction. This provides a useful heterogeneity for interpreting news events. One could envision a collective event like a terrorist attack being discussion across networks on Facebook through this aspect of the status update.

MacKinnon (2004) presaged this type of information flow. Rather than a linear one-to-many conversation between media and audience, Facebook's architecture creates a nonlinear, multidirectional, viral "information community" (10). This multi-directionality allows these communities to fill "information gaps" left by mainstream media outlets and expands the range of issues that can be brought to public attention. To the extent that newsfeeds reflect networks formed by social proximity rather than shared interest, this can provide an important vehicle for cross-cutting conversation (Mutz 2002).

The Problem with Personalizing Politics

While Facebook has the potential to expose users to a more diverse set of views, a more realistic possibility is that Facebook exacerbates the trend towards a polarized view of the world. This is not because Facebook constrains access to the view of others, but because the *architecture of disclosure* is set up to encourage more *disclosure* and less *listening*. For most people, constant communication with people with whom they disagree is unpleasant. If a system allows us to opt out of engaging, we will. Facebook makes it easy to *de-friend* or *ignore* updates from people we do not want to interact with. This can be done anonymously with little effort.

An important element inherent in the power of telling your story in the setting in which that story is being told. Livingstone (2005) claims that in the mass-media environment of the twenty-first century "audiences are on the rise while publics are in retreat" (35). An example of this is the daytime talk show. talk shows in the United States publicize people's most intimate thoughts creating "a public sphere of exhibition" where the goal is not deliberation but display ... less the "conclusion of an argument than an experiment in lifestyles" (12) that "*portrays*

*ordinary people discussing topical issues in public with experts - yet it refers to
its audiences rather than to the public; indeed it is often taken as representing the
antithesis of rational public debate"* (20).

I argue that this applies to Facebook as well. On one level, Facebook provides
a seemingly natural forum to tell and share "stories" and present feelings about
public life. But stories aren't subject to deliberation. Like artwork, feelings on
Facebook are neither true nor untrue. Sontag (1977) notes that photography had
both elements of journalistic truth-telling and poetic license. The photograph
depicts a reality, but that reality is shaped by the artist that asks subjective questions
(what is taken, at what angle, and so on). As she notes: "the camera's ability to
transform reality into something beautiful derives from its relative weakness as a
means of conveying truth" (Sontag 1977: 112).

Facebook encourages the production of more *stories* and more commentary
around how one feels about those stories. When the content of political
conversation is based upon disclosure and connection, it casts a different pall upon
conversations. For starters, explicitly "political" talk is disadvantaged in a setting
that is based on connection, even with intimates, because they run the risk of
excluding or marginalizing. Eliasoph (1998) makes a good point about political
talk being excluded from most public settings because of the fear of offending.

Our desire not to want to talk to the other side, particularly in the American
context, has increased in recent years. Heit and Nicholson (2010) asked people
to rate political figures in terms of their "typicality" and found that the "typical"
Democrat was rated as completely opposite the "typical" Republican (a very strong
.9957 correlation coefficient – 1.0 constitutes a "perfect correlation"). They found
similar assessments of dissimilarity among the labels *liberal* and *conservative*.
Interestingly, people did not assess types of jobs or foods the same way. Hence, a
political label in the United States is highly coded, much more so that in decades
past. As such a public pronouncement on Facebook as "liberal" or "democrat"
means something very specific. Such labels have become *identities* rather than
political ideologies.

Hackett-Fischer (1970) refers to this as the "fallacy of difference" or "a
tendency to conceptualize a group in terms of its special characteristics to the
exclusion of its generic characteristics" (222). Facebook groups encourage an
understanding of things in terms of how they are different (I am opposed to X or I
am for Y), not in terms of the commonalities we all share. Hence the more we see
"the other side" for its differences rather than its similarities, the more we can tell
a story about them as fundamentally flawed and not worth engaging in discourse.

Because identities are deeply personal, they lead to misperceptions in processing
political information. The problem is that when we are performing, our biases and
logical fallacies become more like aesthetic discernment rather than parts of a
rational political argument. Discourse becomes more like art than science. And we
view these performances as credible when we share similar feelings to them. Rather
than allow dissonant views to challenge our own, many of us "double down" on
our original beliefs. Rather than search for truth, individuals see challenges to

opinions as threats to core identity. Rather than engage in what Mutz (2002) calls "cross-cutting dialogues" many simply ignore information that does not fit their pre-existing paradigm. On Facebook, that means looking for the next group.

The architecture of publicness reinforces this confirmation bias by presenting users with a community that allows them to mediate the unpleasant aspects of that community. Without the spontaneous, searching conversations about *the good* or *the right*, political talk becomes an exercise either in presenting a political identity (for example, "liking" a story or video) and waiting for confirmatory or conflicting responses in return. Real time, face-to-face communication allows for citizens to pick up on non-verbal cues, to restate a position that elicited a negative response from the conversation partner But Facebook, whether it be the newsfeed or the group, isn't built for this kind of discourse. A spontaneous rant comes across differently in a status update than it does at the dinner table.

If people judge content as reliable, they will judge it as credible (Johnson and Kaye 1998, Wanta and Hu 1994). As it pertains to politics, Nyhan and Reifler (2010) found that when confronted with evidence that weapons of mass destruction were not found in Iraq, a majority of US conservatives in the study became even more convinced of the veracity of their position.

By its nature, the architecture of disclosure is not interested in the vetting of your political ideas. They want you to engage in their revelation regime and any unpleasant interactions that might dissuade you from posting in the future cuts against their core business model. As a result, discourse on Facebook is more like a presentation. People engage the site not to seek truth, but to perform their identity in the hopes of having it validated by like-minded others. Contradictory evidence only serves as part of the performance – something to be outraged over, rather than something to be digested and considered.

Svensson (2008) refers to this desire to cultivate voice through discourse as a form of *expressive rationality* independent of instrumental or communicative modes of discourse (2009). Rather than view talk as serving a direct political purpose, Svensson emphasized the importance of talk as collective identity formation. This phenomenological approach to discourse is often undervalued when discussing the role of talk online. Perhaps it is not the social networks per se that explains the increased offline engagement on the part of Facebook users; rather, the explanation lies in the spaces to *perform and manage identity* on SNS sites.

When political talk takes place in a forum that caters to your desire to connect, the bias is towards encouraging discourse that keeps you engaged. Much like a public sphere, the architecture of disclosure is built on your continued participation, your self-expression, your voice. But unlike a public sphere, its motivation is market-based. The more you reveal of yourself, the more you can be monetized. As such, understanding that unpleasant interaction decreases your desire to engage in a revelation regime, Facebook targets content to you that reinforces what you already believe, whether you seek it out or not.

Facebook and Passive Politics

This tendency to personalize public space conversely makes it difficult for transgressive voices to break through. While Facebook might create a space for new discourses, its emphasis on disclosure and connection means that social norms are explicit and enforced. Because we know our networks off-line, Facebook helps strengthen social cohesion through face to face relations, common religious institutions and shared values. This is often celebrated as a way to prevent *flaming*, or the "intentional (whether successful or unsuccessful) negative violations of (negotiated, evolving and situated) interactional norms" (O'Sullivan and Flanagin 2003: 84).

Indeed, Facebook's insistence on transparency presumably means that there isn't as much of a space for the *anti-publics* (Cammaerts 2008) that foster ethnic, gender and GLBT-based hatred. While much more heavily regulated in Europe, the transparency requirement has forced Facebook users to be more attuned to what Butler (1997) called "the action that speech performs" (72).

But while nonymous discourse might reduce "anti-publics" it does not eliminate offensiveness. Lerum (2010) wrote about a Facebook group titled "Killing your hooker so you don't have to pay her," which accumulated over 22,000 members in a matter of days. It was shut down by Facebook soon after its creation, but the website CarnalNation.com (2010) claimed to have found 232 Facebook groups that currently have the words "dead hooker" in them: for example, "Dead Hooker Storage," "Accidentally Pissing On A Dead Hooker," and "A Dead Hooker A Day Keeps The Doctor Away."

In my own study of political Facebook groups, I found few instances of overt violence towards marginalized groups. Although there were a number of political Facebook groups that revealed anti-immigrant sentiments, they did not advocate violence. An example of these is a UK group called "Let's make Saint George's Day a massive celebration!"[5] where the group's creator makes veiled references to those who oppose the holiday: "A small minority take offence to Saint George's Day, I say boulderdash to them, this is England, this is our country, if you don't like it then tough as we will celebrate our day."

In a non-mediated public sphere, overt political expression can be seen as inappropriate. In some contexts, an expression of anti-immigrant views at a cocktail party could be seen as boorish and insensitive. The speaker might restrain his/her political views so as not to create tension. For marginal discourses, this truncating has a chilling effect. No one has a problem expressing political views at a dinner party with like-minded individuals. However, cultivating a political resistance identity can at best be uncomfortable and at worst be life threatening.

---

5   Let's make Saint George's Day a massive celebration! (n.d.). In *Facebook* [Group]. Available at: www.facebook.com/posted.php?id=241196401962&share_id. [accessed: 12 August 2010].

I would argue that the emotionalization of politics, more often than not, leads to a passive-politics that is not transgressive and does not challenge true centers of power. Heavily networked individuals might be more interested in politics and more engaged in the political system, but they are not necessarily more critical of it. The ability to violate norms is a central element of political change. Stories that are not simply personal but transgressive and provocative are what make radical pluralism useful for democratic systems. This does happen, but more often than not, the personal leads to the passive.

Facebook is motivated to keep you coming back to the site, so its emphasis will be on the interestingly pleasant or the salaciously unusual or ironic, but not the transgressive. Thus, the *radical transparency* advocated by Zuckerberg might simultaneously strengthen social capital bonds and norms of reciprocity, while at the same time disincentivizing dissent. Having undifferentiated communities that are not primarily based on politics or core identity might have the effect of what Noelle-Neumann (1974) famously called a "spiral of silence" whereby those with norm violating views on public issues choose to remain silent so as not to be isolated from the real-time networks that are being replicated online.

People seek the public visibility on Facebook. And while that visibility might lead to stronger offline network ties, it could also lead to greater levels of social passivity. While Facebook might not have panoptic (few watching the many) tendencies per se, it does have synoptic tendencies (many watching the few) and both types of surveillance are mutually reinforcing (Lyon 2001). Wortham (2011) notes, "When we see our friends sharing a drink without us, we think we have made the wrong decision about how to spend our time" (Online).

Kalyvas (2008) makes a useful distinction between *ordinary politics* which is elite-driven, based upon interest group bargaining, fragmented, characterized by low political participation and concerned with civic privatism, and *extraordinary politics* based upon high collective mobilization, support for some fundamental changes, irregular and informal public spaces and campaigns to change the "status quo." During these moments of extraordinary politics:

> the slumbering popular sovereign wakes up to reaffirm its supreme power of self-determination and self-government and to substantially rearrange or alter the fundamental norms, values, and institutions that regulate ordinary politics. (5)

It would appear that there are times when Facebook helps bring about *extraordinary politics*. Facebook's emphasis on the personal as political doesn't so much ignore extraordinary politics as it does steer the politics of the transgressive towards the personal and away from what Latham and Sassen (2005) call "digital formations" – technology that is rooted in economic, political and social structures. They argue the digital is constitutive of the non-digital. As such, it is important to link these technologies to systems of power because the identities expressed on Facebook are forged within political, economic and social systems. As Latham and Sassen (2005) note, *digital formations* serve to express the result of these systems in unique and interesting ways. However, the mere fact that the digital is constitutive of the non-digital will not change those relations. Technology can be "derivative" of social relations and at other times it can be "transformative" or "constitutive."

As an example, challenges to corporate power among the 250 Facebook groups I analyzed were almost exclusively based on removing negative portrayals of individual groups. One site called "Comedy Central - I.S.R.A.E.L. Attack game is offensive. Remove it"[6] asked Viacom's Comedy Central television channel to take an anti-Semitic online game from its website and a Canadian-based group called "Fox News Red Eye - Fire the hosts"[7] that asked Fox News to fire the hosts of one of its shows for making anti-Canadian remarks.

But this would seem to contradict news media reports of Facebook's impact in democratic revolutions. In the next two chapters, I look at how Facebook groups impacts mobilization efforts. I argue that, rather that view it through the lens of whether it encourages mobilization or not, we examine what types of politics it encourages us to mobilize around. A politics of the personal orients us further towards a mobilization around identity.

---

6   Comedy Central - I.S.R.A.E.L. Attack game is offensive. Remove it. (n.d.). In *Facebook* [Group]. Available at: http://facebook.com/group.php?gid=127691407246175 [accessed: 4 August 2010].

7   Fox News Red Eye - Fire the hosts. (n.d.). In *Facebook* [Group]. Available at: http://facebook.com/group.php?gid=143769525723 [accessed: 15 August 2010].

Chapter 6
The Digital Front Stage and Deliberation

In Chapter 5, I argued that Facebook encourages a personalization of, not a disengagement from, public life. This changes the way we engage with public life. In this chapter, I argue Facebook's *architecture of disclosure* increases our sense of public life as based on personal identity maintenance. What do I mean by identity? Taylor (1982) defines it as a small stable group of individuals characterized by shared values and beliefs, direct and many-sided relations and norms of reciprocity (92). This sharing of values and beliefs is an inherently social yet *personal* (for example, subjective) experience. As Tilly (2002) notes "an identity is simply [a] social experience ... coupled with public representation of that experience" (49). Hence, identity construction contains both public and private elements.

The elevation in politics of the personal identity over public concerns presents us with what Sennett (1974: 240) called a *destructive gemeinschaft*. He defines this as a tendency to view public life through the lens of one's personal feelings rather than through objective criteria. Tonneis (1955) defined *gemeinschaft* societies as those in which people form associations based on kinship, proximity or shared interests. This leads to a politics composed of a narrowed public sphere where politics are based on emotional connections. This politics emphasizes the importance of high-intensity thick-ties and are based on *identity maintenance* and a preoccupation with the self, at the expense of a politics based on *gesellschaft*, or formal and structured associations based on instrumental ends (Tonneis 1955).

Sennett describes a world driven by this destructive *gemeinschaft* as one in which individuals are doggedly pursuing intimacy through self-disclosure. Sennett claims this pursuit of intimacy is ultimately unsatisfying because the need for self-affirmation (for example, the "problem of the self" is unquenchable). It results in a constant loop of disclosure and affirmation that is impossible to sustain. But, more importantly, this drive to *disclose* and *connect* is an inherently personal matter and as such moves individuals away from the impersonal "world of things." It is a *destructive gemeinschaft* because it gives the false impression that "identity may indeed be freely constructed by talking, that there is no 'society' as different from intimate transactions" (1974: 196). Our engagement with public life become deeply personal and intimately wrapped up with our own identities. In this context, it is not that we ignore politics, is that we see the public through the lens of the private.

As we have discussed in past chapters, the "problematizing of the self" (Baumeister 1987) leads to a life lived through the lens of personal identity. Central to understanding the construction and maintenance of identity in the information age requires understanding how individuals manage the flood of information and compare it to their self-concepts. Maslow (1968) discussed identity in terms of higher-order needs. Once basic needs are met, individuals need "self-realization" or a sense of belonging. Gergen (1991) argues that modern society provides us with an excess of material from which to construct identity, a flood of material that *saturates* us in a barrage of social stimulation. Gergen (1991) called this condition *multiphrenia* (73) or the condition of being simultaneously drawn in multiple and conflicting directions by what he called "technologies of social saturation" characterized by increasing personal interactions that:

> saturate us with the voices of humankind - both harmonious and alien ... Social
> saturation furnishes us with a multiplicity of incoherent and unrelated languages of
> the self. For everything we "know to be true" about ourselves, other voices within
> respond with doubt and even derision. This fragmentation of self-conceptions
> corresponds to a multiplicity of incoherent and disconnected relationships. These
> relationships pull us in a myriad of directions, initiating us to play such a variety
> of roles that the very concept of an "authentic self" with knowable characteristics
> recedes from view. (1991: 74)

Rather than rely on a modern view of the self that relies on "reason and observation" (Gergen 1991: 19), we are confronted with the "vertigo of unlimited multiplicity" resulting from this multitude of voices. How do we create a self out of this multitude of choices? Do we go build a cabin in the woods? Go "on the road"? Become a "self-made man" or "good wife"? Bauman (2000) refers to this modern problem as the search for the self in a world that is increasingly *liquid*:

> That work of art which we want to mould out of the friable stuff of life is called
> "identity." Whenever we speak of identity, there is at the back of our minds a
> faint image of harmony, logic, consistency: all those things which the flow of our
> experience seems—to our perpetual despair—so grossly and abominably to lack
> ... The search for identity is the ongoing struggle to arrest or slow down the flow,
> to solidify the fluid, to give form to the formless ... Yet far from slowing the flow,
> let alone stopping it, identities are more like the spots of crust hardening time and
> again on the top of volcanic lava which melt and dissolve again before they have
> time to cool and set. So there is need for another trial, and another—and they can
> be attempted only by clinging desperately to things solid and tangible and thus
> promising duration, whether or not they fit or belong together ... .(83)

A key question for our times is how we make sense of the self in this multiphrenic, liquid world? Increasingly we are coming to understand that the flood of information gets managed through *gemeinschaft* based networks oriented around shared sentiment and emotional support. Mingione (1994) argues that people manage the online information flood by forging even deeper ties with thick-tie, kinship networks. This *liquid modernity* (Bauman 2000) creates more of a desire for some form of social mooring that gives solidity to an increasingly fragmented life. The granular and modular nature of the Web was supposed to untether us from the tribal affiliations of the past and allow us to form global communities. Ideally, our reaction to the fragmentation of postmodern society drives us to form intentional communities by seeking out the identification with likeminded others.

The reality, however, is very different. If anything, Hetherington (1998) argues, the Internet is expanding *gemeinschaft* to include communities based on shared experience. Identity in the pre-Internet era meant fitting into conventional kin/ geographic norms, but postmodern information culture allows for the formation of loose communities of interests or *neo-tribes* defines as "communities of feeling" (49). The promise of the Web is that we can choose our own tribes, a concept McLuhan (1969) called *retribalization*. This process, which he saw as mostly positive, placed the personal and the emotional at the center of political struggle:

> The aloof and dissociated role of the literate man of the Western world is succumbing to the new, intense depth participation engendered by the electronic media and bringing us back in touch with ourselves as well as with one another. But the instant nature of electric-information movement is decentralizing – rather than enlarging – the family of man into a new state of multitudinous tribal existences. Particularly in countries where literate values are deeply institutionalized, this is a highly traumatic process, since the clash of the old segmented visual culture and the new integral electronic culture creates a crisis of identity, a vacuum of the self, which generates tremendous violence – violence that is simply an identity quest, private or corporate, social or commercial. (268)

To resolve this "identity quest" can either mean retreating to familiar identities or branching out and forming "neo-tribes" of shared feeling. Most of the world still selects the strong ties of "multitudinous tribal experiences." The selection of these groups is not as free-flowing as post-modern views would presume. Most of us exist within communities as an amalgam of our inherited kinship and geographic networks with communities of interest. The desire to make an imagined community real through a sovereign claim to territory or the preservation of an ethnic specific national identity helps the individual tether their identity.

My examination of Facebook groups reveals numerous instances where users created groups seeking to be based on these "multitudinous tribal experiences." Often these groups had ethnic and nationalistic overtones. These claims ranged from various groups based on the issues of Catalonian autonomy or Kurdish group pages seeking to educate fellow Kurds on historic events or UK-based groups calling for more public and formal exhibitions of British nationalism, the majority of groups began with the premise of enhancing or preserving the position of their tribe.

Performing Political Identity in a Retribalized World

A traditional approach to political identity formation comes from social identity theory (Huddy 2001, Tajfel and Turner 2004). This approach states that individuals choose primary identities based on varying characteristics of social groups and the prospect of being recognized as a member of that group. Thus individuals develop a "subjective group membership" based in part on a sense that society sees one as belonging to a group (Tajfel 1981: 237). In effect, a political identity has to do with having others accepting a performance of identity as belonging to the group: "In political life ... collective identities always form as combinations of relations with others, representations of those relations, and shared understandings of those relations" (Tilly 2002: 10). To become politically valuable, a social identity must draw clear in-group/out-group boundaries. Implicit in social identity theory is the idea at there is a political value to the group solidarity which comes from a core social identity. It must "close ranks" (Carmichael and Hamilton 1967: 44).

Political identity formation is radically changed by Internet technology. Work on the formation of group attachments online suggests that emotions are strongly associated with community formation. Thelwall et al. (2010) using "sentiment analysis" of BBC discussion forums found that online communities formed around posts/comments that exhibited negative affect. Comments that expressed a negative emotion about a subject were much more likely to begin a long discussion thread when the original post expressed outrage or anger about a subject. This is consistent with social identity theory. The extent to which one affiliates with a recognized social identity group affects their political world view. For example, Kinder and Kam (2009) found that, in the United States, ethnocentric beliefs led to more support for expanded homeland security and national defense funding, border security and reduced spending on foreign aid.

What types of political identities are performed on Facebook? Raab (2009) points to two possibilities – one deriving from *idem* meaning sameness and the other from the Latin *ipse* meaning what differentiates individuals or that which is "constitutive of the human subject" (227–228). We need our own internal sense of self but that sense of self requires us to be assessed by others. We have both a unique identity based on our accumulated experience and a public identity based on our various roles.

Facebook moves us towards presenting those public identities by providing a forum for their expression. To have an identity means having an audience of others to which an identity can be presented. Social networks provide that performance space. The very act of making an identity public poses the possibility that others will resonate with that public presentation. This shared community that forms around a collective experience can either be a temporal expression of collective affirmation or a powerful tool for mobilization. Those who create public political Facebook groups are inviting us into their private political world by allowing fellow users an unfiltered view into their own private political thoughts. This is in many ways a courageous act because disclosure of a political opinion occurs in a nonymous environment.

Inherently, political identity construction is about shared experience forged through the use of symbols and stories. A symbol is defined by Geertz (1973) as "*any object, act, event, quality, or relation, which serves as a vehicle for a conception*" (91). A political identity that is too "constitutive of the human subject" is of little use in actual political mobilization. Identities that are individual or based solely on personality are not identities that can be used for collective action. To be effective in collective action, the *ipse* must see him/her self as an *idem*. That typically means setting the self up as part of a collective that exists in opposition to other collectives. It means constructing a self that uses shared stories to reify boundaries. Collective political identities are built through the strategic use of symbols and stories. Facebook causes presumably gave users the tools to build community around stories.

My examination of Facebook groups revealed numerous examples of symbols typically used for this purpose. One group consisted of a 10,000 page description of the Kurdish festival of NewRoz, a symbol of Kurdish nationalism in Turkey.[1] Nationalist sites particularly in Eastern and Southern Europe followed a similar pattern. One group included in its description a Wikipedia-like narrative of the history of the Herceg-Bosna region, an unrecognized region within the Bosnia-Herzegovinian state, including a description of the crest and flag of this would-be nation-state.[2]

Forging a political identity is about notions of the collective (for example, with which identifiable groups in society do we cast our lot). At issue is how we forge a public identity from our private, distinctive selves? Cohen (1994) argues that the private self *reappropriates* a public identity when we choose from available public identities (gender, nationality, ethnicity or religion). Because Facebook groups can be created and remain on the site over time, these "available public identities" move forward in time without reference to the context in which the group was formed. What emerges is an online supermarket of political groups based on oppositional-identity claims detached from the temporal context and typically based on in-group, out-group dynamics.

The problem is that we are not simply our in-group, ethnic or national selves. In recent years, the idea of a core public identity has been challenged by intersectionality theory approaches that suggest identity is contextual and based on social setting. Identities are *fuzzy* in that the part of the self that matters depends on the interaction. Because public identities are constructed within, not outside, discourse, we need to:

> understand them as produced in specific historical and institutional sites within specific discursive formations and practices, by specific enunciative strategies [and] within the play of specific modalities of power. (Hall 1996 4)

But without this broader context in which we can situate the self, we revert to constructing identities that stand in opposition to the "world of things." This is particularly the case with political identities as displayed on Facebook groups. By

---

1 Newroz. (n.d.). In *Facebook* [Group]. Available at: http://facebook.com/group.php?gid=27822828999 [accessed: 27 July 2010].

2 HR HERCEG - BOSNA /nekad i danas-povijest/ (Herceg-Bosna: Then and Now) (n.d.). In *Facebook* [Group]. Available at: http://es-es.facebook.com/group.php?gid=236694733296&v=app_2373072738&ref=nf [accessed: 12 August 2010].

definition, political identities are communities of interest. They are not entirely time/ space bound like in agrarian societies, but neither are they wedded to meta-narratives like modern societies. On Facebook, they inherit elements of both societies – often taking the form of de-territorialized tribal performances.

Performative Identity and Facebook

Robinson (2007) suggests that rather than a re-articulation of identity and interaction, people bring their offline selves (bodies, personality and so on) into their online interactions along the same lines. Zhao et al. (2008) call Facebook a *nonymous* environment in which identity is known to others in the network. This makes it distinct from other forms of online interaction. Back et al. (2010) find that rather than provide a "positive spin" on personal identity, user profiles are fairly accurate depictions of a user's offline persona, particularly those users who were identified as more extrovert and less neurotic.

But Goffman (1959) suggests that interaction is driven by the way spaces are structured. In face-to-face interaction, we get immediate sensory cues from our environment. These signals, or what Goffman called *frames*, allow us to know appropriate ways to perform (Goffman 1974). Individuals offer information about themselves through verbal and non-verbal cues (Goffman 1959). For Goffman, interactions take place until a "working consensus" occurs where each of the participants have a good understanding of the roles, levels of expertise, and conduct which each is supposed to perform. Deviations from these norms cause dissonance and disruption within social systems. The online world makes performance more challenging because we are absent many of the cues we would use to gauge appropriate performance.

Nevertheless, Facebook as a setting does provide tools for performance. Through photographs, icons, symbols and so on, users can receive cues on appropriate behavior through things like how many people "like" a group, or how many members join. Facebook also provides a range of presentation styles: textual differences, photos, video and narratives. As such we can think of it as a semi-private environment:

> [F]eatures like Mini-Feeds, the Wall and various Applications create social connections and social spaces, but the mass-messaging features included in Groups and Fan Pages are limited and have the feel of afterthoughts rather than core functions. Groups and Apps, in turn, actually illustrate what has arisen as a significant problem of using the site for political purposes: clutter. (Sanson 2008: 174).

Contrary to Mark Zuckerberg's stated desire, our everyday interactions we rely on some element of concealment. Lying, or concealing, on a small scale is essential for managing personal interactions. Different people receive different narratives about who we are. The story you tell of yourself to your boss is different than the story you tell to your spouse. *Just because Facebook is constructing an architecture of disclosure, this does not mean users blindly enter the site willing to bear all.* Even as we share our most intimate details on Facebook, we still engage in concealment. Jurgenson (2011) uses Baudrillard's notions of "obscenity" (the drive to reveal) and "seduction" (the process of concealment), to suggest that Facebook users engage in a process of *reveal* and *conceal* on Facebook. As Jurgensen (2011) explains:

> every instance of knowledge is also an instance of non-knowledge ... each time
> we learn something new (knowledge) the stock of what we don't know (non-
> knowledge) grows ever larger. (Online)

From this perspective, Facebook is not a blatant revelation of our innermost selves to our fellow intimates, it is an exercise in making our friends more intrigued by our "inner experience." Jurgensen echoes Goffman's dramaturgical model of self-presentation and Butler's notion of *performativity* to reinforce the point that *simply being* is a creative endeavor (Online). Jurgenson (2011) claims we can see this when users post small, cryptic updates:

> This process is most clear when someone posts an obscure status update like "ugh"
> or just "am smiling so hard right now" that reveal only half-truths; often in order to
> beg some kind of follow-up response from someone else. (Online)

Jurgenson (forthcoming) makes an important point. An example of how this element of performativity plays out in the political Facebook groups I studied was a group entitled "War"[3] with a single word "why" in the description of the group. Indicative of the performative nature of the group formation is the fact that there was no website or email that users were driven to for more information. The group was simply a means of drawing like-minded users to serve as the audience for the performance of political identity.

All of us communicate for different purposes at different times. In expressive communication, each of us is seeking to present a self to others that helps us achieve goals. Lasswell (1971) identified eight primary human motivations: power, respect, rectitude, affection, wealth, skill, enlightenment and well-being. We can achieve these outcomes if we can manage our impressions in ways that generate these sought after values: for example, physical attractiveness, likability, perception of competence and virtue (Leary 1995).

The problem is that this *impression management* process is not completely under our control, particularly on line. A growing body of literature suggests that we're only partially aware of how the impression we give is perceived by others (Back et al. 2010). For example, Barash et al. (2010) found that while Facebook users were successful at projecting themselves as positive to their network, users underestimated

---

3   Anti-War. (n.d.). In *Facebook* [Group]. Available at: http://facebook.com/group.php?gid=49265202081. [accessed: 17 August 2010].

the extent to which they came across as self-important to other members of their external audience.

Because we are dealing with a mediated network, it is easier for people to present idealized selves to their fellow network members. While individuals are also performing identity in non-mediated settings, a mediated forum like Facebook provides a level of abstraction that makes it difficult to read real-time, non-verbal cues. This distance from real-time social relations can lead to misperceptions regarding group activity. Similarly, Jordan et al. (2011) found that US-based college freshmen on Facebook consistently underestimated how many negative experiences members of their network had over the course of a day and correspondingly overestimated how much fun the members of their network were having.

This perception that the members of our network are having greater levels of fun and happiness dictates how we respond to those in our network. If we want to be legitimated by those in our networks, we are likely to shy away from presenting a contentious or controversial political self. If we do seek to make a political performance, we are likely to choose those subjects that can be personalized. We may indeed present our true selves in profiles (Back et al. 2010), but presenting our political selves is awkward if it is going to alienate others in our network by being too abstract or removed for personalization. Facebook adds the dimension of having to manage identity across a web of undifferentiated associations (for example, family, friends and co-workers).

This begs the question "How do you manage a political identity in a mixed, quasi-public space?" Because political disclosure is another data point that can be used in a consumer profile, Facebook has an incentive to get users to engage politically. In the past, the company has done a number of things to engage users politically. In 2007, Facebook launched the *Causes* application which allows non-profits to create pages to access Facebook's growing user base. The application allowed users to add affiliation with a specific cause to their profile (for example, virtual campaign buttons). As Hart and Greenwell (2009) reported in the *Washington Post*, the site was popular with users. More than 25 million of the then 200 million users supported one of the causes; however, a much smaller fraction ever contributed to the site (185,000), with the majority of causes receiving no donations.

While scholars like Morozov (2011) use this fact as an example of *slacktivism*, it underlies the symbolic importance of public affiliation. We want to project a public self to others. Facebook listed affiliations in *Causes* on its newsfeed, so political engagement is not something many users on Facebook choose to do in private. Similarly, the creation of a Facebook group highlights this desire to be affirmed and legitimates for one's political identity. In this way it is an extension of the "problem of the self" to the political (for example, public) world. At times, this performance of political identity can be used to powerful effect.

Chapter 7
Facebook and Mobilization:
Beyond the Facebook Revolution

Much has been written about whether Facebook represents a positive force for movement activists or whether it detracts from movement activity. Social critics like Eugene Morozov (2011) suggest that Twitter and Facebook might do more harm than good in terms of digital activism. Morozov (2011) refers to the ease with which individuals can create and join communities of interest as *slacktivism*. He suggests that this ease of membership and identification detracts from more serious and coordinated efforts to affect social change. The positive feeling associated with affiliating with a movement might satisfy one's need for social connection without then engaging with formal political power. For Morozov (2011), slacktivism is the "dangerous sibling" of activism. He describes it as:

> a mad shopping binge on the online identity supermarket that is Facebook –
> that makes online activists feel useful and important while having precious little
> political impact (190).

The key example Morozov cites is the Facebook group "Saving the Children of Africa." He notes that although the group only had 1.7 million members, it only raised 12,000 dollars – less than one hundredth of a penny per member. Morozov reflects on this fact:

> It's one thing for existing and committed activists who are risking their lives on a
> daily basis in opposition to the regime to embrace Facebook and Twitter and use
> those platforms to further their existing ends ... It's a completely different thing
> thing when individuals who may have only cursory interest in a given issue (or,
> for that matter, have no interest at all and support a particular cause only out of
> peer pressure) come together and start campaigning to save the world. (186)

White (2010) faults activist organizations themselves for this shortcoming. He decries an obsession with marketing techniques, what he calls *clicktivism*, for the decline in the power of left activism:

> The end result is the degradation of activism into a series of petition drives that
> capitalise on current events. Political engagement becomes a matter of clicking
> a few links. In promoting the illusion that surfing the web can change the world,

clicktivism is to activism as McDonalds is to a slow-cooked meal. It may look like food, but the life-giving nutrients are long gone. (Online)

Morozov (2011) builds on this McDonaldization of activism critique. He proposes that rather than serve as emancipatory tools, the Internet more often serves as a tool for authoritarian control. Morozov argues that transparency usually benefits those in power, rather than serving the marginalized. Morozov makes the point that information, particularly in totalitarian states, is more likely to be used to suppress than to liberate. The control of the powerless over the powerful occurs via *censorship, propaganda,* and *surveillance.*

As an example, Morozov argues that the "Twitter revolution" in Iran was a Western construction. The narrative that SNS sites like Facebook are emancipatory tools is a comforting meme in the Western media, but the reality was that SNS sites were used more effectively to identify protesters, to get personal information about dissidents (thru Facebook) and to put out nationalistic propaganda. In many contexts, Facebook serves more as a form of "intelligence" than a form of organization. In addition, Facebook can serve as a vehicle for legitimating authoritarian regimes by allowing criticism against local conditions while not tolerating dissent of the nation state. Through the proliferation of state-controlled intranets, Internet providers, and portals, citizens can have the illusion of access to the outside world.

Further, Morozov notes that Facebook efforts at collecting user data, what I call their *architecture of disclosure,* could be used by totalitarian states to engage in what he calls *predictive censorship* (98) where access to content might be conditioned upon demographic profile – a university student might be denied access to foreign newspapers but a finance minister might have full access to them. Totalitarian regimes could use Facebook's "like" function to determine whether a user is sharing "dangerous" content.

But the place where Morozov's argument has the most theoretical punch is his observation that totalitarian states can *suppress through distraction* (80). Through Facebook's "reservoir of cheap entertainment" totalitarian regimes can engage in more sophisticated forms of repression. In his review of Morozov's book, Farrell (2011) cites Russia as an example of a society in which mass distraction is prevalent by noting that "the most popular Internet searches on Russian search engines are not for 'what is democracy?' or 'how to protect human rights' but for 'what is love?' and 'how to lose weight" Morzov 2011, 58.

As MacKinnon (2011) notes, totalitarian regimes like China engage in *networked authoritarianism,* a form of authoritarianism not centrally dependent upon censorship. As an example, Zheng (2008) draws a distinction between *voice activism* (critiques of the local state intended to root out corruption that serves as a legitimizing agent for the nation state) and *exit activism* (which challenges the authoritarian system itself and is not tolerated).

Another element of networked authoritarianism is the creation of propaganda spaces and commercial government-controlled spaces. For good measure,

Morozov argues, repressive regimes could also engage in political discourse to control dissent when distraction isn't effective. As an example, totalitarian regimes can hire popular bloggers to serve as mouthpieces for the state. Rather than rely on more crude forms of censorship, the Internet allows repressive regimes asymmetrical power in their efforts to win the framing war.

Thus the *customization of censorship* (97) means that even if repression tries to come out into the light, a whole range of responses are at the disposal of totalitarian governments to combat it. Regimes could use distributed denial of service (DDoS) attacks, install malware, face recognition software, GPS tracking application, data mining or key-stroke recorders. But, Morozov argues, totalitarian regimes need not worry about developing censoring strategies. More and more, nation states are "outsourcing" their censorship to Internet service providers (ISPs). They simply order ISPs to censor with the risk of state sanction and the ISP is likely to "over-censor" to ensure they are in compliance (216).

Faris and Vileneuve (2008) found that places that filter content tend to be places that score poorly on measures of citizen voice and political accountability. Filtering typically occurs either at the level of the local Internet Service Provider or at the International gateway into a nation. Countries block IP addresses, tamper with the DNS addresses, block individual pages, or block keyword seraches. But Zittrain and Palfrey (2008) argue that filtering is not precise science. They argue it is almost impossible to block a "just right" amount of content.

Admittedly, this might be a dour, Manichean view of the world. As Morozov himself quips "technology changes all the time … human nature hardly ever" (315). But it is a view with which web-utopianists must reckon. In my own research on political Facebook groups, a number of them address issues of totalitarianism and repression; however, none of these groups were created from users based in totalitarian countries themselves.

Defending Slacktivism

Christensen (2011) notes that the original use of the term *slacktivism* stood for "slacker activism" and had a positive connotation (2011). Joyce (2010) contends that activists should use digital tools as part of an overall digital strategy advocates for the term "digitally enhanced activism" (57). She argues that tools like Facebook constitute *latent potential* for activism that often goes unused (132).

In a review of Morozov's book, Joyce (2011) notes that dissidents using Facebook cause "dilemma actions" for repressive regimes. If they block the application, they raise awareness within their own nations and internationally, potentially mobilizing apolitical users of the site. But if they allow the site to proceed undisturbed, it can serve as a mobilizing tool as it did in Egypt in 2010. Particularly because applications like Facebook can serve as *proxy public sphere* where none currently exist. As Zuckerman (2010) notes:

Communication tools may not lead to revolution immediately, but they provide a new rhetorical space where a new generation of leaders can think and speak freely. In the long run, this ability to create a new public sphere, parallel to the one controlled by the state, will empower a new generation of social actors, though perhaps not for many years. (Online)

These tools serve as a net positive because they force totalitarian regimes to have to engage with dissidents. Joyce (2011) notes that Internet tools force a "cat and mouse" game between dissidents and authoritarian governments (Online). While most dissidents host sites abroad, authoritarian governments can flood site with *distributed denial of service* (DDoS) attacks. Activists can retaliate with proxy servers and other applications intended to route requests around blocks. Regimes can also use "semantic workarounds" (Sartor 2011: 148) that allow groups to continue to discuss censored to get around filtering software.

Further, activists can often combat these efforts through "little technologies" like cell phones, text messages, CDs or flash drives (Saletan 2011). As an example, Rother (2011) reported that Cuban human-rights blogger Yoani Sanchez would sometimes dictate her blog posts to friends over the phone when Internet access was cut off by the government. As Zittrain and Palfrey (2008) point out, that there are a variety of methods of blocking Internet access. As a result, there are really "Internets" where individuals are more or less restricted access to content based on the country in which they live.

Regardless of nation state, citizens want a public sphere. As an example, Bailard (2011) provided Tanzania (a politically stable African nation) with 75 free hours of Internet access a few months before their general election. She found the subjects used the access to learn more about the political process. In her reflection on the experiment, she notes:

> In developed nations, we have long been inundated with information, particularly political information. So, I can see why we might take for granted the unprecedented opportunity that the Internet provides to access such information. However, imagine yourself in a nation where the ability to access this sort of information has long been severely constrained, and one could perhaps imagine how this new technology may be embraced as an invaluable tool for seeking out and sharing such information. (Bailard 2011: Online)

This highlights a central paradox for nation states: civil society seeks information, but states for various reasons might want to suppress information (Deibert and Rohozinksi: 2008). Etling et al. (2009) found that Egypt, Kuwait and Syria, three regimes central to the Arab Spring events of 2011, each had highly active "networked public spheres," defined as:

> the seamless combination of modes of communication into a single system: face-to-face interaction ... mobile phones, television, newspapers, and multiple

genres of Internet sites (blogs, forums, chat rooms, video sharing, photo sharing, etc.). Increasingly, these comprise an emerging *networked public sphere*, in which the power of elites to control the public agenda and bracket the range of allowable opinions is seriously challenged. (7)

From this perspective, the power of tools like Facebook, inasmuch as they contribute to this "seamless combination" of communication tools, serves as an important link between the formation of a public sphere and mobilization opportunities. As we have discussed in previous chapters, they do not in themselves constitute a public sphere, but serve as important vehicles for building collective identity around theme that emerge from online public spheres.

Tunisian blogger-activist Ben Gharbia notes that the Tunisian government "blocked YouTube and Flickr but didn't block Facebook because too many Tunisians had already gathered there, and cutting them off seemed too risky" (in Saletan 2011: Online). Disclosure and connection are critical in states with limited ability to a public sphere. But even in these states, the "networked public sphere" can be manipulated and corrupted.

Beyond the "Twitter Revolution"

But perhaps the more important question is not whether Facebook encourages activism or not is to ask "what type of activism does Facebook encourage?" Rather than ask whether Facebook increases civic engagement we should ask how/if Facebook changes how we think of civic engagement. If the notion of "what it feels like to be a citizen" (LeBlanc 1999) is changed by Facebook, then we ask in this chapter how Facebook changes "what it feels like to be an activist."

Facebook might changes our conceptions of activism, but there's little discussion of how it does so. Our notions of what it means to be "together" and "connected" online take on significantly different meaning. I argue that Facebook encourages a mobilization over topics that are *personal* and are thus removed from impersonal core power centers and institutional dynamics (Coleman and Blumler 2009). Despite this, there are times when the personal is essential to challenge power, particularly when the "search for the self" is repressed.

The debate over whether the Internet has positive or negative effects on democracy is too broadly drawn. The Internet writ large is neither the great savior of democracy nor is it the handmaiden of totalitarianism. The move beyond an Internet "grand narrative" requires careful analysis of each application and each context. For example, SNS sites like Facebook and Twitter represent different platforms from blogs or Websites that are more decentralized and distributed. Facebook has a unique set of strengths and weaknesses that not only change the ways activists organize, but possibly change the types of things activists organize around.

As an example, blogs serve an entirely different function in mobilization. Because they are more dispersed throughout the Web and attached to single users, blogs have the effect of stimulating public discourse, but are not as effective at mobilizing. Facebook and Twitter, because they are based on social-networks, can lower costs for organizing protest and lessen the need to be physically together to mobilize (Earl and Kimport 2011). While Facebook can help organize a rally, it might not be well suited to provide the discourse space that helps foment the sentiment behind the rally.

This brings us to a dilemma woven throughout this book. Facebook is increasingly where we live, and the architecture of disclosure compels us to live there more often. It is becoming something tantamount to a public sphere. However, because Facebook is not as well suited for deliberation and discourse, it is limited as a "liberation technology" (Diamond 2010). More importantly, it is a private for-profit entity. Its code is not open source. It governance practices are not transparent. As such, democratic movements relying on Facebook for mobilizing are relying on a private-sector platform whose reason for being is not tied to movement activism. Along these lines, Slee (2011) makes the trenchant observation that:

> The commercial Web 2.0 platforms that dominate web traffic are quite different from the archetypal open source software communities (in which copies of the source exist in many places) and even from Wikipedia. They cannot be forked, and we do not get to see the source code for the algorithms that drive them. Using "Wealth of Networks" style logic to discuss how they operate is tempting, but is often inappropriate. (Online)

Facebook's potential for change has to be assessed through this lens. Facebook is not the Internet. It is an application that uses the Internet to build a business model that depends on disclosure and connection, two key elements that traditionally have characterized the public sphere. For all of the benevolence and good intentions of those who work for the company, its primary motivation is monetization. As such, traditional public sphere concerns over privacy and speech are not sacrosanct principles, they are obstacles. This makes Facebook's emergence as a global public sphere problematic. As Giglio (2011) points out, Facebook's terms of service were only available in seven languages in 2011.

As such, dissidents using Facebook as part of a *networked public sphere* to "proclaim the self" is secondary to Facebook's market imperatives. At times Mark Zuckerberg seems to link Facebook's global spread to free speech promotion as a core of his philosophy, as he did on *60 Minutes* in 2010:

> When you give everyone a voice and give people power, the system usually ends up in a really good place. So, what we view our role as, is giving people that power." (Zuckerberg: Online).

It might be an aspiration for Mark Zuckerberg and those who work for the company, but what happens when company values and market imperatives clash? Does the company restrict the ways in which its users can disclose and connect to satisfy the demands of emerging markets? At present, Facebook is in talks to enter the Chinese market. The main point of contention is whether Facebook will calibrate what people are allowed to say on the site. In 2011, seemingly in response to recent protests in the Arab world, China restricted access to the Internet and mobile phone services. This prompted member of Congress in the United States to signal their intention to challenge Facebook if they did indeed enter the Chinese market. Senator Tom Coburn of Oklahoma issued a strong rebuke of Facebook's current plans:

> Blocking content in some countries—but not others—would deeply damage
> Facebook's brand and raise troubling questions about its commitment to human
> rights and Internet freedom. (Online)

Although the odds that the US or European government protests would seriously impact Facebook are remote, Facebook's dalliance with China poses a deeper question. Can traditional public sphere functions like *disclosure* and *connection* exist and thrive in settings where speech is centrally restricted by the state? If so their usefulness of privately produced public spheres is in doubt. Put another way, if China is open to the possibility of a "Facebook-lite" then its power as a public sphere that can serve as a democratizing agent is suspect. The company itself does not subscribe to unrestricted talk on its site. In its terms of service it reserves the right to remove "offensive" content. As of April 2011, sites deemed "offensive" received this message:

> Content that you shared on Facebook has been removed because it violated
> Facebook's Statement of Rights and Responsibilities. Shares that contain
> nudity, or any kind of graphic or sexually suggestive content, are not permitted
> on Facebook. This message serves as a warning. Additional violations may
> result in the termination of your account. Please read the Statement of Rights
> and Responsibilities carefully and refrain from posting abusive material
> in the future. Thanks in advance for your understanding and cooperation.
> (Zimmer 2011: Online)

While Facebook may err towards free speech on its site, this statement reminds us that Facebook is a private, not a public, entity and is thus under no obligation to the polis to create free speech as a right. As such, it can take down content with little prodding or explanation. As an example, in April of 2011, Facebook removed an innocuous photo of two men kissing by claiming it violated its terms of service (Zimmer 2011).

We know that Facebook might make us happier, more trusting and more efficacious, but what may be good for us might not be so good for activism. Levin (2010) argues that because Facebook is based on symmetrical *thick-ties*, it is hard to gain new *weak-tie* adherents because the medium is designed for conversations within a network. It is not as effective for conversations between networks. As such, activist organizations not in a thick-tie network have trouble breaking into these "networks of intimates." On Facebook, following someone you do not know is seen as a social faux-pax, but it is the very thing activist organizations need to build a broad-based constituency.

Mobilization in the Intimate State

But a "network of intimates" is the very thing that makes Facebook a powerful vehicle for mobilization. In the past chapter, I argue that Facebook encourages a politics based on the performance of personal identity. Facebook didn't create a move towards identity politics. Bennett and Segerberg (2011) contend that the growing individualization in society has led to an individualization of politics and mobilization around the personalization of policy issues. A politics of the personal requires more personal forms of collective action. Narrative elements like stories, symbols and narratives take a central role.

What does it mean to mobilize around a politics of the personal? Anderson (1983) argues that communities are "imagined" as defined by the ways in which the constituent members imagine the community to be. Much of the activity on political Facebook groups is an exercise in providing fodder for this imaginary. By shaping member perceptions of what holds the groups together, Facebook groups seem well suited for the task. Facebook serves as a place to park images, ideas and concepts that can help establish a particular sense of what binds people together. As Tilly (2002) argues: "In political life ... collective identities always form as combinations of relations with others, representations of those relations, and shared understandings of those relations" (10).

The political Facebook groups I studied used images, ideas and concepts in a number of ways. For example, two separate groups originating from Turkey sought to reinforce Turkish nationalism in the hearts and minds of followers by posting long biographical accounts of Ataturk, Turkey's national hero. One group posted a 2,100 word biography of Ataturk and encouraged young Turks with a call to action: "Turkish Youth! The first task of the Turkish Independence and the Turkish Republic, is to forever preserve and defend."[1]

As such, it is more accurate to say that Facebook promotes *personal, identity based* mobilization, but not necessarily all forms of mobilizing. The spark for group-based collective action comes from shared experiences and the personal connection of people to one another, what Dawson (1995) called *linked fate*. Facebook allows for the formation of these linked fate networks by allowing people to cultivate their own in-group ties.

---

1   NE MUTLU TÜRK'ÜM DİYENE!!!! (Attaturk until I Die) (n.d.). In *Facebook* [Group]. Available at: http://facebook.com/pages/NE-MUTLU-T%C3%9CRK%C3%9CM-D%C4%B0YENE/362310012309?sk=info [accessed: 5 August 2010].

Facebook is well suited to a global political environment that emphasizes mobilization around identity. Our era of *hyper-globalization* challenges us to rethink our notions of what it means for groups to be a citizen. In a post-industrial, post-Fordist, political economy, our sense of the political has moved from an emphasis on the traditional pluralist politics of claims making, goods allocation and material redistribution towards an inter-subjective politics of group recognition. The politics of *new-social movements* (Larana et al. 1994) signals an inter-subjective turn away from a *unidirectional* issue of government responsiveness to group demands and more a *relational* issue of political identity formation.

Globalization has been defined countless ways by academic and in the popular media. Beck (2000) defines globalization as the "the processes through which sovereign national states are criss-crossed and undermined by transnational actors with varying prospects of power, orientations, identities and networks" (11). The effect of this process is to lift "out social relationships from local contexts of interaction and their restructuring across time and space" (Giddens 1990: 21).

Castells (1998) refers to this changing network of social relationships as *informationalism*, defined as "a mode of development in which the main source of productivity is the qualitative capacity to optimize the combination and use of factors of production on the basis of knowledge and information" (1998: 7). This *informationalism* is not simply an acceleration of existing processes, but a reconfiguration of the global system towards *networks* or social arrangements that "generate, process and apply efficiently knowledge based information" such as flattened hierarchies, just-in time production, flexible labor pools and so on (1998: 66).

Castells (1998) argues that informationalism creates a legitimacy crisis for nation states that find themselves incapable of effectively managing these disjointed flows and instead seek to maintain power through mastering the art of political communication. Castells argues that society is increasingly shaped by the:

> inability of the political system anchored in the nation state to represent citizens in the effective practice of global governance and the ascendance of global governance as an increasingly essential component of national and local governance. (2005: 11)

The implications of this analysis for localities are that it is increasingly difficult to build coalitions through the allocation of material benefits to coalition members. Nation states are placed in a double-bind. Tied to a neoliberal global economy, nations are not as able to listen to constituency demands for redistribution but run the risk of challenges to authority if they do not address constituency concerns through redistribution. "Winning" in a game of pluralist politics made more sense in the 1960s and 1970s, an era of nation-state largesse and fixed capital. However, in an era of global financial retrenchment and "austerity" politics characterized by lower taxes and less public investment, mobilizing around claims for material goods would seem pointless.

Nation states respond to these new social arrangements by creating *network states* (1996). This arrangement is characterized by an increased devolution of responsibilities to sub-national political units and non-governmental organizations, an emphasis on flexibility of governance, shared sovereignty, and greater diversity of contact between government and citizens (Castells 2005: 11). At the local level, the network state produces local regions that house accelerated flows of people, ideas and capital in ways that are increasingly decentralized and difficult to manage for both individuals and the political units that govern them. The contemporary local state is characterized by increased fragmentation and issues that cover multiple decision-making arenas. Global economic, labor, and technological flows have lessened the power and resources of the local state (Sassen 1991).

At the individual level, the complexity and fragmentation of the network society creates tension concerning one's place in the social structure. These struggles for meaning through identity often talk on nationalist tones. As an example, one of the Facebook political groups I examined was created by a Serbian presumably for the expression of Serbian-ethnic pride:

> Many of the Serbian people spitting out of jealousy, envy and greed. Many of us fight over territory, our Kosovo, although they are aware of the fact that the entire nation came from there. Many hate us, and fascinated the hatred toward us, but it only tells how much lower under us. Many envy us because we have a big heart, and you can see in all of our athletes, because there is no better than them! Collect as many Serbian women here, that everyone knows how much we are proud of what we are and where we are, and be just as great patriots as well as our opposite sex! And let us be active in the group!

As Castells points out: "In a world of global flows of wealth, power, and images, the search for identity – collective or individual, ascribed or constructed – becomes the fundamental source of social meaning" (1998: 223). Castells (1997) argues that social meaning is achieved through the development of one of three types of identities: *legitimating*, *resistance* or *project* identity. Each of these identities reflects a reaction of an individual's placement within the networks that comprise new state arrangements. As such, individuals build their own identity on the basis of a process of "networked individualization" where we find those that share our identity disposition (, Wellman and Haythornthwaite 2002).

A *legitimating identity*, rationalizes the activities of the groups in power and allows them to extend their dominance over social actors (Castells 1997). The formation of these types of identities is supported by the infrastructure of the *transnational capitalist class*, consisting of "those who own and control the major corporations and their local affiliates, globalizing bureaucrats and politicians, globalizing professionals, and consumerist elites" (Sklair 2002: 144).

In my research, I found few groups directly performing a legitimating identity. A handful of groups were created in support of neoliberal policies. One US based group called "One Million Strong Against the Stimulus"[2] sought to build a coalition in opposition to President Barack Obama's 2009 Stimulus Spending Bill. Another France-based group called "Counter strike of January 29, 2009"[3] was formed to challenge a large-scale strike over the government's response to a flagging economy. A description of the group noted:

> Once again, the unions called a general strike January 29, 2009. France will again be paralyzed: crowded public transport, congestion on the roads, a day of classes and less for the kids, high school students. Students during exam time who do not know how to organize the day to attend their events ... not to mention the billions of euros that will be missed during the day ... what a mess!

More prevalent in my study were those groups who perceive themselves to be excluded by the effects of the transnational capitalist class. Castells calls these groups formed around a *resistance identity* (Castells 1997). The struggles often take religious or nationalistic overtones: "God, nation, family and community will provide unbreakable, eternal codes around which a counter-offensive will be mounted" (Castells 1997: 66). One site called "Labeling in Catalan"[4] calls on fellow Catalonians to buy local products.

> No company wants to lose a market of millions of consumers and more now with the crisis.
> Now is a good time to buy products only in Catalan.
> Not easy but you can try.
> It is so nice to read the tags: rice, milk, sugar, biscuits, jam, etc. that I put off buying products where Catalan is not present.

As an example, one group called "We Want Military Parades in Argentina"[5] was formed because in the users' view:

---

2   One Million Strong Againgst the Stimulus. (n.d.). In *Facebook* [Group]. Available at: www.facebook.com/posted.php?id=139725785416. [accessed: 5 August 2010].

3   29 Janvier GREVE NATIONALE ! (Counter strike of January 29, 2009) (n.d.). In *Facebook* [Group]. Available at: http://facebook.com/group.php?gid=55916370725. [accessed: 12 August 2010].

4   ETIQUETATGE EN CATALA (Labeling in Catalan) (n.d.). In *Facebook* [Group]. Available at: http://facebook.com/group.php?gid=40693549041&v=wall. [accessed: 14 August 2010].

5   Queremos desfiles militares en la República Argentina. (We want military parades in Argentina) (n.d.). In *Facebook* [Group]. Available at: http://facebook.com/group. php?gid=103442033022855 [accessed: 14 August 2010].

> The parades materialize the military compliance with the Constitution and are a
> symbol showing the people the assurance that their armed forces move and act
> as one man and who share the same love of country.

In both examples, groups were formed to solidify an identity opposed to the
tendencies of the transnational capitalist class to de-emphasize national, regional
and ethnic ties. Castells regarded this as the identity that most individuals would
adopt. However, he did not deny that some would adopt *project identities* or
transformative ideologies that work to change the structure of society. Those
that adopt these identities seek "proactive movements which aim at transforming
society as a whole, rather than merely establishing the conditions for their own
survival in opposition to the dominant actors. Feminism and environmentalism fall
under this category" (1997: 10–12). Castells argues, however, that these identities
are rare. Indeed in my own work, I could not find very few groups formed around
these broader, abstract symbols of collective identity that were not specifically
tied to place.

But none of Castells' three types of identities necessarily move to political
action. García-Bedolla (2005) argues that to create a *mobilizing identity* requires
both efficacy and shared ideology. She defined a *mobilizing identity* as the
development of an efficacious worldview combined with positive outlook towards
one's primary ethnic identification. The emphasis on both components is essential.
Perceptions of the community to which one belongs structures the efficacy and
willingness to get involved what that group gets challenged. As she notes:

> for individuals to choose to act, they must feel they are part of something and
> that that "something" is worthy of political effort. That feeling of attachment
> and group worthiness is what motivates them to act on behalf of the collective.
> (García-Bedolla 2005: 7)

Facebook didn't create identity politics, but I argue it accelerates the trend towards
the politics of the personal. Facebook facilitates politics as performance, what
Alexander (2006) calls *cultural pragmatics*. Drawing from a repertoire of symbols,
scripts, actors, audience, and setting, activists can compel users to action, but the
type of politics that is acted upon is based largely on "small things."

Increasingly, the "performance" of political mobilization is taking place in
intimate settings. Hodkinson and Lincoln (2008) talk about the Internet as a "private
social space" where identity play can be performed in front of a hand-picked set of
friends. In an interesting analysis of teen interaction styles, Lincoln (2004) notes
the increasing importance of the bedroom as a social space. Correspondingly,
many of the performances of political identity on Facebook have the feel of a

solitary individual "getting something off their chest" as if they were engaged in an intimate private conversation. As an example, one group from Colombia was titled (in Spanish) "Ni Cagando, voto por Sebastian Piñera"[6] (even defecating, I won't vote for Sebastian Piñera).

But these performances of "small things" in "intimate settings" can often allow for the development of diasporas that can then be used as part of a broader global movement. They are also chimerical, spontaneous, difficult to predict. No one could predict the Arab Spring. What may seem like an isolated expression of political frustration can spill out through a network and have a collective effect. As Diani and McAdam (2003) notes:

> Persons promoting and/or supporting their actions do so not as atomized individuals, possibly with similar values or social traits, but as actors linked to each other through complex webs of exchanges, either direct or mediated. Social movements are in other words, complex and highly heterogeneous network structures. (1)

While intimate politics takes several forms, a recurring theme in examining political Facebook groups is a politics of exclusion. This is not unique to Facebook. Typically the view is that the Web in general invited radical voices targeted against marginalized groups. Sites like Stormfront.org and New Saxon based their mobilization around a politics of racial exclusion. The Internet provides the perfect forum for quickly expressing group-based dissent. For instance, Potok (2008) reports that White supremacist groups saw a flurry of activity on their sites the night Barack Obama won the US presidential election in 2008.

At first glance it might seem that the nonymous status of Facebook users would undercut its use in hate group activity. In addition, Facebook has active anti-hate speech policies. The reality, however, is that Facebook hate groups are active and can flourish for a while before being taken down. A 2010 report by the Simon Wiesenthal Center found that "hate group" social networking sites increased 20 percent from the previous year to 11,500. The Facebook groups found by the center included "national kick a ginger day" and "I love curry bashing." (Simon Wiesenthal Center 2009).

A turn towards the intimate in politics might seem problematic but Butler (1997) suggests that eliminate these noxious discourses could move them further underground, paradoxically giving them more power. Providing these views might provide a space for these dissonant views to be performed and expressed without further action. As a result, activism becomes incidental rather than structural, ephemeral.

---

6 Ni Cagando, voto por Sebastian Pinera. (Even defecating, I won't vote for Pinera) (n.d.). (n.d.). In *Facebook* [Group]. Available at: http://facebook.com/group. php?gid=158624085790. [accessed: 27 July 2010].

More often, groups emerge that are not "hate groups," but express a sense in which their nation is "under siege" by external threats. The Tea Party movement in the United States is a good example of these types of communities where solidarity is forged by a shared belief of American superiority being challenged by a range of internal and external threats (Barreto and Parker 2011). These ethnic specific, nationalistic movements are efforts (often unintentional) to forge a collective identity using symbols, language, discourses. When done intentionally, movement activists used these tools to recruit, retain, mobilize and motivate members. Through sharing stories and framing events in the world "out there" activists can form specific *cultures of resistance* (Oboler 1994).

The Middle East and Private Mobilization

The events across the Arab world in the spring of 2011 are prime examples of how the politics of the personal can create these cultures of resistance. Nowhere did the power of mobilizing seem as apparent as in the Egyptian protests of 2011. Facebook's celebrated status as a tool for activism is a direct results of the Egyptian revolution of 2011. An indication of how connected Facebook has become to the successful protests, an Egyptian father Jamal Ibrahim named his first-born daughter "Facebook."

This intimate act of naming a first-born "Facebook" is ironic, being Facebook's ability to unleash the power of the personal. Perhaps more ironic is the name of the Facebook group that is credited with galvanizing the Egyptian protests of 2011. A group based upon one person's story called "I am Khaled Said" was instrumental in galvanizing Egyptian youth behind a mass-movement.

The group was started in the wake of the death of Khaled Said, a 28-year-old businessman, in Alexandria in June. He was beaten by police in the street in front of a host of spectators who took cell phone photos and circulated them online. He was murdered presumably because he had uncovered evidence that identified corruption within the Egyptian government. When the Egyptian government spread a false story about why Said was murdered and attempted to use it in court, the "We are all Khaled Said" Facebook page was formed.

At the time, the site's administrator was anonymous. The page focused on Said, interspersing video of his life with gruesome images of his death. In a matter of months, the site had 500,000 followers (Preston 2011). The movement began through an initial call for strikes and protests against wages and working conditions through a Facebook group called "April 6 youth movement." The page, created in 2006, was formed to call a strike on that day to show solidarity with workers striking for higher wages in the city of Al-Mahalla Al-Kobra; 70,000 people joined the group almost immediately. The founder, Israa Abdel Fattah, was detained for two weeks after creating the site. Soon after, the April 6th movement Facebook page was transformed into a hub for activists. The first action coordinated through the site was a series of synchronized labor protests on January 25, 2010. This group served as the basis for later protest activity.

El Fattah (in Saletan 2011) notes that Facebook was effective at "build(ing) a narrative about revolution" (Online) that the regime was responsible for nation's ills. The "We Are All Khaled Said Facebook" group credited with sparking the Egyptian pro-Democracy protests of 2011 provided a narrative that individual Egyptians were not alone in their political views. They could voice public outrage in a forum that was difficult for the repressive government to shut down. The proliferation of cell phone in Egypt allowed for the sharing of this site detailing the beating of Kahed Said, a 28-year-old Egyptian businessman. The collective outrage at this act spread quickly on Facebook, garnering 1 million followers by June 2011 (Zhuo et al. 2011).

The Khalid Said page highlights the power of Facebook to mobilize through a *politics of the personal*. Few of the sites that motivated these movements spoke directly of revolution. Indeed in my 250 groups, I identified very few groups with "revolutionary" motives. This might be a case of quality over quantity, but few groups specifically asked visitors to engage in any form of protest action.

Inherent in the idea of Facebook as an aid to activists is the sousveillance it can provide. As a forum for building a public sphere its effect may be limited. But as a space where oppressed voices can perform politics through the use of stories and symbols, Facebook has the potential to be of great use. It is in these very places where "the personal" is held in low regard that Facebook can be used to foster social change. By combining offline, street-level protest activity with narratives and symbols that represent the marginalization and oppression of a people, Facebook's personalization of politics can foment social movement activity.

In the wake of the 2011 "Arab Spring," news headlines in the United States and Europe grabbed onto a narrative that gave central importance to SNS in fostering regime changes in Egypt and Tunisia. Headlines like "Can Facebook topple Egyptian authoritarianism?" were not uncommon. Zhuo et al. (2011) argue that the mobilization on the part of Egyptian protesters came from the ability to access to SNS sites like Twitter and Facebook on mobile phones rather than on personal computers whose access was blocked by the government. The phones turned out to be important tools for the protests because they could be recharged quickly by plugging them into streetlamps.

The cell phone has radically changes Facebook's role in mobilization. A 2010 Pew survey of 16 nations found that in 2002, only 45 percent of those surveyed worldwide owned cell phones. By 2010, that number had jumped to 81 percent – a much faster rate than the growth in the percent that use a computer (Pew Research Center 2010). By far, the largest growth in cell phone ownership was in developing countries. For example in 2002, according to Pew, 35 percent of those surveyed in Jordan had a cell phone. By 2010, that number was 94 percent (Pew Research Center 2010). Similarly, in Kenya, 9 percent had cell phones in 2002, by 2010, 65 percent of Kenyans had cell phones. By contrast, the growth in computer ownership worldwide only increased from 32 percent to 50 percent over the same 8-year period (Pew Research Center 2010).

Curiously, Pew found this phenomenon was driven almost exclusively by young people between 18 and 29 years of age. The differences in cell phone ownership by age group were stark. For example, in China in 2010, 83 percent of 18 to 29 year olds surveyed by Pew had a cell phone but only 16 percent of those 50 years and over did. Similar disparities in cell phone ownership by age were found in countries like Poland where 90 percent of 18–29 year olds owned a cell phone whereas only 25 percent of those 50 and over owned a cell phone (Pew Research Center 2010). In Russia 78 percent of 18–29 year olds owned a cell phone whereas only 18 percent of those 50 and over owned a cell phone (Pew Research Center 2010).

The ubiquity of smart phones has redefined the ability to extend the *politics of the personal* to different communities of interest. Zhuo et al. (2011) claims that the Arab Spring resulted largely from move away from traditional groups to a "networked individualism" (Wellman and Hampton 1999) that exhibited a turn to social networks, the proliferation of a high-speed Internet and the emergence of mobile devices.

The smart phone allowed people in Tahrir Square and throughout the Arab world to take video, upload them to YouTube and share them on Facebook and Twitter. For example, in Tunisia, cell phones allowed for video to be transmitted of the self-immolation of Mohamed Bouazizi, a fruit vendor who burned himself to death in response to being abused by the policy. This highly personal, emotional act was then transmitted to the rest of Tunisia via YouTube and Facebook sparking protests. Cellphones then captured and transmitted video of the initial protests in Sidi Bouzidin which make international journalists pay attention.

The capacity of smart phones to create dense, youth-driven networks based on a shared *politics of the personal* helped galvanize a nation against totalitarian rule. Zhuo et al. (2011) found Facebook helped maintain both strong and weak tie networks in ways traditional media could not. Facebook served as a source of pan-Arab mobilization through groups like "Progressive Youth of Tunisia" and the Serbian "Center for Applied Nonviolent Action and Strategies" that translated identity politics into mobilization through shared experiences with strikes and blogging.

The very act of Facebook mobilization can become an identity in and of itself. A large gap in Internet use existed between the college-educated and non-college-educated throughout the developing world. The gaps were particularly large in the Middle East and North Africa. For example, 88 percent of college educated Jordanians use Internet as opposed to 20 percent of Jordanians without a college degree (Pew Research Center 2010). In Egypt 71 percent of those with college degrees used the Internet while only 9 percent of those without college educations did the same.

Facebook was especially popular among young educated Egyptians. Egypt's 5 million Facebook users constitute the highest adoption rate in the Middle-

East or North Africa (Preston 2011). Not surprisingly, many of these same young, college-educated, Egyptians were the driving force behind the Egyptian revolution. Being connected to an educated, networked transnational community online gave the protesters a sense of identity. Zhuo et al. (2011) dubbed them *the Facebook generation*: a modern "neo-tribe" still rooted in ethnic identity but opposed to traditional society and norms. Evidence of this effort to connect to this transnational community were the numerous signs in English created by Egyptian protesters and the English language Facebook pages, both intended to speak to a transnational audience.

This ability to transcend geographic boundaries allowed for the development of a "diasporic public sphere" (Smith 2003). In the Egypt example, Howard et al. (2011) looked at over 3 million tweets containing seven popular Twitter *hashtag* codes – #egypt, #libya, #sidibouzid (Tunisia), #feb14 (Bahrain), #morocco, #yemen, and #algeria. He found the majority of the usage of these hashtags taking place outside the Middle East. This broader community sharing information about the protests prompted Internet-savvy Egyptians and Tunisians to further try to capture this attention to get a hearing for their issues with the government.

This public sphere evolved from social/economic discussions in 2008 to explicitly political discussions in 2010–2011. Nahawi (2011) studied the discussions that emerged in the millions of conversations on *Facebook*, *Twitter* and other social networking sites and found a shift in conversation from an emphasis on economic issues, particularly a resistance to privatizing national industries, towards a political discussion that more identity emphasized themes like "Arab unification" and an expanded role for the Muslim Brotherhood.

Granted, one can overdraw the importance of these diasporic public spheres. Despite the excitement of the 2009 "Twitter revolution" in Iran, most Twitter conversations about the protests took place outside Iran, among Western diasporic communities and was less of a mobilization tool (Morozov 2011). But it is undeniable that the Internet did help focus the protest movements by documenting the death of Neda Agha-Sultan, a Iranian demonstrator whose death at the hands of police galvanized large numbers of Iranian youth. Her murder traveled through YouTube and was eventually picked up by mass-media outlets, *Al Jazeera* in particular. Further, Facebook played a limited role in the Iranian elections of 2009. The challenger Mousavi tried to use Facebook but the government shut down the service.

But the success of Egypt's movement is not due to Facebook alone, but the development of a broad *networked public sphere*. In a country with limited Internet access, there are more cell phones (82 million) than people (80 million) and an estimated 160,000 bloggers (Preston 2011). The Egyptian movement was not oriented around one blog or Facebook page. Facebook pages like "El Shaheed" (The Martyr), Twitter hashtags like #*jan25* and #*Egypt*, Tweeters like @ Dancefromiraq, @Sandmonkey, @waelabbas and 'BloggerSeif' and anonymous bloggers, "Egyptian Chronicles" and "Baheyya" were all part of the movement's spread (*The Economist* 2011).

Facebook's emphasis on creating a "network of intimates" is exactly what is needed for mobilizing totalitarian states. While Facebook's encouragement of a "retreat to the personal" might be a problem in Western democracies, it is exactly what's needed in totalitarian regimes where "problematizing the self" might be an important corrective to a regimes that do not regard "the self" as important. The architecture of revelation might be a problem unique to liberal societies. A "problem of the self" means a "prioritizing of the self" over other ways of defining identity, be it social position or religious adherence. In places where identity construction is constricted, a vehicle that allows for challenging these conventions is important and useful.

The "problem of the self" in modernity in the West is encapsulated by Sartre's pronouncement in *Being and Nothingness* that he was "condemned to be free" (415). The Facebook solution to this question is to revel in the company of others through *disclosure* and *connection*. Throughout the book, I've discussed the limitations of this approach as it relates to politics in democratic states, particularly in the United States and Europe. But in totalitarian states where the "problem of the self" is a forced "negation of the self," either through theocracy or totalitarian control, the possibility of disclosure and connection, particularly the collective identity it can foment, can work as a primary tool for liberation, particularly because individuals in repressed regimes are more likely to have their personal sphere intruded upon by the public sphere. As such, "talk" on Facebook might be shaped by an urgent need to proclaim the value of the self.

Chapter 8

Privacy in the Age of Personal Politics

In 2010, Alex Pentland and his colleagues the Massachusetts Institute of Technology (MIT) conducted a study with 100 students living in an on-campus dormitory. They students were given smartphones that tracked their daily movements. The information gleaned from their phones was uploaded into a database that provided researchers with data on the students' location, call log, and text message log. Each of the student's phones would scan every six minutes for any other phone issued to one of the subjects that came within a 10-foot radius. This allowed the team to model a host of relationships and produce a fascinating set of findings including this one:

> Almost a third of the students changed their political opinions during the three months. Their changing political ideas were related to face-to-face contact with project participants of differing views, rather than to friends or traditional campaign advertising, the analysis showed. (Hotz 2011: Online)

This move towards *social computing* is revolutionizing social science. What used to be a "data problem" is being solved by subjects volunteering vast amounts of information about themselves. In 2009, the average US citizen consumed 34 gigabytes of information per day, 3.5 times more than in 1980 (Bohn and Short 2009). But as important is the ability to maintain the vast wealth of data users create. The world's servers in 2008 processed 9.57 zettabytes, or 10 million million gigabytes of information (Bohn et al. 2011).

The willing submission of vast reams of data is increasing scientists' predictive power by giving them more access to data thereby increasing "fit" of behavioral models. Acquisti and Gross (2009) used online data to predict nearly 5 million social social security numbers, or 8.5 percent of the people born in the United States between 1989 and 2003. Jernigan and Mistree (2009) used 4,000 Facebook profiles to build a model that predicted with 78 percent accuracy whether the profile belonged to a gay male.

Similarly companies can learn a great deal about product success by examining online data. Dewan and Ramaprasad (2009) found that "blog buzz" was a strong predictor of record sales. Asur and Huberman (2010) found that a movie's Twitter mentions during its opening weekend almost perfectly predict how well a movie will do. The information gleaned from using online devices to gather data on users is valuable to both scholars and marketers. For marketers, it is tantamount to what Anderson (2008) posited in a provocative *Wired Magazine* article called *The End of Theory* where he posited that the scientific model was becoming obsolete because of the vast reams of online data that could simply tell scientists and companies how an individual would behave with such predictive certainty that theoretical models were no longer necessary to drive prediction.

As it pertains to marketing, the "end of theory" means that rather than speculate as to what types of products users will want to buy, companies can cull enough data to simply know it with almost complete certainty. Businesses are savvy to the value of the power of social computing. Narayanan and Shmatikov (2008) found that Netflix user data can be *de-anonymized* by identifying a user's pattern of movie rating and recommending. By comparing Netflix data with Twitter accounts and Flickr accounts, Narayanan and Shmatikov were able to identify the user in 20 percent of cases even when the information had been stripped of identifiers. While this is far from "the end of theory," it suggests an increased merging between our private-consumer self and our entire self.

Facebook is part of a broader trend in social network analysis. Phone companies can identify "influentials" based on how quickly they are called back, whether they call people late at night and whether the calls they make are long and the calls they receive are short (*The Economist* 2010). If a company can identify nodes in a network, they can target who is most likely to persuade others. Banks in the United States and Europe are experimenting with using network analysis to determine if a borrower is a good risk, a phenomenon (*The Economist* 2010) called *online redlining*. If the borrower is opening a business and no one in his network is in that business, banks can make an educated guess the person's proposal constitutes a bad credit risk. Markoff (2008) describes this process:

> The students' data is but a bubble in a vast sea of digital information being recorded by an ever thicker web of sensors, from phones to GPS units to the tags in office ID badges that capture our movements and interactions. Coupled with information already gathered from sources like Web surfing and credit cards, the data is the basis for an emerging field called collective intelligence. (Online)

Lanier (2011) argues that contemporary data mining is not simply about targeting products that companies think consumers will want to buy. Companies are also concerned with how to persuade you, using a vast set of tools to analyze which pitches were most effective to create *persuasion profiles*. This sorting of online users into different profile runs the risk of "giving us back to ourselves," but filtering the type of content we receive. Kambara (2010) predicts the advent of the *Semantic Web*, or a Web that attempts to contextualize your engagement with the Web (for example, personally customized Google search profiles) will reorient our online, and possible offline, life towards *latent networks* of interest learned from the aggregating of content into interests.

This move to predict what users want based on past behavior and consumer profiles has profound implications for society. Rather than use the networks to determine your consumption patterns, the *Semantic Web* signals a move towards creating networks based upon our patterns of consumption. To use Marxist language, the broader project of the social graph could possibly be to render indistinct *exchange value* (monetary value) and use value (intrinsic value). Vaidhyanathan's (2009) argues that the "Googlization" of information creates a market logic of information dissemination geared towards consumption and not other more worthy aims:

> we are not Google's customers: we are its product ... We—our fancies, fetishes, predilections, and preferences—are what Google sells to advertisers. When we use Google to find things on the Web, Google uses our Web searches to find out things about us (3).

The increasing proliferation of mobile phone is increasing how much of *a product* we can become. The cell phone is a portable data collection device. It can collect data on where people go on a daily basis. That data can be *geo-tagged* to other types of data to identify a user's whereabouts and the reason for being there. Smartphones turn mobile devices into mini computers. Now calls, SMS texts, photos and video, Web searches, status updates, and so on can be executed and collected by phone. Unlike a conventional landline telephone, a mobile phone usually is used by only one person, and it stays with that person everywhere, throughout the day.

Barabási (2010) argues that these new technologies have exponentially increased our predictive power to explain human behavior. As an example, González et al. (2008) looked at 16 million records of call data from 100 European users to construct a model whereby they could forecast future whereabouts with over 90 percent accuracy. Isaacman et al. (2011) looked at millions of anonymous mobile call records from NY and LA to study commuting habits and found that New Yorkers traveled less than Los Angelinos during the winter but that people in both cities traveled less. MacKerron (2011) measured emotion in the UK using an iPhone app called *mappiness* that had users record their moods and would record the person's GPS location and noise levels. He found that the "the U.K.'s happiest time is 8 p.m. Saturday and its unhappiest day is Tuesday" (Hotz 2011: Online).

The Fully Specified Self

Social scientists that engage in econometric modeling speak of models being fully-specified when each variable that could possibly be affecting a causal relationship are identified. In reality, full specification is next to impossible to achieve since there is so much variation in the social world. But in principle, once a model is fully specified, this issue is simply collecting enough data to "smooth out" anomalies.

A critique of social science research, when compared to behavioral science is that you cannot control for all the possible "noise" in the world that can impact a researcher's model. There would be no way to know if the "treatment" accounted for change because there is too much "randomness" in the world and there is too much variation for a model to apply to any one person. But through the plethora of data collection devices at our disposal, users can capture enough data to create models of their own individual behavior. When the subject of study becomes the individual and there are hundreds of thousands of data points at a researcher's disposal, our models of reality get closer and closer to becoming and shaping reality.

We are using this vast amount of storage capacity to attempt to create *specified-selves*. A specified self is one whose past behavior can be mapped out and quantified in such a way that the self becomes predictable and potentially manageable. Pariser (2011) detailed this as the *personalization* of the Web. This pesonalization process is highly impersonal. Scholars aren't interested in the individuals per se, but rather they want to look at the individual as part of a broader pattern of relationships. Similarly, companies are not interested in the totality of individuals, they are simply looking for patterns in behavior to determine the best ways to market products.

But what of this *specified-self* as a political subject? Do we become predictable and managed? Perhaps, but more important are the ways in which we willingly submit to the process of *fully specifying ourselves*. We develop norms and habits that reinforce the routine, the predictable. Facebook can play a central role in this self-specification process. Just as scholars are seeking to take the randomness out of explaining the social world, are we drawn to Facebook because it helps take the "statistical noise" and "randomness" out of our own lives?

At one extreme of this trend are those that fully embrace the idea of fully specifying themselves and sharing that with the rest of the online world. Berlin performance artist Christian Heller created a wiki where he posts every intimate aspect of his life at the Website: *futur.plomlompom.de*. He uploads his daily schedule to a public wiki – his meals, where he goes, his thoughts, and so on (Jolly 2011). Similarly, New York-based graphic designer Nicholas Felton uses online tools to create annual reports of trips had taken, what he eats, books he read and so on, and turns them into publically accessible info-graphic reports. An example is the data point: "I attended 20 birthday parties: average age 31 years old." (*Bits Blog* 2010: Online).

These examples highlight a trend towards *body hacking* or using online tools to collect and report on vast amounts of personal data (Dembrosky 2011). The types of data kept by individuals range from fitness updates, heart rate, body temperature, blood pressure, mood or vitamin levels in the blood stream. This idea of *self-quantification* (Dembrosky 2011) has attracted enough of a following to merit yearly conferences on the subject. The practice can go to what might seem absurd extremes as evidenced by this recollection by Lisa Betts-LaCroix on her husband's reaction to the birth of their child: 'I was giving birth to our son, and instead of holding my hand and hugging me he was sitting in the corner entering the time between my contractions into a spreadsheet" (Dembrosky 2011: Online).

Advocates of this movement see it as emancipatory: as a way to improve the self through monitoring the self. While the members of this nascent movement are the earliest of adopters, devices used to capture this information will soon be small and ubiquitous enough to be worn on the body or included as smartphone applications. Users can then sync their vital data to their Facebook account if they choose to tell others of their status. Conceivably, Facebook status updates might completely circumvent the presentation of self and simply report objective "moods" to your network without your vetting.

This extreme revelation is unusual and it reveals a deep human need to differentiate oneself, to be noticed. Disclosing oneself does open one up to criticism and ridicule, even when it is within the relative safety of Facebook. However, this turn towards "the personal" as "data" is a luxury of the privileged. Only those with the time, resources and skill to collect data on oneself can leverage it for personal benefit. In addition, these users are employing "technologies of the self" (Foucault et al. 1988) to collect data on their own personal achievement, something far removed from question sources of power. These *self-quantifiers* could be seen as garnering more control over the self, but they also serve as *passive subjects* who do not fear the state using public data to oppress or control then in some way. Were these self-quantifiers collecting public data for public purposes that were more challenging of state authority, their revelation might go beyond annoyance to physical harm.

The view that the self-quantification movement is a means of self-improvement has a great deal of attraction for companies that make money out of user data. If we can see "post-privacy'" as the new norm, then we will be less susceptible to the meme that Facebook is taking something valuable from us. Ferris (2011 in Dembrosky) suggests this might become modal in the very near future:

> I think, as soon as the next 12 or 24 months, that people will have to opt out of
> self-tracking, as opposed to opt in," he says, "much like GPS and geo tagging,"
> a feature of smartphones that records users' geographic location automatically
> for use in various consumer mobile applications. (Online)

This "post-privacy" thinking emphasizes the importance of reputation management over privacy. In this new era, individuals simply accept that their lives will be forever public and simply work to use the Web to achieve personal goals. Many of the devices used in the *self-quantification* movement have a "gaming" element that motivates users to meet goals by sharing their personal data and "winning" if they hit certain targets. This all seems innocuous. *Self-quantifiers* are willingly submitting their data online. There is no formal coercion. This practice is in line with Mark Zuckerberg's thought on the subject:

> Given that the world is moving towards more sharing of information, making
> sure that it happens in a bottom-up way, with people inputting their information
> themselves and having control over how their information interacts with
> the system, as opposed to a centralized way, through it being tracked in
> some surveillance system. I think it's critical for the world. (Zuckerberg in
> Kirkpatrick 2010: 323)

Primarily because Facebook's allure is its sense of the personal; we behave in intimate, private ways in what is essentially a public space. Facebook and other SNS sites have created a public context in which we feel free to reveal our intimate selves to others, something traditionally reserved for private life. Our sense of "the private" becomes overtaken by stronger impulses within ourselves to connect and disclose.

As an extreme example, in June 2011, US Congressman Anthony Weiner was caught engaging in sexually explicit correspondence with a number of women on Facebook and Twitter. The Congressman's dalliances would usually begin with women that sought to "friend" the Congressman on Facebook or "follow" the Congressman on Twitter. In one example, the Congressman engaged in 220 Facebook messages with one woman who sought to "friend" the Congressman. Discussions about politics very quickly turned towards a flirtatious relationship between the woman and the newly married congressman. This explicit chatter could only occur under an *architecture of disclosure* that gave users the impression of a private forum. But these forums are anything but private. Political opponents of the Congressman were soon able to uncover this trail of flirtatious *tweets* and messages and embarrass the Congressman into resigning his seat.

In some ways, it is amazing that someone whose life is devoted to cultivating a public image could be so drawn into Facebook's *architecture of disclosure* that they fail to recognize the deeply public nature of the correspondence. The Congressman, a public figure, had wandered so deeply into the personal space that Facebook creates that he equated his salacious flirtations online to private one-on-one conversations.

Broadbent (2009) argues that social media enhances intimacy by closing the gap between public and private life that developed during the industrial age. She calls it the "democratization of intimacy" through real time connection. Indeed sexting, the very personal act of sending easily reproducible nude pictures or explicit SMS messages to others, has exploded in recent years (Wysocki and Childers 2011).

A core problem with this increased sense of a "specified self" is that it is an illusion. It is impossible to eliminate the randomness and spontaneity from life, particularly when we engage with public life. Most of us seek to connect with actual human people, but we would like those interactions to be on our terms, freed from the messiness and drudgery of everyday life. But more importantly our own openness to randomness and spontaneous acts is what makes us challenging political subjects. Without these appreciations for contingency, we are easily pacified by the powerful.

What emerges is a disconnect between our perception of our technologically enhanced lives that give us the illusion of control and the reality that control in impossible. Facebook, in particular, give the illusion of control over our social life. We pick the what, when and who of our engagement. We don't want the virtual world to replace our engagement, we want it to serve as the lens through which we have that engagement. For example, Wysocki and Childers (2011) found that SNS sites like Facebook served as venues for initiating offline infidelity:

> While social networking sites are increasingly being used for social contact, people continue to be more interested in real-life partners, rather than online partners. It seems that, at some point in a relationship, we need the physical, face-to-face contact. (238–239)

This desire to connect in a medium that seems intensely personal and intimate and free of the complications of face-to-face relationships lulls us into believing that "escape" from our day-to-day relationships is something that we can control. Facebook provides us with the false perception that we can customize our personal lives. The truth is far different. To extend the infidelity example, the American Academy of Matrimonial Lawyers reported that 81 percent have used a SNS site as evidence against a client over the last five years (Italie 2010: Online).

Granted, few will have sympathy for those announcing infidelity on Facebook. People have some personal responsibility for what they post online. But privacy conceded willingly is still a concession: a concession that has implications for both private and public life. There are a number of reasons to want to maintain personal privacy. Tavani (2008) refers to privacy as a "nonintrusion into space, noninterference into choices, noninterference into ones thoughts and personal identity, and access to persona information" (135–141). Wang et al. (1998) elaborated a taxonomy for online privacy concerns. They identified improper acquisition (access, collection, monitoring), use (analysis, transfer) and storage of data as well as privacy invasion (unwanted solicitation) as reasons for concerns. As such, privacy breaches can engender real harms: harassment, theft and social stigma through embarrassment.

Facebook faces a difficult challenge. It can reasonably protect its users from the first two possibilities (harassment and theft) but the more difficult challenge is keeping users from opting out because of social stigma through embarrassment (for example, managing (and thereby reducing) their disclosure). The challenge here is the speed with which Facebook has been adopted. User behavior in what we might call "early Facebook" was highly revelatory. Early Facebook users were more open with their information. While "early adopters" claimed that privacy was a central concern for users of Facebook (Lenhart and Madden 2007), empirical evidence suggests few users actually change the privacy settings. For example, Kolek and Saunders (2008) found that only 11 percent of college students they were studying had restricted access to their profiles. Tufekci (2008a) found the majority of Facebook users used their real names and sizeable numbers of users included phone numbers and addresses.

It's not that users aren't concerned with privacy. It is that there are dual interests at stake: disclosure/connection and personal protection. But those two don't necessarily jibe. In an early study on Facebook, Acquisti and Gross (2006) found that privacy concerns were not necessarily related to how much content young people shared on the site. Thus, high-disclosure users were not necessarily more concerned about privacy than low-disclosure users. The effect is a vast sea of personal information:

> personal information people share – profiles, activities, beliefs, whereabouts, status, preferences, etc. – represent a level of communication that neither has to be told, nor has to be asked for. It is just "out there," untold and unasked, but something that is part of the socializing in mediated publics. (Albrechtslund 2008: Online)

The challenge for the Facebook user is that few know how their information is used. When informed, users are less interested in keeping login status and inactive time private, but many more in the study wanted things like usage statistics and number of conversations (Patil et al. 2011). In those areas, users did seek out and often use higher privacy controls. But higher-frequency users were more likely to have relaxed settings.

However, as I have argued in this book, the sharing of information is not just "out there," but coerced from users in subtle ways. Facebook's architecture is focused on disclosure. When compared with MySpace, users didn't reveal as much (Jones et al. 2008). Hinduja and Patchin (2008) found few people on MySpace offered contact information. This willingness to make ourselves public is problematic for political subjects, particularly in places where personal freedom is curtailed. In these contexts, anonymity is an important tool of resistance.

The Virtues of Anonymity

Part of the success of a movement in the face of a hostile regime is the protection that anonymity provides. But this presents a paradox. The veil of anonymity gives dissidents freedom to speak their mind, but it removes the very personalization that allows people to connect to one another. People need a sense of the personal to be motivated towards action. As such, it is difficult to find political movements comprised of anonymous participants.

This freedom to connect and share personal stories on Facebook created a "much needed public sphere where citizens 'meet' to mingle and discuss issues that matter to them." (Sifry 2011: Online). While Facebook groups were effective used in spreading word of labor strikes and galvanizing youth around the personal story of Khaled Said, it took the efforts of a great number of anonymous bloggers that created the civic society needed for protest to occur. Protest activist requires the formation of a *collective civic consciousness* (Chryssochoou 1998) that can only occur in totalitarian states if a level of anonymity is afforded to its citizens.

Hirschkind (2011) notes that anonymous Egyptian bloggers pioneered: "forms of political critique and interaction that can mediate and encompass the heterogeneity of religious and social commitments that constitute Egypt's contemporary political terrain" (Online). Marshall (1964) notes that voice is an essential component of effective citizenship. A politics rooted in intimacy and *the personal* takes on special meaning in regimes where vibrant civic society is denied. Hirschkind (2011) finds that the revolution in Egypt was the culmination of two decades of offline mobilization augmented by a decade of online civic society building, largely through anonymous bloggers.

The primary advantage of a *politics of the personal* is the ability to quickly disseminate content through pre-existing networks, but it is not as effective in providing the discourse space to cultivate a counter-sphere to the formal state. As an example, the *We Are All Khaled Said* Facebook group was created by Google's head of marketing operations in the Middle East, Wael Ghonim. When his identity was discovered, Egyptian authorities had him arrested on January 27 and Ghonim was held for two weeks.

Google was proactive in challenging the detention. The next day after Ghonim's arrest, the Egyptian government shut down all mobile and Internet communication. Google sought to keep information flowing by creating *speak2tweet* where activists who still had access to phone lines could "call in" tweets about conditions in the country. In addition, Google pressed the US government to pressure Egypt to restore Internet access. Immediately Google made clear that Ghonim would welcome him back to his old job.

By contrast, Facebook seemed reluctant to get involved. In November of 2010, Facebook took down the page citing its policy of not allowing anonymous page administrators. Even when US Senator Richard Durbin sent Facebook a letter asking for an exception to its policy, Facebook refused (Giglio 2011). Richard Allen, Facebook's director of policy for Europe, worked behind the scenes to keep Wael Ghonim's Facebook page up. The company ultimately found a loophole in its policy, adhering to its policy against anonymity but suggesting the site could be administered by a current user. As Richard Allen noted in a correspondence to concerned activists:

> People must use the profile of a real person to admin the page or risk it being taken down at any time. *It is not important to us who that real person is* (my emphasis) as long as their account appears genuine. So if they can offer a real person as admin then the page can be restored. (Allen in Giglio 2011: Online)

This workaround solved the immediate problem. Ghonim was removed as admin for the group and an NGO activist with a Facebook account became the admin so the site could be restored. Giglio (2011) noted that the lag time associated with Facebook's efforts to aid the nascent revolution aggravated the relationship between Facebook and NGO's in Egypt. Nadine Wahab, the US-based activist who became the admin for the *Khaled Said* group expressed frustration with Facebook's efforts: "Facebook helped. But it was almost like they were hesitant to help. They don't understand, or they didn't understand, the power of Facebook in all this" (Giglio 2011: Online).

Ultimately Facebook's did release a statement regarding the *Khaled Said* page but it was ambivalent about giving itself credit:

Mr. Ghonim is a hero and, like all true heroes, he diminishes his own role and gives credit to others. We've witnessed brave people of all ages coming together to effect a profound nonviolent change in their country. Certainly, technology was a vital tool in their efforts but we believe their bravery and determination mattered most. (Schrage: 2011: Online)

Why the reluctance to waive rules an allow anonymity in this specific case? Why the carefully worded language giving credit to "brave people of all ages coming together"? It is because Facebook, as a business, is primarily about revealing the self. It is based on the *problem of the self*, or how to encourage people to disclose and connect to their personal communities. The language regarding making the world better off through *radical transparency* could be a genuine belief of the company and its founder. At the same time, an adherence to this principle is a key financial driver.

But "the problem of the self" is not always a core principle in the public sphere. At times, to uphold the rights of the individual may mean transcending the confines of the personal. In the *We Are Khaled Said* group example, maintaining anonymity was tantamount to speaking for the whole. By not being identifiable, Wahlid Ghonim could allow Khaled Said's murder to stand for the whole. It becomes a public act, an invitation for others to identify with a martyred symbol. Ceding anonymity to have to identify with the page hence becomes a private act. By claiming ownership of a group, it becomes the group's, not the people's.

A core challenge that Facebook poses is rendering *the private* less valuable as a political tool. There is a political value to removing oneself, detaching from the cause of movement one is pursuing. While passion, identification and emotion play a central role in public life, so does anonymity or "living one's life as in a cloud." I turn to this in the next section.

Privacy in the Age of the Personal

Privacy and anonymity are also important in democratic societies. Schoenberg (2010) argues the Internet in general, and Facebook in particular, makes it difficult for us to forget. The vast flowing stream of data "out there" about us cognitively locks us in to an identity we have been cultivating over time. The ability to quickly process data means our past can be recalled making it difficult to reconstitute ourselves into new selves.

But the central challenge for democratic politics is not that we are losing the ability to forget, it is that we are we are losing our ability to see the detached, structural, world "out there." This is not to say that we are unaware that the world "out there" exists, but rather we are losing the capacity to see that world through anything other than the lens of the personal. By looking at the world through the lens of the personal, we lose the capacity to situate our private selves in this broader "world of things." C. Wright Mills (1959) argued that good citizenship required the acquisition of socially relevant knowledge that helps individuals foster what sociologist C. Wright Mills referred to as the *sociological imagination* (Mills 1959). Mills argued that what good-citizens needed was:

> a quality of mind that will help them to use information and to develop reason in order to achieve lucid summations of what is going on in the world and of what may be happening within themselves. (5)

Those imbued with the sociological imagination are able to "grasp history and biography and the relations between the two in society" (Mills 1959: 6). Mills lists three questions he feels are central to this imagination:

1. What is the structure of this particular society as a whole?
2. Where does this society stand in human history? What are the mechanics by which it is changing?
3. What varieties of men and women now prevail in this society? What varieties are coming to prevail? (6)

Primarily because Facebook's allure is its intimacy, users are cued in to engage the public, not through an ability to rationally "grasp history and biography" but to expect the public to be like the private Facebook network, a realm of controlled disclosure and connection. By doing so, we fail to grasp the larger structural dynamics at play that affect our lives. As such we are given a space where we can indulge the world of the personal without the tools needed to engage the larger structural dynamics that inform it. To do this requires having spaces where we can be detached, anonymous and removed from our immediate world of connections and feelings.

The Coming Privacy Backlash

In May 2011, 6 million users in the United States quit Facebook. In addition, the company posted losses of users in Canada, the UK, Russia and Norway (Popkin 2011). While some of the loss can be explained by the "loss of cool" associated with Facebook's growing ubiquity, a meme is also developing regarding Facebook that it is unconcerned with protecting user privacy.

The growing concern over privacy is exacerbated in developing countries by high profile incidents of people making unwise choices. United States Congressman Anthony Weiner's Facebook transgressions had the salacious quality that keeps a story in the headlines for weeks. In light of the scandal, the website Lifehacker released a simple application called "Internet Shame Insurance" designed to send user warning messages before they posted material. The comments include prompts like this one: "Everyone can see this. Including your grandma, your priest and your thought-controlling government" (Pash 2011: Online).

Facebook's appeal comes from the fact that the virtues of disclosure and connection outweigh the virtues of privacy for many users. But if there is an imbalance towards the personal, it occurs because we haven't yet developed a set of norms for online behavior. The London-based artist Nico Muhly created YouTube video to advertise his opera *Two Boys*. In the video, one of the members of the troupe went on the streets of London and sought to engage in online Facebook behavior offline. The performer asked people he had just casually met to be his "friend" by showing them photos, asked people if he could "poke" them, placed a "like" placard on random objects and people and asked merchants if he could write on their "wall." The public reaction highlighted the absurdity of behaving offline the same way you behave online. But as it pertains to politics, we are still negotiating how to relate to the "world out there."

Chapter 9
Friending the Nation-State:
Social Networking and Power

Leading up to the 2008 US presidential election, 2.4 million people signed up to become "friends" with candidate Barack Obama on Facebook. By comparison, only 624,000 people signed up to be friends with his challenger, John McCain (Wasow 2008). What they received for their Facebook "friendship" were standard updates on campaign events, positions of the candidate and responses to the news cycle. But mixed in with this type of traditional political information were personal anecdotes about the candidate, like the listing of his favorite bands on his profile page, which included Miles Davis, John Coltrane, Bob Dylan, Stevie Wonder, J.S. Bach, and the Fugees, leaving one prominent US blogger to comment that this selection made him appear as the "very model of the modern non-threatening black man" (Yglesias 2007).

Facebook's architecture of disclosure gives candidates an unprecedented ability to construct their self-presentations. By disclosing seemingly "personal" information and/or observations, candidates are able to appear as "a real person." As an example, Cory Booker, the charismatic mayor of Newark, New Jersey, actively uses Facebook and Twitter to interact with supporters. As of October of 2011, Mayor Booker had over 1.1 million followers on Twitter, and over 53,000 "likes" on Facebook. Booker's Facebook posts seem like those of any friend you might have. On the site, he challenges President Obama to a game of one-on-one basketball, shares words of wisdom, and jokes that he will personally pull over any citizen that litters.

While few of Cory Booker's followers genuinely think he is their friend, the presence of political figures on Facebook sends a message about how elected officials should act. Crawford (2009) distinguishes between "reciprocal listening" where public officials use social media to engage in a dialogue with constituents, and "delegated listening" where public officials "outsource" their online listening to staff members but do not actively respond. Politicians can choose to use these tools either way. Then UK Prime Minister Gordon Brown's *Downing Street* Twitter feed sought to engage in "reciprocal listening" by responding to constituent posts on his Twitter feed while US President Obama's feel was simply used for information dissemination and hence looked more like "delegated listening" (Crawford 2009: 530).

Crawford notes that the increased use of these social media tools as discourse spaces puts added pressure on politicians to *perform* in these spaces. As such, politicians must carefully manage their identities in social networking spaces.

But a site like Facebook that is entirely based around disclosure and connection demands a much more intimate and informal style of communication than does mass media. Politicians who aren't able to cultivate an "authentic" style are disadvantaged on Facebook. As Wilson (2009) notes:

> Users of social media expect, rightly or wrongly, a much more conversational and unaffected style of political communication ... there is visible frustration on services like Twitter and Facebook when politicians will not engage in the dialogue that many users take to be the key function these spaces afford. (Online)

This puts politicians in a precarious position. Aware of the distinction between public and private (or at least campaigning and governing) some politicians might like to keep a formal distance between themselves and their constituents. The notion that revealing too much of yourself as a public figure is unseemly seems a quaint, naive notion. By maintaining a presence in social media networks, which is a must for politicians today, politicians are expected to be *personal*. If they fail to appear *personal*, they will lose followers and run the risk of alienating the very people they are seeking to reach.

There is some evidence that appealing to others on Facebook has a positive effect on candidate success. Williams and Gulati (2007) found that the size of online supporter networks affected vote share in 2006 US midterms. According to their data, incumbents added 1.1 percent to their vote share by doubling their number of supporters on Facebook and open seat candidates added 3 percent to their vote total by doing the same thing. That open seat candidates could expand their vote share three times as much as incumbents by becoming popular on Facebook signals that SNS applications, at least in 2006, can "challenge the power of elite hierarchies to determine and organise knowledge and practice" (Jarrett 2008: Online).

The Architecture of Faux-Revelation

But in most cases, this "challenge to the power of elite hierarchies" is all a mirage. Facebook and Twitter pages for politicians are maintained by staff (for example, characterized by *delegated listening*) (Crawford 2009). Much like with pop stars, often candidates and officeholders will have staffers and advisers that handle "Internet messaging" for them. Politics in these social networking spaces is more often an exercise in managing the impression these faux "friends" have of the candidate. The result is more often than not Web 1.5 or the use of SNS sites to manage communication rather than to create an honest dialogue (Jackson and Lilleker 2009). In their study of Danish parliamentary elections, Andersen and Medaglia (2009) echo the Web 1.5 thesis. In a survey of followers of the two main candidates on Facebook they found "friends" on the site were already predisposed to support the candidate. As such, the main goal was to gather information about the candidate rather than engage in a dialogue with the candidates.

Similarly in my own research on Facebook groups, the vast majority of users that created groups were using candidates as symbols to perform political identity. Groups either served as homages to current or former candidates or served as personal diatribes against a candidate. As an example, one site from the US called simply "Ronald Reagan," was created as homage to the former US president:[1]

> This group is for all people, Republicans and Democrats alike, who love Ronald Reagan. The fact is that he was the single most greatest president of our time. His policies, beliefs, and actions led America to flourish in his time in office. I do believe that he could get us out of these bad times if he were here today. I also believe that no matter how many years pass, his legacy will live on forever, and President Reagan will always have an impact. God Bless!

Another example is a group formed called "We love Gonzi and The Nationalist Party and we don't hate anyone" created "for all those people who love our dear Prime Minister, Dr Lawrence Gonzi and The Nationalist Party."[2] A pro-Italian Prime Minister Silvio Berlusconi group called "children can come out, the communists are gone" revealed appreciation for the prime minister through verse:

> There is a big dream
> Who lives in us
> We are people of freedom,
> President we're with you
> Thank goodness that's Silvio

Other groups were created to express strong negative feelings against a candidate. A group called: "I will oppose the government of Piñera!" was created to oppose the Chilean President:[3]

> Piñera was elected with 51.6% of the votes validly cast, will be the new President of the Republic since 11 March 2010, as people aware of our social reality, we must join forces, we are a strong opposition and we will not let you destroy our DIGNITY.

---

1   Ronald Reagan!!! (n.d.). In *Facebook* [Group]. Available at: http://facebook.com/group.php?gid=6351184990. [accessed: 11 August 2010].

2   We love Gonzi and The Nationalist Party and we don't hate anyone. (n.d.). In *Facebook* [Group] http://facebook.com/group.php?gid=285525932379&amp%3Bref=mf. [accessed: 9 August 2010].

3   Seré OPOSICIÓN al Gobierno de Piñera! (I am against the government of Pineda) (n.d.). In *Facebook* [Group]. Available at: http://facebook.com/group.php?gid=75064020224. [accessed: 9 August 2010].

Another group called "I bet I can get at least 10,000 or more ppl who dislike Mikhael Saakashvili" was created so the user could express his strong dislike for the Georgian president:[4]

> The President of Georgia, Mikheil Saakashvili is an asshole that's what i think!
> If u agree with me and dislike Misha join my group and let's make it to 10,000
> to proof that he is a real asshole!

These sites are genuine expressions of love or hate towards public figures. However, they also highlight what Marlin-Bennett (2011) calls a "flattening of emotion" towards public figures. These extreme expressions of admiration or hatred towards public figures personalize the state in ways that place emphasis on the figurehead rather than on the state itself. What makes Facebook powerful for politicians is the ability to enter into this intimate setting and give people a sense that *public life* is indistinct from personal life. To be able to tap into the intimacy of the private for political purposes is a powerful tool. But formal politics can never truly be personal, at least at the national level. Lacking in political communication between candidate and constituency is the sense of interactivity, or a dialectical form of communication between parties where communication is built upon previous messages. An elected official who serves hundreds of thousands if not millions of constituents cannot engage in this process of reciprocal listening.

President Obama is the classic example of the state as friend. He far surpassed the sitting president in the number of friends. As of October of 2008, the US President has over 23 million "likes' on his Facebook wall. By comparison, former President George W. Bush has slightly more than 1.6 million likes on his wall. Levenshus (2010) notes that a core theme of the Obama online strategy was to use the personal as a "hook" to engaging citizens. The purpose was to use Facebook as a "feeder system" to move people into offline campaign activities (donating money, hosting events, voting) (325). A prime way of doing this was to create a "you centered" campaign (328) that empowered "volunteers and gave them a sense of ownership and control in the campaign" (328).

The campaign used a variety of tools to achieve these ends. They created a Facebook profile page that generated millions of "friends." That page was used for mass messaging and combined with email lists to serve as the basis for initial supporter contact. In addition, supporters could download a Facebook app that would directly send messages to friends as they visited their profile. In addition, they fostered the development of a network of local Facebook groups created by field organizers (Levenshus 2010).

This sense of personal control was mediated by a clear top-down strategy (Exley 2008). The campaign created *MyBarackObama*, a "walled garden" social

---

4   I bet I can get at least 10,000 or more ppl who dislike Mikhael Saakashvili. (n.d.). In *Facebook* [Group]. Available at: http://facebook.com/group.php?gid=23523679816 [accessed: 15 August 2010].

network mostly for activists, the site provided activist tools to organize (house parties, fundraising drives) to be used before the formal campaign came into an area. At the beginning of the process, it gave volunteers a way to channel their excitement, and when formal staff came in, they had a pool of volunteers from which they could draw.

To get people committed, politicians have mastered the art of personalizing themselves. While this has always been a part of politics, it becomes hyper-personalized online. If the presumed distance between public officials and private citizens hadn't fallen before Facebook, it has been entirely decimated since its widespread adoption. This impetus to be personal changes the nature of political communication. Political communication between elected official and constituent must be informal. As one US media consultant notes:

> "Facebook is the thing that we do while we're at work, and we do it as a distraction from work. We don't do it as extra work," said J.P. Freire, a consultant at New Media Strategies. "Messages that work are 'Pay attention to this thing,' or 'Weigh in on this thing,' or 'Give us money.' Things that don't work are 'Read this white paper.'" (Friere in Phillip 2011: Online)

But this emphasis on political engagement as transactional (give us money) or opinion based ("What do you think about this?") reduces politics to the realm of "small things" at the expense of the "world out there" that requires a different type of communication built around "reflection and listening." The emphasis of politics on Facebook becomes an exercise in evaluating the candidates' or politicians' status based on the "brand" they have constructed and whether it fits the users' personal preferences.

Facebook provides an unprecedented opportunity to get people personally interested and excited about public life. But ultimately the same *politics of the personal* that excited users lets them down when the realization that public governance cannot be personal. Moreover, it creates the impression that politicians can be, and should be, our *friends* or our *enemies*. The problem is that the nation state isn't *personal*. It shouldn't be our friend or our *enemy*. We shouldn't want to "connect" with it, or have it be an intimate to which we "disclose." Nor should we see it as something we simply "rant over."

The Power of the Private Self

The problem with conflating the public with the personal is that the process of disclosure and connection is asymmetrical. It ignores the fact that in the realm of the political, mystery has its virtues. Scott (1992) argues for the value of *hidden transcripts* as a tool for resisting power-based hegemonic discourses. In *Weapons of the Weak: Everyday Forms of Peasant Resistance* (1992) James Scott highlights the lived experience of cultural subordination. He differentiates between *public transcripts* or the "open interaction between subordinates and those who dominate" (2) and *hidden transcripts* or the discourse that takes place "beyond the direct observation of powerholders" (4). In his work, he saw a clear dividing line between the formal public life of the subordinated and the private life lived of the subordinated lived in kitchens, alleys and private spaces. Domination has much to do with the ability of the state to gain access to this *hidden transcript*.

Rather than simply accept the hegemonic discourse of the powerful, the dominated keep their critiques ensconced in the private realm. Scott notes that "the more menacing the power, the thicker the mask" (3). In order to avoid conflict with the powerful, the powerless adopt a formal, meek and respectful deferential public language. However, beneath the surface lies an informal, boisterous and critical assessment of formal power. Here, dissent and resistance can foment and while not expressed in public, always lie beneath the surface. But because this discourse in not public, the presumption is compliance. It is not simply the dominated's only recourse for dissent, it is a powerful and deliberate strategic tactic to maintain one's sense of dignity and power. When this hidden transcript suddenly becomes public, the results are often spontaneous and unpredictable revolutions like the Arab spring revolts.

It is conceivable that the aim of a *radical transparency* project is to do away with all forms of public transcripts, a sort of postmodern, cosmopolitan, identity free-for-all where no social norms exists and people are free to be their private selves in public without fear of retribution or recrimination. But can a medium build around market-based connection and disclosure accommodate discourses that challenge these core premises, particularly in ways that inform public decisions?

Even in democratic states, sites like Facebook and Google peel layers off the hidden transcript. Law enforcement officials are increasingly using Facebook in criminal investigations. As an example, Google got 4,601 requests for user data from the US government July–December 2010 and complied with 94 percent of those requests (Google 2011). By comparison, Google received 1,162 user data requests from the United Kingdom and complied with 72 percent of them (Google.com 2011).

Facebook is particularly useful as a law enforcement tool. According to a Reuters report "at least two dozen warrants have been granted by federal judges to search the Facebook accounts of suspects. In addition, another 11 warrants have been authorized by federal agencies this year alone, nearly double that for 2010" (Roberts 2011: Online). One example of the usefulness of Facebook for the state is facial recognition. Rather than attempt to build a "database of faces" that would require users to submit data to law enforcement in ways that would raise privacy concerns, Facebook has created a platform where users create a "database of faces" for law enforcement. Through "tagging" photos, users unwittingly aid the state in its law enforcement efforts. This led Manjoo (2011) to note about Facebook: "the government couldn't have built a better facial database if it tried" (Online).

Perhaps the most pernicious effect of the divide between public and private evidenced by *an architecture of disclosure* is the removal of cognitive barriers between the public and hidden transcript. This provides something of a paradox. A good nation state communicates with its publics. Facebook seems an excellent vehicle for establishing a dialogue between the state and its citizens in a non-threatening context. Removing this barrier means that politicians can talk with the public without needing the news media. The old maxim "never pick fights with people who buy ink by the barrel" doesn't apply anymore.

Facebook and Mendacity

On a deeper level, Facebook's emphasis on connection creates expectations about the political that cannot be met. We cannot expect our political system to act like our friends or enemies. As an example, we want honesty from our friends, but we can't have honesty from the state. Martin Jay (2010) makes a provocative case for the virtues of *mendacity* in politics, not in a Machiavellian, instrumental way, but as a baseline assumption that the *public sphere* is a place where we negotiate difference and as such cannot have the same level of intimacy and authenticity that the private sphere exhibits.

He notes that the United States differs from Europe in general by insisting on a Republican tradition of civic virtue and puritan self-examination. In the US, politicians are expected to be open and transparent. George Washington is to be commended because he "did not tell a lie." Abraham Lincoln was lionized as "honest Abe." This insistence that Americans "tell the truth" is not as expected in European political life.

Referencing Carl Schmidt, Jay argues that he thought it is a mistake of categorization, and perhaps even a dangerous one at that, to reduce "the political" to anything else, such as the social, the economic, the aesthetic, the moral or the legal (76–86). The subordination of the political (the public) to other realms weakened its value. The expectation that the political should act as these other institutions do diminished its ability to "tell lies to power," to resist intolerance, religious and political. Jay (2010) quotes Hannah Arendt:

> the democracy of everyday life, which is rightly admired by egalitarian visitors, does not arise from sincerity. It is based on the pretense that we must speak to each other as if social standings were a matter of indifference in our views of each other. (Arendt in Jay 2010: 172)

Here Arendt is speaking mainly about the intrusion of scientific rationality and the search for universal covering laws into the realm of "the political" where pluralist, dialogic dissensus is required. Introducing modes of thought that are oriented towards "truth" overwhelm such debate at the expense of "listening to others" and arriving at what Rawls called an overlapping consensus about public life.

The same critique could be made in the opposite direction about how Facebook reorients our sense of "the public." To the extent that we expect "the public" to be about the personal, about disclosure and connection, we grow distasteful of those forums that do not provide us with those things. The expectation that public life can be about disclosing and affirming/connecting undermines the real work of politics which involves reasoning, listening and arriving at a possibly distasteful consensus. But because we've dissociated "the political" from politics that we've grown jaded and disappointed with it. As Arendt noted (in Jay):

> it is never simple to separate the noble from the vulgar, the great ambitions from
> the petty egotistical calculations, the trenchant language of truth from the sophistry
> of manipulation and seduction ... there grows up around the political, as a result, a
> longing that in a certain sense is impossible to fulfill. (in Jay 2010: 169)

The impertinence with this reality of politics doesn't necessarily mean people exit the process. It means they approach it with the same expectations they have for their private relations – "transparency, integrity, honesty and truthfulness" (169) – and evaluate candidates accordingly. But the reality is that politics is about the messy distinction between the public good and a "plurality of interests" (110). But our inability to see that leads us to "see politics as deeply theatrical, and habitually chastise our opponents for 'playing politics,' as if that were somehow a betrayal of what they should be doing" (7–8).

This is not to say that citizens in the US think politicians are honest. More to the point, we expect that politicians are trying to *connect* with us and *disclose* to us and that their behavior should elicit strong feelings of hatred or love for them. As such, we evaluate candidates based on their ability to engage in a process of *reveal* and *conceal* drawing us in with half details, but seeking to disclose to us and connection with us the entire time.

Political institutional structures in different countries might serve to buffer against this personalization. The personalization of politics in the United States is part of a decades'-long process begun with the advent of television. In the United States, the phenomenon of *candidate-centered campaigns* (as opposed to *party-centered campaigns* in most European democracies) (Agranoff 1976) has been the norm for quite a while. In this instance, party-centered parliamentary systems might serve to buffer against this personalization by creating fewer incentives and expectations that political candidates would engage in a process of *connection* and *disclosure*. However, to the extent that more and more of our interactions globally develop norms of intimacy, we begin to lose sight of the fact that when agents of the state perform on Facebook, they are not *friends* but agents of power who have a vested interest in concealing.

Chapter 10
Conclusions: How to Listen on Facebook

In 2011, the California State Senate considered Senate Bill 242, a measure introduced by Sen. Ellen Corbett to place privacy protections on SNS sites like Facebook. The measure required firms to remove personal information from sites if requested by the user and allow parents to edit their children's content. The measure included a $10,000 fine for non-compliance. In effect, the legislation sought to subvert the architecture of disclosure by requiring social networking sites to establish strict default privacy setting that would reveal the name and hometown of the user/customer and would restrict a broad range of information like: "home addresses, telephone numbers, driver's license numbers, social security numbers, mother's maiden names, bank account numbers and credit card numbers" (McGreevy 2011). In addition, the measure would require sites to remove personal identifying information within 96 hours of a user request or if requested by the parent of a minor.

The bill ultimately deadlocked in the state Senate 16–16, partly in result to the opposition by Google, Facebook, Twitter, Yahoo, Skype, eHarmony and Match. com (McCreevey 2011). The position taken by the companies was rooted in a free speech and non-government interference in the private market argument. A Facebook spokesperson noted:

> (California State) Senator Corbett is arguing for unnecessary regulations that ignore the extraordinary lengths that companies like ours go to in order to protect individuals' privacy and give them the tools to determine for themselves how much information they wish to share online. (Noyes in McGreevy 2011: Online)

This is a logical response for a private business to make against regulations that might impede their business practices. Data protection works against Facebook's core business model. But the efforts of companies like Facebook highlight an important distinction between public and private life. Facebook incentive is to support legislation that prohibits external, non-Facebook actors from accessing user data while resisting legislation that curtails how Facebook can use the data.

Facebook and other SNS sites do not object to all forms of nation-state or international legislation. As an example, ICANN, the international organization charged with regulating the global Internet, is essentially charged with making cyberspace safe for firms, not for the public (Mathiason et al. 2004).

Other jurisdictions are enacting policies that aid the architecture of disclosure by regulating the possible repercussions of acting on Facebook posts. In 2010, Germany moved to ban employer use of Facebook to look up interviewee profiles

(O'Hear 2010). These forms of privacy protection that facilitates *disclosure* and *connection* by ensuring that users can engage with their network without fear of repercussion from future employers unwittingly supports Facebook's core business.

It is a business model that draws us towards a different self, a digital self that ideally would be free from external constraints on user's ability and desire to disclose. But a digital footprint in which we are encouraged to disclose our private selves rather than perceive our digital self to be a public self, has repercussions for our behavior as public citizens. If we are performing our identity on Facebook, we have choices as to how that performance is carried out. If we are telling the story of ourselves on Facebook, that story can appear as a carefully crafted autobiography where we are keenly aware of how our identity can appear to a vast audience of others. Or it can appear as messier, less-edited, decontextualized fragments of a life.

It is problematic for us to present the former on Facebook because unlike an autobiography, Facebook does not present us as a coherent narrative. It presents us as a stream of decontextualized fragments. In reality, we are multiple identities and can function effectively as different selves in different roles. A person who wants to "blow off steam" can also be a highly effective and competent employee. But employers might turn to "gut assessments" (which can often be wrong, especially if employee and employer do not share the same cultural norms). They might also turn to *psychometrics* to determine whether a potential employee is statistically likely to do the job based on the behavior of their digital Facebook selves.

Facebook must manage the perception that these fragments of a user's *digital self* presented on Facebook can be picked up and reconstituted by others with ill effects for the user. Facebook wants to manage the reconstitution process because it is their product. From their perspectives, efforts to legislatively curtail how Facebook can use their users' data is tantamount to the state enacting a legal *taking* of Facebook's private property.

This is not the way we think of Facebook. Sifry (2009) poses an interesting puzzle central to Facebook's future: "Is Facebook more like a town hall or a private mall?" If we deem it to be more like a town hall, it is entirely appropriate to think of Facebook users as digital citizens and their content as a form of property. And, if that is the case, then digital citizens have rights. The extent of these rights can be debated, but they serve as a basis for how users should treat their participation on Facebook going forward. In this context, Facebook is like a nation state and users have the ability to create the terms for how their property can be used and disseminated. They can determine rules for what can and cannot be said. But for this to work in practice, Facebook must belong to the users. It must be "public."

In reality, Facebook is private. It is not a nation state. Its CEO is not elected by the users. It is not a cooperative with user ownership of the company. As such, Facebook is more like a "private mall" where the mall operators have the ability to set the terms for speech. As such, our expectations should be akin to what DeRosa (2011) calls digital feudalism:

... the land many live on is owned by someone else, be it Facebook or Twitter or Tumblr, or some other service that offers up free land and the content provided by the renter of that land essentially becomes owned by the platform that owns the land (Online).

Sorting out this distinction is essential to determining how the state should respond to Facebook. Should the nation-state see Facebook as a supplement to the public sphere or should it see it as a threat to public communication? The answer perhaps lies somewhere in between. This middle-ground approach suggests that Facebook could provide a useful discourse space, but the state could adopt legislation that curtails Facebook's ability to collect and use data. Evidence of the importance companies like Facebook place upon maintaining this architecture of disclosure is their strong lobbying efforts against privacy legislation in the United States, as the "do not track" legislation example can attest.

Facebook's Challenge from the State

Can nation states constrain Facebook? One step taken is the EU's Data Protection Directive. This directive states that user data must be "freely given, specific and informed" (Article 2(h) of Directive 95/46/EC) in addition, the EU has also issued an E-Privacy Directive (Directive 2002/58 on Privacy and Electronic Communications) that forbids the surveillance and interception of electronic data without user consent. In addition, the directive forbids the storing of electronic data without both consent and 'clear and comprehensive information" about why the data is being collected. In response to the testing of user tracking software being tested by BT, a UK-based digital carrier, Viviane Reding, the EU's telecom commissioner, made explicit the EU's position on the use of digital information:

> European privacy rules are crystal clear: a person's information can only be used with their prior consent. We cannot give up this basic principle, and have all our exchanges monitored, surveyed and stored in exchange for a promise of "more relevant" advertising! I will not shy away from taking action where an EU country falls short of this duty. (Meller 2011: Online)

But this strong statement was simply a warning, albeit one that could lead to litigation in the European Court of Justice. However, Facebook operates internationally. Addressing challenges with how Facebook uses information requires a global response. That response, however, is unlikely to be coordinated. For example, the United States has done little in the way of protection for user data on social networking sites. Congressional advocates in the United States have asked the Federal Trade Commission to establish guidelines for social networking sites to help users understand how their information is used by these sites.

Some of this recalcitrance is changing, however. Government agencies in the US and Europe have fired rhetorical salvos at Facebook over their June 2011 decision to adopt *facial recognition software* to help users tag photos. The *Congressional Privacy Caucus* in the United States Congress issued a strong rebuke to Facebook of the adoption of the technology. In particular the chairman, Representative Edward Markey of Massachusetts, challenged Facebook's "opt out" policy as it related to the facial recognition technology:

> Requiring users to disable this feature after they've already been included by Facebook is no substitute for an opt-in process ... If this new feature is as useful as Facebook claims, it should be able to stand on its own, without an automatic sign-up that changes users' privacy settings without their permission. (in Olivarez-Giles 2011: Online)

In November of 2011 the *New York Times* reported that the United States Federal Trade Commission reached an agreement with Facebook wherein the company would agree to 20 years of "privacy audits" and would be restricted from making public information a user had originally shared privately on the site without permission from the user (Cain-Miller 2011). The state, however, is not the major threat to Facebook's business. Government regulation is a minor challenge when compared with larger societal trends that may work against Facebook's architecture of disclosure.

The Challenge for Facebook from Its Market Model

While Facebook is estimated to have more than one billion users by the end of 2011, Manjoo (2011) speculates that we might be in an era of "peak Facebook" citing a meager global growth rate of 1.7 percent in May of 2011. He notes that in May of 2011, Facebook lost users in the US and Europe and was relying on increases of users in developing countries for its growth, with most of the new growth coming from Latin America and Asia.

Can Facebook rely on the developing world for its continued growth? The prospect of China's 420 million Internet users (and growing exponentially) as a potential market is a big part of Facebook's future growth. Access to that market, however, is not assured. As such, it has to find other users to expose to its *architecture of disclosure*. Manjoo (2011) likens a developing world business model to an imperialist state, whereby an early phase of conquering nations has now moved into a governing phase. While the Facebook as nation-state metaphor has its flaws, it is particularly apt in explaining how Facebook plans to accommodate future growth.

Its current emphasis on trying to become ubiquitous among the users it currently has through the social graph has its limits. Offering a "like" button in all corners of the Web can help "squeeze out" more disclosure from its user base. But that user base only has so much it can disclose, and more importantly, only has so much disposable income with which it can consume. Hence, Facebook has to expand the number of users.

Perhaps we are seeing the beginnings of cracks in the *architecture of disclosure*. An October 2010 survey conducted by *Vanity Fair* magazine found that 36 percent of US respondents reported social media use as their largest "waste of time," a higher percentage than those who reported TV viewing as their greatest time waster (Dolliver 2010: Online).

Facebook's business is to populate a network for you. But it is conceivable that Facebook has "tapped out" its existing networks. It is conceivable that we have reached a point where, at least in the US and Europe, those attracted to Facebook have signed up and those people's networks have pretty much been populated. Facebook is no longer an "emerging technology." It has arrived. It is hard to conceive that there are many adults left who just discovered Facebook and are busily searching old high-school friends. What if most of the people drawn to Facebook have already "found their friends"?

The Architecture of Disclosure and Cultural Context

Cultural resistance to the architecture of disclosure poses significant business challenges to Facebook. For instance, what does Facebook do about Japan? Japan is one of the most developed economies in the world. However, forays into the Japanese market have thus far fallen flat. The International Telecommunications Union (2011) estimates there are over 100 million Internet users in Japan, making it the third largest Internet market in the world.

Tabuchi (2011) reported in the *New York Times* on a survey done by MMD in 2010 where 89 percent of Japanese respondents reported reluctance in disclosing their real names on the Web. Instead, Japanese users appear to be drawn to the potential anonymity of the Web. As such, SNS sites that use pseudonyms are more popular in Japan. Rather than use the Web to bolster offline friendships, Japanese users seek to create a distinct online life (Tabuchi 2011). In effect, these users are not as drawn to the "architecture of disclosure" as North American and European users seem to be. Facebook's response has been to try to shoehorn the architecture of disclosure into the Japanese context. Tabuchi notes that in Japan in early 2011, users were presented with this message on Facebook: "Facebook values real-life connections ... Please use your real name" (Tabuchi 2011, Online).

The last two years has seen an explosion of global SNS use, a phenomenon largely driven by young people. A 2010 Pew Global Attitudes survey found that while the United States had the highest rate of SNS use (46 percent of those surveyed use social networking sites) the rest of the world is catching up. The next three countries in proliferation of SNS use were Poland (43 percent), Britain (43 percent) and South Korea (40 percent) (Pew Research Center 2010).

The spread of SNS use was largely driven by people under 30 who used SNs' at significantly higher levels than those over 30. In Germany for instance, 86 percent of people under 30 used SNS but only 8 percent of those 50 and older used the site (Pew Research Center 2010). The gaps are not the result of differences in Internet use. Older people use the Internet, but they use the Internet for different reasons.

Low use, according to Pew, was largely the result of low access and not an unwillingness to use SNS sites. For example, 19 percent of Kenyans use SNS, but only 5 percent of Kenyans with Internet access "just used the Internet". . Lowest rates were found in Indonesia (6 percent) and Pakistan (3 percent) but that is largely due to lack of Internet access (Pew Research Center 2010).

Butler (2010) graphed the then 500 million Facebook users based on the geographic distribution of friends. What it revealed was that Facebook in 2010 was very much a phenomenon of the West. The map reveals obvious facts. Autocratic regimes have significantly less Facebook adoption (Burma, North Korea). Other, what one might call semi-authoritarian regimes, places, like China for instance, are dark because of a preference for other networks (for example, the state-sponsored *Ren Ren* in China). Democratic states like Brazil and India, at the moment, have a preference for the social networking service Orkut over Facebook. Eastley (2010) observed the existence of a *Facebook curtain* that parallels the old Soviet Bloc states including China, Facebook's biggest unclaimed prize. There are a number of reasons for Facebook's failure to spread globally at a faster rate from a lack of interest (Brazil, Japan) to a lack of Internet penetration (Indonesia), to censorship (Iran, Pakistan) to the presence of a state-sponsored alternative (China).

Some of these issues are greater challenges than others. In Brazil, Orkut's early foothold means finding your friends online requires establishing an Orkut account. A shift in Facebook's favor would require a *great migration* to Facebook. Seemingly, as Facebook expands, it will offer its service in a wider range of languages. The bigger challenge for Facebook is how to penetrate into markets that have low penetration rates. Internet World Statistics (2011) notes that over half of the nations in the world have Internet penetration rates that are lower than 25 percent and many African, particularly Sub-Saharan Africa, have penetration rates below 1 percent. In addition, countries like China have banned Facebook, keeping its 420 million potential users (and growing exponentially) from Facebook's architecture of disclosure.

Beyond Facebook?

Dear Facebook, heard twitter is replacing you. karma is a bitch! Sincerely, Myspace.

In October of 2011, this "tweet" bounced around Twitter for a few days. Is it prescient? Is Facebook destined to go the way of MySpace? Will the "next big thing" overtake it? Alternatives to Facebook are slowly emerging. Diaspora, a

San Francisco-based company, has developed an alternative to Facebook (an "anti-Facebook) designed to give users more control over their data. For example, the site allows users to select whom they share data with and allow users to maintain ownership over their photos. An *alpha* version of the site went live in late September of 2011. While popular with the digerati, Diaspora is unlikely to significantly challenge Facebook's hegemony.

But a more serious challenge to Facebook comes from Google. In June of 2011, Google launched Google+, a social networking site that allows users to use an expanded set of tools like video chat and group messaging, but with a smaller, more segmented set of friends. Although reviews of Google+ are mixed, one application that received praise is the *circles* feature. Through circles, Google+ allows you to group people based on shared interests or proximity. The set of friends on Google+ is extracted from your Google contacts, but they can be placed into clusters of groups based on shared interests. The initial launch of Google+ provided users with templates for categorization. New users could place contacts into "empty circles" called Friends, Acquaintances, Family and Following.

Google+ builds its social network around this "Google circle" premise. You can share content through the sparks feature, and have instant group chats with the "hangouts" feature. In addition, Google in 2011 added features that mirrored Facebook's architecture of disclosure. In March of 2011, Google introduced a "+1" option on its search applications. The button allows you to recommend pages to your Google contacts, much like the Facebook "like" button. The +1 button allows Google to capture one more stream of user data it can sell to advertisers. So even if the Facebook empire sunsets, other applications will arrive to take its place.

Facebook's Response

While Facebook may appear a juggernaut, there are threats to its market growth. Wu (2010) suggests that Internet companies are playing with new business models like providing higher quality of service for a fee and allocating greater bandwith to those who pay more. Conceivably, Facebook could change its business model to de-emphasize the *architecture of disclosure*. It could for instance charge users who do not wish to have their data shared. Indeed, a model that is based almost exclusively on ad-revenue is dependent upon the vagaries of the market. Facebook took in roughly four billion dollars in advertising revenue in 2011: this constitutes about 90 percent of its total revenue (Horn 2011).

But if Facebook's recent activity is any indication, they are expanding, rather than constraining, the *architecture of disclosure*. Facebook has responded to the increased competition from Google by enacting changes of its own. In September of 2011, Facebook added slight but important modifications to its site. Among them were changes that made it easier for Facebook users to place their friends into groups, like the *Circles* application in Google+ and a *subscribe* button that allowed users to follow others much as one does on Twitter. Facebook also changed its newsfeed. Rather than simply provide a scroll of feeds in chronological order, Facebook created a "top stories" section (for example, the most popular stories), denoted with a blue tab in the corner of the update, at the top of the newsfeed. Recent updates continued under the "top stories" tab.

In September of 2011, Facebook announced a number of changes at its F8 conference. The biggest of these changes was Facebook's new "Timeline" feature. The feature serves as an "enhanced profile" that enlarges the profile picture but also allows users (and visitors) to see a "timeline" of their Facebook participation, from their earliest posts and pictures to the current time. This arc of participation is mapped out for users to see. The timeline feature is sorted by years and months and allows users to click on a specific date and see Facebook activity from that time. They can also add content to their timeline, making the site serve as a virtual scrapbook. While this undoubtedly enhances the appeal of the site to many, it places past user activity into public view. While users can "limit the audience for past posts," it uses the opt-out feature to gain the largest possible share of participation to its new site.

In addition, the company has also added a Twitter-like ticker that will be populated by what Facebook calls "lightweight" content (cooking, listening to music, and so on) shared through the *open graph*. So when a network member listens to music on the music application *Spotify* it will appear on the ticker and will provide easy access to the media the user's "friend" is sharing.

Facebook and Listening

Mark Zuckerberg hailed these new changes as providing users with "frictionless experiences." But friction is an essential element of democratic life. More important for the future of democratic citizenship is that users learn to "listen" on Facebook. Listening is a precondition for cooperation. Without the ability to understand the needs of the other, we are incapable of engaging in sustained action. We have different preconditions to listen. We can think of listening and disclosing as a dialectical process.

At its best, Facebook as a political tool provides a platform for the airing of marginalized voices. While the medium might also fragment discourse spaces in ways that may inhibit cross-cutting deliberation (Mutz 2006), the greater concern highlighted in this book is the impact on our self, on if and how we distinguish between the personal work of our networks and the public "world of things" (Arendt 1958).

The data on political Facebook groups I have presented points to an engagement with public issues that comes from a deeply personal and performative position. Rather than focus on how the architecture of Facebook encourages network formation based on homogeneity (Boyd and Ellison 2007), I have made the case that Facebook's encouragement of constant disclosure makes political engagement on the Web intimately personal. As such, the vast majority of ways in which people engage with the political on Facebook reinforces this demand for public life to be like private life: informal, agentic, revelatory and authentic. In addition, it also structures political talk in ways that are performative rather than deliberative, expressive rather than dialogic.

The impulse to *disclose* and *connect* is central to who we are as human beings; we feel a strong pull towards these otherwise virtuous traits. We are drawn to them because they are often pleasant, familiar, and comfortable. However, their overuse diminishes their value. While much of this is good and important, the health of democratic societies relies upon more than simply proclaiming our political selves. It requires cultivating habits of democratic attention (Bickford 1996) and, in particular, cultivating habits of talking to strangers (Allen 2006).

Moon (2002) draws an important distinction between democracy and democratic practices (online voting, e-democracy, submitting comments) which are tools of democracy but are not democracy itself. Similarly, Facebook's ability to *disclose* and *connect* might create an image of a public sphere, but does not necessarily make it one. Marlin-Bennett (2011) warns of the dangers of conflating the agora with the polis:

> Having an additional marketplace for ideas in the guise of information technologies does not make society more democratic because simply having the ideas out there does not mean that people are engaged in meaningful democratic deliberation ... more talk does not necessarily mean more democracy. (138)

This creates a serious problem for democratic life. Facebook exacerbates a move away from a deliberative democracy by making it easier to occupy ourselves with our personal spheres. Twenge and Campbell (2009) suggest that Facebook encourages narcissistic behavior and devalues friendships by allowing users to opt in or out of dialogue with their friends. This ability to "unfriend" or "mute" a friend when it is convenient changes the underlying nature of friend relations in ways that affect offline interaction. Constant contact might not have the mutually beneficial effects of friendship if online friends can selectively ignore each other.

Deresiewicz (2011) argues that Facebook represents a long-term diminishing of *friendship* obligation. He notes that classical notions of friendship included virtue, seeking mutual improvement and developing intense personal bonds.

> Facebook's very premise—and promise—is that it makes our friendship circles visible. There they are, my friends, all in the same place. Except, of course, they're not in the same place, or, rather, they're not my friends. They're simulacra of my friends, little dehydrated packets of images and information, no more my friends than a set of baseball cards is the New York Mets ... What we have, instead of community, is, if we're lucky, a "sense" of community— the feeling without the structure; a private emotion, not a collective experience. And now friendship, which arose to its present importance as a replacement for community, is going the same way. We have "friends," just as we belong to

"communities." Scanning my Facebook page gives me, precisely, a "sense" of
connection. Not an actual connection, just a sense. (Online)

Deresiewicz's emphasis on the importance of sustained and intense contact as a
centerpiece of friendship translates to the political realm as well. Bickford (1996)
recasts Aristotle's notion of friendship into a "politics of attention" that requires us
to develop the habits of *listening* to a wide range of groups in a democratic society.
Vibrant functioning democracy requires the cultivation of *voice* for marginalized
groups and that voice requires a polis that is willing to listen.

   Allen (2006) argues that embracing classical notions of friendship is the only
thing that can work against the inter-group, inter-racial distrust that threatens
democratic societies. She reminds us how the classical notion of friendship instills
in us obligations that are needed for community and nation building:

> ... friendship is not an emotion, but a practice, a set of hard-won, complicated
> habits that are used to bridge trouble, difficulty, and differences of personality,
> experience, and aspiration. Friendship is not easy, nor is democracy. Friendship
> begins in the recognition that friends have a shared life—not a "common" nor
> an identical life—only one with common events, climates, built-environments,
> fixations of the imagination, and social structures. (xxi)

Friendship for Allen is a precondition for addressing collective problems.
Friendship cues us into the reality of our shared existence and our need to mutually
address problems like climate change, economic inequality, and so on. This filial
responsibility to one another does not mean we are "friends with everyone" but
rather that we strive to take this relationship seriously, to be better and to strive to
help our friends become better.

   Indeed, recent scholarship has emphasized the importance of the density and
duration of inter-group contact in changing attitudes towards the other. Intimate
contacts, such as friendship and love relationships, increase empathy and reduce
stereotypes (Ellison and Powers 1994, Aberson et al. 2004, Martin et al. 2003).
Pettigrew argues that "friendship potential is an essential, not merely a facilitating
condition for positive intergroup contact" (1998: 76). Facebook impoverishes
political discourse to the extent that Facebook reinforces our own personal stories
at the expense of listening to the personal stories of diverse others.

   SNS provides a steady, ambient stream of information (status updates, tweets,
and so on.) You cannot disclose if you are listening, and vice versa. Listening
takes more effort because there are more codes to unpack when you engage with
publics different from your own. This process of listening is central to democracy.
The great danger in this for democratic life is the illusion of personal engagement,
when in reality we are engaging with pre-selected publics; we can "tune out" and
not be really involved in the practice of listening. As Crawford (2009) puts it:

> If the hours are long, a worker can perform a kind of presence, using the ambient awareness of the goings-on in the lives of their loved ones to feel connected, despite being physically removed in an office or work site. At the same time, they may come to feel an increasing expectation that they should be using these services, regularly updating and never away too long. If they are not paying attention, are they still a maximally effective student, worker, partner or parent? (532)

Crawford (2009) points out that the research on the Web has privileged voice as the key narrative for justifying online participation. She ties this to the early "techno-utopian" libertarian ethos of the Web which emphasized the expression of personal beliefs and preferences over collaborative goals. Voice can be democratic participation when we "speak truth to power." But very often voice is an excuse to avoid listening. To the extent that we preference voice over the hard work of "being fully present" in public life, we are impoverished.

As an example, in May of 2011, Facebook announced that they are using Microsoft's *PhotoDNA* software to cull through the 200 million images uploaded to its site to identify and remove illegal images of child pornography (Bishop 2011). Rather than rely on "the crowd" as before, Facebook can now take the job of eliminating offensive material from the community and entrust it to an algorithm. Undoubtedly this will reduce the number of offensive photographs, and that outweighs any costs to not having the service. But it also takes the unpleasant work of "turning in" rule-breakers. In a sense, it blinds us to the fact that the behavior happens in the world "out there." It diminishes our need to listen for inappropriate behavior within our communities.

But in reality these things do happen in the world out there. If there was ever an opportunity to have the conversation about this unpleasant reality, it has been eliminated. It would be difficult to find anyone who would object to not having to be responsible for identifying pedophiles. But that is the point. Eliminating the use of "the crowd" to remove these photographs gives the illusion that the problem has disappeared, when it has not. It eliminates for us the need to listen for problems in our community. The response to pedophilia is a *public issue* that citizens should "be listening for" by being able to "grasp history and biography and the relations between the two" (Mills 1959: 6).

In reality everyone is both a listener and a discloser online. But Facebook elevates the practice of "presenting oneself" to others at the expense of more subtle and equally important social roles. Disclosure is a means of connecting, but connection requires the engagement of those who aren't speaking. This hyper-emphasis on "joining-in" and being a "content creator" undervalues the role of discretion, contingency and reflection in public discourse.

Crawford echoes this theme by advocates for placing more value on *lurkers* in political discourse. They constitute the "audience" that encourages others to make contributions. However, she notes that the very term "lurker" connotes something untoward and duplicitous. But lurkers, she notes, are *the public* that makes voice possible. As such, there have been efforts to reframe the role of lurkers in online communication into 'peripheral participants' (Zhang and Storck 2001) and as 'non-public participants' (Preece et al. 2004). For her part, Crawford (2009) advocates the use of the term *listening in* (528) as one would a radio or television program as an important dimension of creating an ideal online discourse space.

Creating an Architecture of Listening

How can we create a social networking future that includes listening and paying attention to the other? What we pay attention to is a historically and socially bound process. As Crawford (2009) notes:

> Along with new technological forms of display, communication, recording and
> playback come new forms of looking, listening and interacting; they afford new
> ways of focusing as well as defocusing attention. In doing so, they also become part
> of the ongoing reconstruction of the limits of human capacities. They contribute to
> the sense of what is possible, as well as to the qualities of being. (239)

The answer thus lies in changing the architecture of Facebook and other SNS sites. Facebook is not simply a platform for communication. It is part of a connected and evolving system of interactions. Facebook has its own ecology. Therefore, presumptions that changes in the system are linear or predictable are bound to be wrong. Facebook as a system is complex with multiple feedback looks. If we look at Facebook as a system, we emphasize the interactions between users in a complex system rather than the users themselves.

If we think of Facebook as a system, the core question becomes how the system gets managed to produce desired behavior. Does Facebook organize itself among the personal network to such an extent that it fails to account for larger systemic changes? Systems can be organized along a number of different pathways, but if Facebook moves down a path of *disclosure* and *connection* it may lack *resilience* when societal needs change. Systems designed for revelation leave a lot on the table. These systems are caught in a constant treadmill of expanding platforms and trying to introduce new ways to get people to disclose more information. There is an upper limit to how much you can get individuals to reveal about themselves.

There may be a point at which an emphasis on "the personal" becomes so pervasive it harms the system. An indication of this is the face that 6 million users left Facebook in May of 2011 (Manjoo 2011). Is there a tipping point of disclosure and connection become so pervasive that it creates disincentives for people to join? As with natural systems, dynamics that are undermining the system do not appear until it is too late. As Folke (2010) points out "the clear lake seems hardly affected by fertilizer runoff until a critical threshold is passed, at which point the water abruptly goes turbid" (42). It is hard to know if we have we arrived at "peak Facebook," but an important question to ask is whether Facebook's model is sustainable into the future. The question for Facebook users going forward is how to build a *resilient* Facebook or a *resilient* social network alternative.

Poteete et al. (2010) highlights how members of complex systems can effectively manage common-pool resources. Systems that cultivate habits of listening might not need to be as aggressive in tracking your every move. A system that builds on, and seeks to leverage, our desires to listen to others can bring us closer towards collaborative problem-solving. This might mean the development of a "public Facebook" subsidized by the state or by philanthropic organizations and oriented towards non-market, non-individualist ends. If as behavioral economics suggests, we can structure choice to lead to preferred outcomes, is it possible to create an *architecture of listening*? Could we create networks around cooperation, rather than connection? The social network *Jumo* is an example of a social network build around social causes, rather than personal networks. Creating networks that emphasize problem-solving might provide some appeal to users. Rilling and Sanfey (2011) found that cooperation lights up "pleasure centers" in our brain.

Applications that incentivize "listening to the other" could be a challenge to Facebook but would not replace it. A cluster of the population may have little interest in listening to others, but simply want to disclose (narcissists). Another group is more interested in listening rather than disclosing (lurkers). But what of the majority of people in the middle, those who want to engage in both disclosing and listening? MacKinnon (2011) calls for an Internet "magna carta" moment. But much of what is needed from citizens extends beyond creating more egalitarian frameworks for the Internet. An enhancement of a democratic polity is populating SNS sites with users that see themselves as flexible and contingent. If users engaged Facebook sites with more reflection about how people respond to their updates, mixed tones, shared content that might be seen as out of the norm, engaged with diverse others outside their personal networks, the site might be more useful in creating effective citizens. But to do this requires actions outside Facebook. It requires citizens that break out of their secure, contingent political selves.

Bibliography

Aberson, C.L., Shoemaker, C. and Tomolillo, C.M. 2004. Implicit bias and contact: The role of interethnic friendships. *Journal of Social Psychology*, 144, 335–347.

Acquisti, A. and Gross, R. 2006. Imagined communities: Awareness, information sharing, and privacy on the Facebook. In *Privacy Enhancing Technologies*, edited by G. Danezis and P. Golle. Berlin: Springer, 36–58.

Acquisti, A. and Gross, R. 2009. Predicting social security numbers from public data. *Proceedings of the National Academy of Sciences*, 106(27), 10975.

Adorno, T. 1978. *Minima Moralia: Reflections from Damaged Life*. Translated by E.F.N. Jephcott. London: Verso.

Agranoff, R. 1976. *The Management of Electoral Campaigns*. Boston: Holbrook Press.

Albrechtslund, A. 2008. Online social networking as participatory surveillance. *First Monday*, 13(3).

Alexander, J.C. 2004. Cultural pragmatics: Social performance between ritual and strategy. *Sociological Theory*, 22(4), 527–573.

Allen, D.S. 2006. *Talking to Strangers: Anxieties of Citizenship since Brown v. Board of Education*. Chicago: University of Chicago Press.

Allfacebook.com. 2009. *Google Now Indexes 620 Million Facebook Groups*. [Online]. Available at: http://allfacebook.com/google-now-indexes-620-million-facebook-groups-2010–02 [accessed: 8 September 2011].

Andersen, K. and Medaglia, R. 2009. The use of Facebook in national election campaigns: Politics as usual? In *Electronic Participation*, edited by A. McKintosh and E. Tambouris. Berlin: Springer, 101–111.

Anderson, B. 1983. *Imagined Communities: Reflections on the Origin and Spread of Nationalism*. London: Verso, 60, 73–82.

Anderson, C. 2008. The end of theory. *Wired Magazine*. [Online, July]. Available at: http://wired.com/science/discoveries/magazine/16–07/pb_theory. [accessed: 12 September 2011].

Andrejevic, M. 2009. *iSpy: Surveillance and Power in the Interactive Era*. Lawrence: University of Kansas.

Appadurai, A. 1996. *Modernity at Large: Cultural Dimensions of Globalization*. Minneapolis: University of Minnesota Press.

Aral, S., Muchnik, L. and Sundararajan, A. 2009. Distinguishing influence-based contagion from homophily-driven diffusion in dynamic networks. *Proceedings of the National Academy of Sciences*, 106(51), 21544.

Arendt, H. 1958. *The Human Condition*. Chicago: University of Chicago Press.

Arrington, M. 2007. 85 Percent of College Students Use FaceBook. *TechCrunch. com* [Online, 7 September]. Available at: http://techcrunch.com/2005/09/07/85-of-college-students-use-facebook/ [accessed: 11 September 2011].

Asur, S. and Huberman, B.A. 2010. Predicting the future with social media. In 2010 IEEE/WIC/ACM International Conference on Web Intelligence and Intelligent Agent Technology. York University, Toronto, Canada.

Back, M.D., Stopfer, J.M., Vazire, S., Gaddis, S., Schmukle, S.C., Egloff, B. and Gosling, S. 2010. Facebook profiles reflect actual personality, not self-idealization. *Psychological Science*, 21(3), 372–374.

Bagui, L. and Parker, M.B. 2009. Mobilising an Obama Nation using Web 2.0: Yes We Can. *Informatics and Design Papers and Reports. Paper 27*. Available at: http://dk.cput.ac.za/inf_papers/27. [accessed: July 12 2011].

Bailard, C. 2011. *A Field Experiment on the Internet's Effect in an African Election: Savvier Citizens, Disaffected Voters, or Both?* Available at: http://themonkeycage. org/wp-content/uploads/2011/05/bailard_tanzania_experiment.pdf. [accessed: 24 August 2011].

Bailard, C. 2011. The Political Relevance of the Internet in Developing Countries. *The Monkey Cage Blog*. [Online, 5 October]. Available at: http://themonkeycage. org/blog/2011/05/10/the-political-relevance-of-the-internet-in-developing-countries/ [accessed: 11 September 2011].

Baker, J.R. and Moore, S.M. 2010. Creation and validation of the personal blogging style scale. *Cyberpsychology, Behavior, and Social Networking*, 14(6), 379–385.

Baldassarri, D. and Gelman, A. 2008. Partisans without constraint: Political polarization and trends in American public opinion. *American Journal of Sociology*, 114, 408–446.

Barabási, A.L. 2010. *Bursts: The Hidden Pattern Behind Everything We Do*. New York: EP Dutton.

Barash, V., Ducheneaut, N., Isaacs, E. and Bellotti, V. 2010. Faceplant: Impression (mis)Management in Facebook Status Updates. Proceedings of 4th International AAAI Conference on Weblogs and Social Media (ICWSM), Washington, DC, May 23–26.

Bargh, J.A., McKenna, K. and Fitzsimons, G.M. 2002. Can you see the real me? Activation and expression of the "true self" on the Internet. *Journal of Social Issues*, 58(1), 33–48.

Barlow, J.P. 1996. *A Declaration of the Independence of Cyberspace*. [Online]. Available at: http://editions-hache.com/essais/pdf/barlow1.pdf. [accessed: 12 October 2011].

Barreto, M. and C. Parker. 2011. The Tea Party and the Anti-Immigration Debate in 2010. Western Political Science Association Annual Conference (San Antonio, TX).

Barry, A. 2001. *Political Machines: Governing a Technological Society*. London: Athlone Press.

Bartels, L.M. 1996. Uninformed votes: Information effects in presidential elections. *American Journal of Political Science*, 40(1), 194–230.

Bartky, S.L. 1988. Foucault, femininity, and the modernisation of patriarchal power. In *Feminism and Foucault*, edited by I. Diamond and L. Quiaby. Boston: Northern University Press.

Bauman, Z. 1992. *Intimations of Postmodernity*. London: Routledge.

Bauman, Z. 2000. *Liquid Modernity*. Cambridge: Polity Press.

Baumeister, R.F. 1987. How the self became a problem: A psychological review of historical research. *Journal of Personality and Social Psychology*, 52(1), 163.

Bauwens, M. 2005. *The Political Economy of Peer Production*. [Online]. Available at: http://informatik.uni-leipzig.de/~graebe/Texte/Bauwens-06.pdf [accessed: 23 September 2011].

Beck, U. 2000. *What Is Globalization?* Cambridge: Polity Press.

Benhabib, S. 1996. *Democracy and Difference: Contesting the Boundaries of the Political*. Cambridge: Cambridge University Press.

Benkler, Y. 2006. *The Wealth of Networks: How Social Production Transforms Markets and Freedom*. New Haven: Yale University Press.

Bennett, W.L. and Segerberg, A. 2011. Digital media and the personalization of collective action. *Information, Communication and Society*, 14(6), 270–299.

Berger, J. and Milkman, K. 2010. *Social transmission, emotion, and the virality of online content*. Wharton Research Paper. [Online]. Available at: http://marketing.wharton.upenn.edu/documents/research/virality.pdf. [accessed: 19 October 2011].

Berry, W. and Pollan, M. 2009. *Bringing it to the Table: On Farming and Food*. Berkeley, CA: Counterpoint Press.

Beshears, J. and Weller, B. 2010. Public policy and saving for retirement: The "autosave" features of the Pension Protection Act of 2006. In *Better Living through Economics*, edited by J. Siegfried. Cambridge: Harvard University Press, 274–291.

Bessière, K. 2010. Effects of internet use on health and depression: A longitudinal study. *Journal of Medical Internet Research*, 12(1), 6.

Bickford, S. 1996. *The Dissonance of Democracy: Listening, Conflict, and Citizenship*. Ithaca, NY: Cornell University Press.

Bishop, J. 2011. Facebook to use Microsoft's PhotoDNA Technology to combat Child Pornography. *Geek Wire*. [Online]. Available at: http://geekwire.com/2011/facebook-adopts-microsofts-photodna-combat-child-pornography. [accessed: 5 September 2011].

Blair, A.M. 2010. *Too Much to Know: Managing Scholarly Information Before the Modern Age*. Cambridge, MA: Yale University Press.

Bodle, R. 2011. Regimes of sharing. *Information, Communication and Society*, 14(3), 320–337.

Bohn, R.E. and Short, J.E. 2009. *How Much Information?* Global Information Industry Center at the School of International Relations and Pacific Studies, UC San Diego.

Bohn, R., Short, J. and Baru, C. 2011. *How Much Information? 2010 Report on Enterprise Server Information*. San Diego: Global Information Industry Center at the School of International Relations and Pacific Studies, UC San Diego. [Online]. Available at: http://hmi.ucsd.edu/howmuchinfo_research_report_ consum_2010.php. [Accessed 12 September 2011].

Borgmann, A. 1987. *Technology and the Character of Contemporary Life: A Philosophical Inquiry*. Chicago: University of Chicago Press. Bourdieu, P. 1986. The forms of capital. In *Readings in Economic Sociology*, edited by N.W. Biggart. Oxford: Blackwell, 280–291.Bourdieu, P. 1991. *Language and Symbolic Power*. Translated by G. Raymond and M. Adamson. Cambridge, MA: Harvard University Press.

Boyd, D. 2007. Social network sites: Public, private, or what? *Knowledge Tree*, 13. [Online, May]. Available at: http://kt.flexiblelearning.net.au/tkt2007/?page_ id=28. [accessed: 29 August 2011].

Boyd, D. 2010. White flight in networked publics: How race and class shaped American teen engagement with MySpace and Facebook. In *Digital Race Anthology*, edited by L. Nakamura and P. Chow-White. London: Routledge.

Boyd, D. and Heer, J. 2006. Profiles as Conversation: Networked Identity Performance on Friendster. Proceedings of Thirty-Ninth Hawai'i International Conference on System Sciences. Los Alamitos, CA: IEEE, January 4–7.

Boyd, D.M. and Ellison, N.B. 2008. Social network sites: Definition, history, and scholarship. *Journal of Computer-Mediated Communication*, 13(1), 210–230.

Boyd, D.M. and Hargittai, E. 2010. Facebook privacy settings: Who cares? *First Monday*, 15(8). August.

Boyle, K. and Johnson, T.J. 2010. MySpace is your space? Examining self-presentation of MySpace users. *Computers in Human Behavior*, 26(6), 1392–1399.

Brand, S. 1987. *The Media Lab: Inventing the Future at MIT*. New York: Viking-Penguin.

Broadbent, S. 2009. How the Internet Enables Intimacy. *TED: Ideas Worth Spreading*. [Online, Nov 2009]. Available at: http://ted.com/talks/stefana_broadbent_how_ the_internet_enables_intimacy.html. [accessed: 12 October 2011].

Brownstein, R. 2011. Pulling apart. *National Journal*, February (16), 18–43.

Brundidge, J. 2006. The Contribution of the Internet to the Heterogeneity of Political Discussion Networks: Does the Medium Matter? Paper presented at the annual meeting of the International Communication Association, Dresden International Congress Centre, Dresden, Germany.

Buffardi, L.E. and Campbell, W.K. 2008. Narcissism and social networking web sites. *Personality and Social Psychology Bulletin*, 34(10), 1303.

Butler, J. 1997. *Excitable Speech: A Politics of the Performative*. New York: Routledge.

Butler, P. 2010. Visualizing Friendship. *The Facebook Blog*. [Online]. Available at: http://facebook.com/note.php?note_id=469716398919. [accessed: 12 October 2011].

Cain-Miller, Claire. 2011. FTC Said to Be Near Facebook Privacy Deal. *New York Times*. [Online, 10 November]. Available at: http://nytimes.com/2011/11/11/

technology/facebook-is-said-to-be-near-ftc-settlement-on-privacy.html?_
r=1&partner=rss&emc=rss. [Accessed 11 November 2011].

Cammaerts, B. 2008. Critiques on the participatory potentials of Web 2.0. *Communication, Culture and Critique*, 1(4), 358–377.

Carmichael, S. and Hamilton, C.V. 1967. *Black Power: The Politics of Liberation in America*. New York: Vintage.

CarnalNation.com. 2010. *Facebook Full of Wannabe Murderers?* [Online]. Available at: http://carnalnation.com/content/47650/898/facebook-full-wannabe-murderers. [accessed: 11 September 2011].

Carpentier, N. and Cammaerts, B. 2006. Hegemony, democracy, agonism and journalism: An interview with Chantal Mouffe. *Journalism Studies*, 7(6), 964–975.

Carpentier, N. 2007. Theoretical frameworks for participatory media. In *Media Technologies and Democracy in an Enlarged Europe*, edited by N. Carpentier et al. Tartu: University of Tartu Press 105–122.

Carr, N. 2008. Is Google making us stupid? Why you can't read the way you used to. *Atlantic Monthly*, 302(1), 56–63.

Carr, A. 2010. A Delete Button for the Internet: Tool Removes Personal Info from Google, Facebook. *Fast Company*. [Online]. Available at: http://fastcompany.com/1709756/privacy-company-offers-delete-button-for-the-internet-removes-personal-info-from-google-face. [accessed: 12 August 2011].Cascio, J. 2005. The Rise of the Participatory Panopticon. *Worldchanging.com* [Online]. Available at: http:// worldchanging. com/archives/002651. [accessed: 4 September 2011].

Castaneda, C. 1991. *Journey to Ixtlan*. New York: Washington Square Press.

Castells, M. 1998. *The Information Age: Economy, Society and Culture. Volume III: End of Millennium*. Oxford: Blackwell.

Castells, M. 2000. *The Rise of the Network Society*. London: Blackwell Publishing.

Castells, M. 2007. Communication, power and counter-power in the network society. *International Journal of Communication*, 1(1), 238–266.

Castells, M. 2009. *The Power of Identity: The Information Age: Economy, Society, and Culture*. London: Wiley-Blackwell.

Chandler, D. 1998. *Personal Homepages and the Construction of Identities on the Web*. [Online]. Available at: http://aber.ac.uk/~dgc/Webident.html. [accessed: 12 September 2011].

Chen, W., and B. Wellman. 2005. Charting digital divides: Comparing socioeconomic, gender, life stage, and rural-urban Internet access and use in five countries." *Transforming Enterprise, MIT Press, Cambridge*: 467–497.

Christakis, N.A. and Fowler, J.H. 2009. *Connected: The Surprising Power of Our Social Networks and How They Shape Our Lives*. New York: Little, Brown and Company.

Christensen, H.S. 2011. Political activities on the Internet: Slacktivism or political participation by other means? *First Monday*, 16(2–7).

Cohen, A. 1994. *Self Consciousness: An Alternative Anthropology of Identity*. London: Routledge.

Cohen, N.S. 2008. The valorization of surveillance: Towards a political economy of Facebook. *Democratic Communiqué*, 22(1), 5–22.

Cohen, S. and Taylor, L. 1992. *Escape Attempts: The Theory and Practice of Resistance to Everyday Life*. New York: Psychology Press.

Coleman, S. 2005. Blogs and the new politics of listening. *Political Quarterly*, 76(2), 273–280.

Coleman, S. and Blumler, J.G. 2009. *The Internet and Democratic Citizenship: Theory, Practice and Policy*. Cambridge: Cambridge University Press.

Converse, P. 1975. Public Opinion and voting behavior. In *Handbook of Political Science*, edited by F.W. Greenstein and N.W. Polsby. Reading, MA: Addison-Wesley, 75–169.

Couldry, N. 2010. *Why Voice Matters: Culture and Politics after Neoliberalism*. London: Sage Publications.

Crawford, K. 2009. Following you: Disciplines of listening in social media. *Continuum: Journal of Media and Cultural Studies*, 23(4), 525–535.

Chryssochoou, D. 1998. *Democracy and integration theory in the 1990s: a study in European polity-formation*. Jean Monnet Working Papers in Comparative and International Politics,

Dahlberg, L. 2007. The Internet, deliberative democracy, and power: Radicalizing the public sphere. *International Journal of Media and Cultural Politics*, 3(1), 47–64.

Dahlgren, P. 1991. Introduction. In *Communication and Citizenship*, edited by P.Dahlgren and C. Sparks. London: Routledge, 1–24.

Dahlgren, P. 2005. The Internet, public spheres, and political communication: dispersion and deliberation." *Political Communication* 22(2): 147–162.

Davis, A. 2010. New media and fat democracy: The paradox of online participation. *New Media and Society*, 12(5), 745–761.

Dawson, M.C. 1995. *Behind the Mule: Race and Class in African-American Politics*. Princeton, NJ: Princeton University Press.

Deibert, R. and Rohozinski, R. 2008. Good for liberty, bad for security? Internet securitization and global civil society. In *Access Denied: The Practice and Policy of Internet Filtering*, edited by R. Deibert et al. Cambridge, MA: MIT Press, 123–151.

Delli Carpini, M.X. and Keeter, S. 1997. *What Americans Know about Politics and Why It Matters*. New Haven, CT: Yale University Press.

DeLong, B. 2010. What Future Does Facebook Have? *Brad Delong's Blog*. [Online]. Available at: http://delong.typepad.com/sdj/2011/01/wht-future-does-facebook-have.html. [accessed: 19 July 2011].

Dembrosky, A. 2011. Invasion of the Body Hackers. *Financial Times*. [Online, 11 June]. http://ft.com/intl/cms/s/2/3ccb11a0–923b-11e0–9e00–00144feab49a. html#axzz1bRkyCj5C. [accessed: 11 June 2011].

Deresiewicz, W. 2011. *Faux Friendship*. Fort Worth, TX: Fountainhead Press.

DeRosa, A. 2011. The Death of Platforms. *Reuters Blog.* [Online]. Available at: http://soupsoup.tumblr.com/post/2800255638/the-death-of-platforms. [accessed: 19 September 2011].

Detmer, D.E. 2010. Activating a full architectural model: Improving health through robust population health records. *Journal of the American Medical Informatics Association,* 17(4), 367–369.

Dewan, S. and Ramaprasad, J. 2009. Chicken and Egg? Interplay between Music Blog Buzz and Album Sales. PACIS 2009 Proceedings, Paper 87.

Dewey, J. 1991. *The Public and Its Problems.* Athens: Swallow Press.

Diamond, L. 2010. Liberation technology. *Journal of Democracy,* 21(3), 69–83.

Diani, M. and McAdam, D. 2003. *Social Movements and Networks: Relational Approaches to Collective Action.* Oxford: Oxford University Press.

DiMaggio, P., Hargittai, E., Celeste, C. and Shafer, S. 2004. From unequal access to differentiated use: A literature review and agenda for research on digital inequality. In *Social inequality,* edited by K. Neckerman. New York: Russell Sage Foundation, 355–400.

Dolliver, M. 2010. Social Networking: A Waste of Time. *AdWeek.* [Online, 7 October]. Available at: http://adweek.com/news/technology/social-networking-waste-time-10348. [accessed: 10 October 2011].

Donath, J. 2007. Signals in social supernets. *Journal of Computer-Mediated Communication,* 13(1). [Online]. Available at: http://jcmc.indiana.edu/vol13/issue1/donath.html. [accessed: 4 September 2011].

Donath, J. and Boyd, D. 2004. Public displays of connection. *BT Technology Journal,* 22(4), 71–82.

Dreyfus, S. and Dreyfus, H. 1980. *A Five-stage Model of the Mental Activities Involved in Directed Skill Acquisition.* Berkeley Operations Research Center Report. Berkeley: University of California.

Dryzek, J.S. 1990. *Discursive Democracy.* Cambridge: Cambridge University Press.

Duflo, E. and Banerjee, A. 2011. *Poor Economics: A Radical Rethinking of the Way to Fight Global Poverty.* London: Public Affairs.

Dunbar, R. 1998. *Grooming, Gossip, and the Evolution of Language.* Cambridge, MA: Harvard University Press.

Dunbar, R. 2010. *How Many Friends Does One Person Need: Dunbar's Number and Other Evolutionary Quirks.* Cambridge, MA: Harvard University Press.

Dwyer, C. 2007. Digital Relationships in the "MySpace" Generation: Results from a Qualitative Study. Proceedings of the 40th Hawaii International Conference on System Sciences (HICSS), Hawaii, 2007.

Dwyer, C., Hiltz, S.R. and Passerini, K. 2007. Trust and privacy concern within social networking sites: A comparison of Facebook and MySpace. In Proceedings of AMCIS. Keystone, CO, March 1. [Online]. Available at: http://csis.pace.edu/~dwyer/research/DwyerAMCIS2007.pdf. [accessed: 12 September 2011].

Earl, J. and Kimport, K. 2011. *Digitally Enabled Social Change: Activism in the Internet Age.* Cambridge, MA: MIT Press.

Earl, J. and Schussman, A. 2003. The new site of activism: On-line organizations, movement entrepreneurs, and the changing location of social movement decision-making. *Research in Social Movements, Conflict, and Change*, 24(1), 155–187.

Eastin, M.S. and LaRose, R. 2000. Internet self-efficacy and the psychology of the digital divide. *Journal of Computer-Mediated Communication* 6(1).

Eastley, W. 2010. Instead of the Iron Curtain, the Facebook Curtain. *Aid Watch*. [Online]. Available at: http://aidwatchers.com/2010/12/instead-of-the-iron-curtain-the-facebook-curtain/[accessed: 9 September 2011].

Edinburgh Napier University. 2011. *Facebook Stress Linked to Number of Friends*. [Online]. Available at: http://napier.ac.uk/media/Pages/NewsDetails.aspx?NewsID=187. [accessed: 9 September 2011].

Eliasoph, N. 1998. *Avoiding Politics: How Americans Produce Apathy in Everyday Life*. Cambridge: Cambridge University Press.

Ellison, C.G. and Powers, D.A. 1994. The contact hypothesis and racial attitudes among black Americans. *Social Science Quarterly*, 75(3), 385–400.

Ellison, N.B., Steinfield, C. and Lampe, C. 2007. The benefits of Facebook "friends:" Social capital and college students' use of online social network sites. *Journal of Computer-Mediated Communication*, 12(4), 1143–1168.

Etling, B., Kelly, J., Faris, R. and Palfrey, J. 2009. *Mapping the Arabic Blogosphere: Politics, Culture, and Dissent*. Internet and Democracy Project. Berkeley: University of California, Berkman Center for Internet and Society.

Exley, Z. 2008. The New Organizers, What's Really behind Obama's Ground Game. *Huffington Post*. [Online, 8 October]. Available at: http://huffingtonpost.com/zack-exley/the-new-organizers-part-1_b_132782.html. [accessed: 12 September 2011].

Facebook Data Team. 2010. What's on Your Mind? *Facebook blog*. [Online]. Available at: http://facebook.com/note.php?note_id=477517358858. [accessed: 17 October 2011].

Facebook.com. 2011. Statistics. *Facebook Blog*. [Online]. Available at: http://facebook.com/press/info.php?statistics. [accessed: 9 October 2011].

Faris, R. and Villeneuve, N. 2008. Measuring global Internet filtering. In *Access Denied: The Practice and Policy of Global Internet Filtering*, edited by R. Deibert et al. Cambridge, MA: MIT Press, 5–28.

Farrell, H. 2011. The Internet and the Obama Camapaign. *The Monkey Cage Blog*. [Online 10, February]. Available at: http://www.timeshighereducation.co.uk/story.asp?storycode=415096 [accessed: 11 November 2011].

Farrell, H. 2011. Review of: The Net Delusion. Times Higher Education. [Online]. Available at: http://themonkeycage.org/blog/2008/12/11/the_internet_and_the_obama_cam/ [accessed: 11 September 2011].

Feezell, J.T., Conroy, M. and Guerrero, M. 2009. Facebook is fostering political engagement: A study of online social networking groups and offline participation. American Political Science Association meeting, Toronto, Canada.

Fitzpatrick, B. 2007. Thoughts on the Social Graph. *Bradfitz.com* [Online]. Available at: http://bradfitz.com/social-graph-problem/. [accessed: 9 September 2011].

Flacy, M. 2011. Nearly 300,000 status Updates Are Posted to Facebook every Minute. *Digital Trends*. [Online, 7 October]. Available at: http://digitaltrends.com/social-media/nearly-300000-status-updates-are-posted-to-facebook-every-minute. [accessed: 9 October 2011].

Fletcher, D. 2010. How Facebook is Redefining Privacy. *Time Magazine*. [Online, 20 May]. Available at: http://time.com/time/magazine/article/0,9171,1990798,00. html. [accessed: 9 August 2011].

Flyvbjerg, B. 2001. *Making Social Science Matter: Why Social Inquiry Fails and How It Can Succeed Again*. Cambridge: Cambridge University Press.

Fogg, B. and Eckles, D. 2007. The behavior chain for online participation: how successful web services structure persuasion. In Proceedings of the 2nd International Conference on Persuasive Technology. 199–209.

Folke, C. 2010. On resilience: SEED global reset. *Seed Magazine*, 43, 40–41.

Foucault, M. 1977. *Discipline and Punish*. London: Penguin Books.

Foucault, M. 1980. *Power/Knowledge: Selected Interviews and Other Writings*. New York: Pantheon Books.

Foucault, M. 1982. The subject and power. In *Beyond Structuralism and Hermeneutics*. Translated by H. Dreyfus and P. Rabinow. Chicago: University of Chicago Press.Foucault, M., Martin, L.H. and Gutman, H. 1988. *Technologies of the Self*. Amherst, MA: University of Massachusetts Press.

Fowler, G. and A. Das. 2011. Facebook Numbers Feed IPO Outlook. *Wall Street Journal*. [Online, 1 May]. Available at: http://online.wsj.com/article/SB1 0001424052748704436004576297310274876624.html?mod=WSJ_hp_ LEFTWhatsNewsCollection. Accessed [9 September 2011].

Franzen, J. 2011. Liking is For Cowards. Go for What Hurts. *New York Times*. [Online, 29 May]. Available at: http://nytimes.com/2011/05/29/opinion/29franzen. html?pagewanted=3and_r=3andemc=eta1. [accessed: 9 October 2011].

Friedman, M. 1953. The methodology of positive economics. In *Essays in Positive Economics*. Edited by M. Friedman. Chicago: University of Chicago Press: 3–43.

Frohlich, N. and Oppenheimer, J. 1998. Some consequences of e-mail vs. face-to-face communication in experiment. *Journal of Economic Behavior and Organization*, 35(3), 389–403.

Galimberti, C. and Riva, G. 2001. Actors, artifacts and inter-actions: Outline for a social psychology of cyberspace. In *Towards Cyberpsychology: Mind, Cognitions and Society in the Internet Age*, edited by C. Galimberti. Washington, D.C.: IOS Press, 3–18.

Galston, W. 1991. *Liberal Purposes: Goods, Virtues, and Duties in the Liberal State*. Cambridge: Cambridge University Press.

García-Bedolla, L. 2005. *Fluid Borders: Latino Power, Identity, and Politics in Los Angeles*. Berkeley: University of California Press.

Geertz, C. 1973. *The Interpretation of Cultures*. New York: Basic Books.

Gelles, M. 2010. Facebook's Grand Plan for the Future. *Financial Times*. [Online, 3 December]. Available at: http://ft.com/intl/cms/s/2/57933bb8-fcd9–11df-ae2d-00144feab49a.html#axzz1blsIN5U2. [accessed: 9 October 2011].

Gergen, K.J. 1991. *The Saturated Self: Dilemmas of Identity in Contemporary Life*. New York: Basic Books.

Gerodimos, R. 2010. New media, new citizens: The terms and conditions of online youth civic engagement. Doctoral thesis. Bournemouth University, UK. September 2010.

Ghosh, P. 2011. Facebook's Postponed IPO: A Wise and Patient Strategy. *International Business Times*. [Online, 21 September]. Available at: http://ibtimes.com/articles/217614/20110921/facebook-ipo-delay-postponement-zynga-groupon-apple-google.htm. [accessed: 17 October 2011].

Gibson, G. 2010. Google's Earth. *New York Times*. [Online, 1 September]. Available at: www.nytimes.com/2010/09/01/opinion/01gibson.html [accessed: 9 October 2011].

Giddens, A. 1990. *The Consequences of Modernity*. Stanford, CA: Stanford University Press.

Giglio, M. 2011. Middle East Uprising: Facebook's Secret Role in Egypt. *The Daily Beast*. [Online, 24 February]. Available: http://thedailybeast.com/articles/2011/02/24/middle-east-uprising-facebooks-back-channel-diplomacy.html. [accessed: 11 July 2011].

Gilbert, E., Bergstrom, T. and Karahalios, K. 2009. Blogs Are Echo Chambers: Blogs Are Echo Chambers. In Proceedings of HICSS, 2009, 1–10.

Gladwell, M. 2010. Twitter, Facebook, and Social Activism. *The New Yorker*. [Online, 4 October]. Available at: www.newyorker.com/reporting/2010/10/04/101004fa_fact_gladwell. [accessed: 9 October 2011].

Glennerster, R. and Kremer, M. 2011. Small Changes, Big Results: Behavioral Economics at Work in Poor Countries. *Boston Review*. [Online, March–April]. Available at: http://bostonreview.net/BR36.2/glennerster_kremer_behavioral_economics_global_development.php. [accessed: 11 August 2011].

Goel, S., Mason, W. and Watts, D.J. 2010. Real and perceived attitude agreement in social networks. *Journal of Personality and Social Psychology*, 99(4), 611–621.

Goffman, E. 1959. *The Presentation of Self in Everyday Life*. Garden City: Doubleday.

Goffman, E. 1974. *Frame Analysis: An Essay on the Organization of Experience*. Cambridge, MA: Harvard University Press.

Golder, S.A., Wilkinson, D.M. and Huberman, B.A. 2007. Rhythms of social interaction: Messaging within a massive online network. *Communities and Technologies*, 41–66.

Goldhaber-Fiebert, J.D., Blumenkranz, E. and Garber, A.M. 2010. *Committing to Exercise: Contract Design for Virtuous Habit Formation*. National Bureau of Economic Research Working Paper 16624.

Goldsmith, J.L. and Wu, T. 2006. *Who Controls the Internet: Illusions of a Borderless World*. Oxford: Oxford University Press.

González, M.C., Hidalgo, C.A. and Barabási, A.L. 2008. Understanding individual human mobility patterns. *Nature*, 453(7196), 779–782.

Google. 2011. *Transparency Report: United Kingdom. July to December 2010.* [Online]. Available at: http://google.com/transparencyreport/governmentrequests/GB/ [accessed: 14 October 2011].

Google. 2011. *Transparency Report: United States. July to December 2010.* [Online]. Available at: http://google.com/transparencyreport/governmentrequests/US/?p=2010–06andt=USER_DATA_REQUEST. [accessed: 14 October 2011].

Gould, E. 2008. It's not a revolution if nobody loses. *Technology Review*. [Online, September/October]. Available at: http://technologyreview.com/Infotech/21251/ [accessed: 19 October 2011].

Granovetter, M.S. 1973. The strength of weak ties. *American Journal of Sociology*, 1360–1380.

Habermas, J. 1973. What does a crisis mean today? Legitimation problems in late capitalism. *Social Research*, 40(4), 643–67.

Habermas, J. 1975. *Legitimation Crisis*. New York: Beacon Press.

Hackett-Fischer, D. 1970. *Historians' Fallacies*. New York: Harper and Row.

Hall, S. 1996. Introduction: Who needs identity? In *Questions of Cultural Identity*, edited by S. Hall and P. DuGay. London: Sage, 1–18.

Hampton, K.N., Goulet, L.S., Rainie L. and Purcell, K. 2011. Social networking sites and our lives. Pew Research Center's Internet and American Project, Washington, DC.

Hansell, M. 2008. Zuckerberg's Law of Information Sharing. *New York Times Bits Blog*. [Online, 11 November]. Available at: http://bits.blogs.nytimes.com/2008/11/06/zuckerbergs-law-of-information-sharing/. [accessed: 9 September 2011].

Hargittai, E. 2002. Second-level digital divide: Differences in people's online skills. *First Monday*, 7(4), 1–20.

Hargittai, E. 2007. Whose space? Differences among users and non-users of social network sites. *Journal of Computer-Mediated Communication*, 13(1), 276–297.

Hargittai, E. and Hinnant, A. 2008. Digital inequality: Differences in young adults' use of the Internet. *Communication Research*, 35(5), 602–621.Hargittai, E., Gallo, J. and Kane, M. 2008. Cross-ideological discussions among conservative and liberal bloggers. *Public Choice*, 134(1–2), 67.

Hart, K., and M. Greenwell. 2009. To nonprofits seeking cash, Facebook app isn't so green." *The Washington Post*. [Online, 22 April]. Available at: http://www.washingtonpost.com/wp-dyn/content/article/2009/04/21/AR2009042103786.html. [accessed: 11 October 2011].

Harris, J. and Kamvar, S. 2009. *We Feel Fine: An Almanac of Human Emotion.* New York: Scribner.

Hassani, S.N. 2006. Locating digital divides at home, work, and everywhere else. *Poetics*, 34(4–5), 250–272.

Heidegger, M. 1978. *Being and Time*. London: Wiley-Blackwell.

Heit, E. and Nicholson, S.P. 2010. The opposite of Republican: Polarization and political categorization. *Cognitive Science*, 34(8), 1503–16.

Hendry, J. and Goodall, K.E. 2010. Facebook and the commercialisation of personal information: Some questions of provider-to-user privacy. In *Dimension of Technology Regulation*, edited by M. Goodwin, B.J. Koops and R. Leenes. Nijmegen: Wolf Le-gal Publishers, 39–62.

Heppner, W.L. and Kernis, M.H. 2007. "Quiet ego" functioning: The complementary roles of mindfulness, authenticity, and secure high self-esteem. *Psychological Inquiry*, 18(4), 248–251.

Hetherington, K. 1998. *Expressions of Identity: Space, Performance, Politics.* London: Sage Publications.

Hibbing, J. R, and E. 2002. Theiss-Morse. *Stealth Democracy: Americans' Beliefs About How Government Should Work.* Cambridge: Cambridge University Press,

Himelboim, I. 2010. Civil society and online political discourse: The network structure of unrestricted discussions. *Communication Research*, 38(5), 634–659.

Hindman, M. 2009. *The Myth of Digital Democracy*. Princeton: Princeton University Press.

Hinduja, S. and Patchin, J.W. 2008. Personal information of adolescents on the Internet: A quantitative content analysis of MySpace. *Journal of Adolescence*, 31(1), 125–146.

Hodkinson, P. and Lincoln, S. 2008. Online journals as virtual bedrooms? *Young*, 16(1), 27.

Hofstetter, R., Shriver, S. and Nair, H. 2010. Social Ties and User Generated Content: Evidence from an Online Social Network. Stanford Graduate School of Business Research Paper No. 2083. [Online]. Available at: SSRN: http://ssrn. com/abstract=1915634. [accessed: 9 October 2011].

Holland, D.C. and Quinn, N. 1987. *Cultural Models in Language and Thought.* Cambridge: Cambridge University Press.

Horn, L. 2011. How Facebook Earned 1.86 Billion in Ad Revenue in 2010. *PC Magazine.* [Online]. http://pcmag.com/article2/0,2817,2375926,00. asp#fbid=ci1OUQdb7IP [accessed: 9 October 2011].

Hotz, R.L. 2011. The Really Smart Phone. *Wall Street Journal.* [Online, 23 April]. Available at: http://online.wsj.com/article_ email/SB10001424052748704547604576263261679848814- lMyQjAxMTAxMDIwNDEyNDQyWj.html. [accessed: 11 October 2011].

Howard, P., Rainie, R. and Jones, S. 2001. Days and nights on the Internet. *American Behavioral Scientist*, 45(3), 383.

Howe, J. 2006. The rise of crowdsourcing. *Wired.* [Online, 14 June]. Available online: http://www. wired. com/wired/archive/14.06/crowds. html. [accessed: 18 September 2011].

Hsu, M., Bhatt, M., Adolphs, R., Tranel, D. and Camerer, C.F. 2005. Neural systems responding to degrees of uncertainty in human decision-making. *Science*, 310(5754), 1680.

Huddy, L. 2001. From social to political identity: A critical examination of social identity theory. *Political Psychology*, 22(1), 127–156.

Ibrahim, Y. 2010. Social networking sites (sns) and the "narcissistic turn." The politics of self-exposure. In *Collaborative Technologies and Applications for Interactive Information Design: Emerging Trends in User Experiences*, edited by S. Rummler and K.B. Ng. Pennsylvania: IGI Group.

Internet Telecommunications Union. 2010. *Definitions of World Telecommunication/ ICT Indicators*. [Online, March]. Available at: http://itu.int/ITU-D/ict/material/ TelecomICT_Indicators_Definition_March2010_for_web.pdf. [accessed: 30 July 2011].

InternetWorldStats.com. 2011. Internet Users in Europe. [Online]. Available at: http://internetworldstats.com/stats4.htm. [accessed: 9 October 2011].

Isaacman, S., Becker, R., Kobourov, S., Martonosi, M., Rowland, J. and Varshavsky, A. 2011. Ranges of human mobility in Los Angeles and New York. In Pervasive Computing and Communications Workshops (PERCOM Workshops), 2011 IEEE International, 88–93.

Italie, D. 2010. Divorce Lawyers: Facebook Tops in Online Evidence. *Associated Press*. [Online, 29 June]. Available at: http://usatoday.com/tech/news/2010–06– 29-facebook-divorce_N.htm. [accessed: 9 October 2011].

Jackson, N.A. and Lilleker, D.G. 2009. Building an architecture of participation? Political parties and Web 2.0 in Britain. *Journal of Information Technology and Politics*, 6(3), 232–250.

Jarrett, K. 2008. Interactivity is Evil! A critical investigation of Web 2.0. *First Monday*, 13(3), 34–41.

Jay, M. 2010. *The Virtues of Mendacity: On Lying in Politics*. Charlottesville: University of Virginia Press.

Jenkins, H. 2006. *Convergence Culture: Where Old and New Media Collide*. New York: NYU Press.

Jernigan, C. and Mistree, B. 2009. Gaydar: Facebook friendships expose sexual orientation. *First Monday*, 14(10).

Johnson, T.J. and Kaye, B.K. 1998. Cruising is believing: Comparing Internet and traditional sources on media credibility measures. *Journalism and Mass Communication Quarterly*, 75(2), 325–340.

Jolly, C. 2011. Survey Results: Online Privacy and Your Queasy Button. *CBC Spark*. [Online, 2 June]. Available at: http://cbc.ca/spark/2011/06/help-us-out-online- privacy-and-your-queasy-button/ [accessed: 11 October 2011].

Jones, S., Millermaier, S., Goya-Martinez, M. and Schuler, J. 2008. Whose space is MySpace? A content analysis of MySpace profiles. *First Monday*, 13(9).

Jordan, A.H., Monin, B., Dweck, C.S., Lovett, B.J., John, O.P. and Gross, J.J. 2011. Misery has more company than people think: underestimating the prevalence of others' negative emotions. *Personality and Social Psychology Bulletin*, 37(1), 120–135.

Joyce, M. 2011. The Net Delusion Reviewed. *Meta Activism Project Blog.* [Online, 26 March]. Available at: http://meta-activism.org/2011/02/net-delusion-reviewslacktivism/. [accessed: 9 October 2011].

Joyce, M.C. 2010. *Digital Activism Decoded: The New Mechanics of Change.* Washington, DC: Intl Debate Education Association.

Jurgenson, N. 2011. Rethinking Privacy and Publicity on Social Media. *Cyborgology.* [Online, 30 June]. Available at: http://thesocietypages.org/cyborgology/2011/06/30/rethinking-privacy-and-publicity-on-social-media-part-i/. [accessed: 14 October 2011].

Kahne, J. and Middaugh, E. 2009. Democracy for Some: The Civic Opportunity Gap in High School. Circle Working Paper 59, College Park, MD: The Center for Information and Research on Civic Learning and Engagement.

Kahne, J., Middaugh, E., Lee, N. and Feezell, J. 2010. *McCarthur Network on Youth and Participatory Politics.* [Online]. Available at: http://ypp.dmlcentral.net/sites/all/files/publications/Online-Diversity.pdf. [accessed: 9 September 2011].

Kalyvas, A. 2008. *Democracy and the Politics of the Extraordinary: Max Weber, Carl Schmitt, and Hannah Arendt.* Cambridge: Cambridge University Press.

Kambara, K. 2010. Identity and the Semantic Web. *ThickCulture.* [Online, 8 April]. Available at: http://thesocietypages.org/thickculture/2010/04/08/identity-semantic-web/. [accessed: 9 September 2011].

Kao, G. 2000. Group images and possible selves among adolescents: Linking stereotypes to expectations by race and ethnicity. *Sociological Forum*, 15(3), 407–430.

Katz, J. 1997. The Digital Citizen, Wired. [Online, 5 December], Available at: http://hotwired.lycos,com/special/citizen/. [accessed: 14 September 2011].

Keen, A. 2007. *The Cult of the Amateur: How Today's Internet Is Killing Our Culture.* New York: Crown.

Kinder, D.R. and Sears, D.O. 1985. Public opinion and political action. In *Handbook of Social Psychology*, edited by G. Lindzey and E. Aronson. New York: Random House, 659–741.

Kinder, D.R. and Kam, C.D. 2009. *Us against Them: Ethnocentric Foundations of American Opinion.* Chicago: University of Chicago Press.

King, C.S., Feltey, K.M. and Susel, B.O.N. 1998. The question of participation: Toward authentic public participation in public administration. *Public Administration Review.* 317–326.

Kingdon, J.W. 1984. *Agendas, Alternatives, and Public Policies.* Longman.

Kirkpatrick, D. 2010. *The Facebook Effect: The Inside Story of the Company That Is Connecting the World.* New York: Virgin Books.

Kock, N. 2004. The psychobiological model: Towards a new theory of computer-mediated communication based on Darwinian evolution. *Organization Science*, 15(3), 327–348.

Kolek, E.A. and Saunders, D. 2008. Online disclosure: An empirical examination of undergraduate Facebook profiles. *NASPA Journal*, 45 (1), 1–25.

Konrath, S.H., O'Brien, E.H. and Hsing, C. 2011. Changes in dispositional empathy in American college students over time: A meta-analysis. *Personality and Social Psychology Review*, 15(2), 180.

Koskela, H. 2004. Webcams, tv shows and mobile phones: empowering exhibitionism. *Surveillance & Society* 2(2/3), 199–215.

Krämer, N.C. and Winter, S. 2008. Impression Management 2.0. *Journal of Media Psychology: Theories, Methods, and Applications*, 20(3), 106–116.

Krienen, F.M., Tu, P.C. and Buckner, R.L. 2010. Clan mentality: Evidence that the medial prefrontal cortex responds to close others. *Journal of Neuroscience*, 30(41), 13906–13915.

Kushin, M.J. and Kitchener, K. 2009. Getting political on social network sites: Exploring online political discourse on Facebook. *First Monday*, 14(11).

Lanier, J. 2011. *You Are Not a Gadget: A Manifesto*. New York: Vintage.

Larana, E., Johnston, H. and Gusfield, J.R. 1994. *New Social Movements: From Ideology to Identity*. Philadelphia: Temple University Press.

Lasswell, H.D. 1971. *A Pre-View of the Policy Sciences*. New York: American Elsevier Publishing.

Latham, R. and Sassen, S. 2005. *Digital Formations: IT and New Architectures in the Global Realm*. Princeton: Princeton University Press.

Lau, R.R. and Redlawsk, D.P. 1997. Voting correctly. *American Political Science Review*, 91(3), 585–598.

Laurenceau, J.P., Barrett, L.F. and Pietromonaco, P.R. 1998. Intimacy as an interpersonal process: The importance of self-disclosure, partner disclosure, and perceived partner responsiveness in interpersonal exchanges. *Journal of Personality and Social Psychology*, 74(5), 1238.

Lawrence, E., Sides, J. and Farrell, H. 2010. Self-segregation or deliberation? Blog readership, participation, and polarization in American politics. *Perspectives on Politics*, 8(1), 141–157.

Lazarsfeld, P. and Menzel, H. 1963. Mass media and personal influence. In *The Science of Communication*, edited by W. Schramm. New York: Basic Books.

Leary, M.R. 1995. *Self-Presentation: Impression Management and Interpersonal Behaviour*. Dubuque: Brown and Benchmark.

LeBlanc, R.M. 1999. *Bicycle Citizens: The Political World of the Japanese Housewife*. Berkeley: University of California Press.

Ledbetter, A.M., Mazer, J.P., DeGroot, J.M., Mao, Y., Meyer, K.R. and Swafford, B. 2011. Attitudes toward online social connection and self-disclosure as predictors of Facebook communication and relational closeness. *Communication Research*, 38(1), 27–53.

Lee, J. 2011. A Call to Take Back the Internet from Corporations. *New York Times Bits Blog*. [Online, 12 July]. Available at: http://bits.blogs.nytimes.com/2011/07/12/a-call-to-take-back-the-internet-from-corporations/ [accessed: 9 October 2011].

Lenhart, A. and Madden, M. 2007. Teens, privacy and online social networks. Pew Internet and American Life Project, Washington, DC.

Lenhart, A., K. Purcell, A. Smith and K. Zickuhr. 2010. Social media and mobile Internet use among teens and young adults. Pew Research Center, Washington, DC.

Lerum, K. 2010. Making Hate Fun: Facebook Users Continue to Joke En Masse about Killing 'Hookers." *Sexuality and Society Blog.* [Online, 12 February]. Available at: http://thesocietypages.org/sexuality/2010/02/12/making-hate-fun-facebook-users-continue-to-joke-en-mass-about-killing-hookers/ [Accessed: 15 July 2011].

Lessig, L. 2004. *Free culture: How Big Media Uses Technology and the Law to Lock Down Culture and Control Creativity.* New York: Penguin.

Leuprecht, P. 2005. Brave new digital world-reflections on the world summit on the information society. *Revue Québécoise de Droit International,* 18, 41.

Levenshus, A. 2010. Online relationship management in a presidential campaign: A case study of the Obama campaign's management of its Internet-integrated grassroots effort. *Journal of Public Relations Research, 22*(3), 313–335.

Levi, A. 2011. Zynga, Facebook Spark 51 Percent Jump in Value of Top Web Startups. *Bloomberg.* [Online, 7 April]. Available at: http://bloomberg.com/news/2011-04-07/zynga-facebook-spur-51-jump-in-private-market-valuations-of-web-startups.html. [accessed: 9 October 2011].

Levin, A. 2010. The Trouble with Facebook for Organizing. *BookBlog.* [Online, 7 August]. Available at: http://alevin.com/?p=2425. [accessed: 9 September 2011].

Lewin, T. 2010. If Your Kids Are Awake, They're Probably Online. *New York Times.* [Online 20 January]. Available at: http://nytimes.com/2010/01/20/education/20wired.html. [accessed: 11 July 2011].

Lincoln, S. 2004. Teenage girls "bedroom culture: codes versus zones." In *After Subculture,* edited by A. Bennett and K. Kahn-Harris. London: Palgrave, 94–106.

Liszkiewicz, A.J.P. 2010. Cultivated Play: Farmville. *Media Commons.* [Online]. Available at: http://mediacommons.futureofthebook.org/content/cultivated-play-farmville. [accessed: 28 July 2011].

Livingstone, S. and Helsper, E. 2007. Gradations in digital inclusion: Children, young people and the digital divide. *New Media and Society,* 9(4), 671–696.

Livingstone, S.M. 2005. *Audiences and Publics: When Cultural Engagement Matters for the Public Sphere.* Bristol: Intellect Ltd.

London, S. 1995. Teledemocracy vs. deliberative democracy: A comparative look at two models of public talk. *Journal of Interpersonal Computing and Technology,* 3(2), 33–55.

Lupinska-Dubicka, A. and Druzdzel, M.J. 2008. Analyzing Certain Temporal Dependences in Netflix Data. [Online]. Accessible at: www.pitt.edu/~druzdzel/psfiles/zeszyty08.pdf. [accessed: 28 July 2011].

Lyon, D. 1994. *The Electronic Eye: The Rise of Surveillance Society.* Minneapolis: University of Minnesota Press.

Lyon, D. 2001. *Surveillance Society.* Buckingham: Open University Press.

McAdam, D. 1986. Recruitment to high-risk activism: The case of freedom summer. *American Journal of Sociology,* 92(1), 64–90.

McConnell, B. and Huba, J. 2003. *Creating Customer Evangelists: How Loyal Customers Become a Volunteer Sales Force*. Chicago: Kaplan Publishing.

McGreevy, P. 2011. Online Privacy Bill Fails to Pass State Senate. *Los Angeles Times*. [Online, 28 May]. Available at: http://articles.latimes.com/2011/may/28/local/la-me-social-networking-20110528-32. [accessed: 13 October 2011].

MacIntyre, A.C. 1981. *After Virtue*. London: Duckworth.

MacKerron, G. 2011. Happiness economics from 35,000 feet. *Journal of Economic Surveys*. doi: 10.1111/j.1467-6419.2010.00672.x.

MacKinnon, R. 2004. The world-wide conversation: online participatory media and international news. *The Joan Shorenstein Center on the Press, Politics and Public Policy-Working Paper Series*.

MacKinnon, R. 2011. China's "networked authoritarianism." *Journal of Democracy*, 22(2), 32–46.

McKenna, K. and Bargh, J.A. 2000. Plan 9 from cyberspace: The implications of the Internet for personality and social psychology. *Personality and Social Psychology Review*, 4(1), 57.

McLuhan, M. 1969. *Playboy* Interview: Marshall McLuhan: A Candid Conversation with the High Priest of Popcult and Metaphysician of Media. *Playboy*, March, 233–269.

Madden, M. and Smith, A. 2010. Reputation management and social media. Pew Internet and American Life Project, Washington, DC.

Manago, A.M., Graham, M., Greenfield, P. and Salimkhan, G. 2008. Self-presentation and gender on MySpace. *Journal of Applied Developmental Psychology*, 29(6), 446–458.

Manjoo, F. 2011. Has Facebook Peaked? *Slate.com* [Online, 14 June]. http://slate.com/articles/technology/technology/2011/06/has_facebook_peaked.html. [accessed: 28 September 2011].

Manjoo, F. 2011. Smile, You're On Everyone's Camera. *Slate.com* [Online, 13 July]. Available at: http://slate.com/articles/technology/technology/2011/07/smile_youre_on_everyones_camera.html. [accessed: 28 September 2011].

Marichal, J. 2010. Political Facebook Groups: Micro-Activism and the Digital Front Stage. *Internet, Politics, Policy 2010: An Impact Assessment*. [Online]. Available at: http://microsites.oii.ox.ac.uk/ipp2010/programme/115. [accessed: 13 October 2011].Markoff, J. 2008. You're Leaving a Digital Trail. What about Privacy? *New York Times*. [Online, 30 November]. Available at: http://nytimes.com/2008/11/30/business/30privacy.html?pagewanted=all. [accessed: 13 October 2011].

Markus, H. and Nurius, P. 1986. Possible selves. *American Psychologist*, 41(9), 954–969.

Marlin-Bennett, R. 2011. I hear America tweeting and other themes for a virtual polis: rethinking democracy in the global infotech age. *Journal of Information Technology and Politics*, 8(2), 129–145.

Marshall, T.H. 1964. Class, Citizenship and Social Development. New York: Columbia University Press.

Martin, J.N., Bradford, L.J., Drzewiecka, J.A. and Chitgopekar, A.S. 2003. Intercultural dating patterns among young white U.S. Americans: Have they changed in the past 20 years? *The Harvard Journal of Communications*, 14(1), 53–73.

Maslow, A.H. 1968. *Toward a Psychology of Being*. New York: Van Nostrand Reinhold.

Mathiason, J., Mueller, M., Klein, H., Holitscher, M. and McKnight, L. 2004. *Internet Governance: The State of Play: The Internet Governance Project*. [Online]. Available at: http://internetgovernance.org/pdf/ig-sop-final.pdf. [accessed: 19 October 2011].

Matsuba, M.K. 2006. Searching for self and relationships online. *CyberPsychology and Behavior*, 9(3), 275–284.

Mayer-Schönberger, V. 2009. *Delete: The Virtue of Forgetting in the Digital Age*. Princeton: Princeton University Press.

Mazer, J.P., Murphy, R.E. and Simonds, C.J. 2007. I'll see you on "Facebook": The effects of computer-mediated teacher self-disclosure on student motivation, affective learning, and classroom climate. *Communication Education*, 56(1), 1–17.

Mehdizadeh, S. 2010. Self-presentation 2.0: Narcissism and self-esteem on Facebook. *Cyberpsychology, Behavior, and Social Networking*, 13(4), 357–364.

Meller, P. 2011. EU Sues UK Government over Treatment of Phorm. *PC World*. [Online, 14 April]. Available at: http://pcworld.com/article/163079/eu_sues_uk_government_over_treatment_of_phorm.html. [accessed: 19 October 2011].

Metzger, M.J. and Pure, R.A. 2009. Privacy management in Facebook: An application and extension of Communication Privacy Management theory to online social networking. Paper presented at the 95th Annual National Communication Association Convention, Chicago, IL.

Miller, T. 1993. *The Well-Tempered Self: Citizenship, Culture, and the Postmodern Subject*. Baltimore: Johns Hopkins University Press.

Mills, C.W. 1959. *The Sociological Imagination*. New York: Oxford University Press.

Mingione, E. 1994. Life strategies and social economies in the post Fordist age. *International Journal of Urban and Regional Research*, 18(1), 24–45.

Mitchell, J. 2011. Making Photo Tagging Easier. *Facebook Blog*. [Online, 30 June]. Available at: http://blog.facebook.com/blog.php?post=467145887130. [accessed: 19 October 2011].

Moon, M.J. 2002. The evolution of e-government among municipalities: Rhetoric or reality? *Public Administration Review*, 62(4), 424–433.

Morozov, E. 2011. *The Net Delusion: How Not to Liberate the World*. New York: Public Affairs.

Mouffe, C. 1992. *Dimensions of Radical Democracy: Pluralism, Citizenship, Community*. New York: Verso.

Mutz, D.C. 2002. The consequences of cross-cutting networks for political participation. *American Journal of Political Science*, 46(4), 838–855.

Mutz, D.C. 2006. *Hearing the Other Side: Deliberative versus Participatory Democracy*. Cambridge: Cambridge University Press.

Nakamura, L. 2002. *Cybertypes: Race, Ethnicity, and Identity on the Internet*. New York: Psychology Press.

Narayanan, A. and Shmatikov, V. 2008. Robust De-Anonymization of Large Sparse Datasets. In IEEE Symposium on Security and Privacy, Spring 2008, 111–125.

New York Times. 2010. An Annual Report on One Man's Life. *Bits Blog*. [Online, 9 February]. Available at: http://bits.blogs.nytimes.com/2010/02/09/an-annual-report-on-one-mans-life/ [accessed: 11 October 2011].

Nock, S.L. 1993. *The Costs of Privacy: Surveillance and Reputation in America*. New York: Aldine De Gruyter.

Noelle-Neumann, E. 1974. The spiral of silence: A theory of public opinion. *Journal of Communication*, 24(2), 43–51.

Nosko, A., Wood, E. and Molema, S. 2010. All about me: Disclosure in online social networking profiles: The case of Facebook. *Computers in Human Behavior*, 26(3), 406–418.

Nussbaum, M. 2001. *Upheavals of Thought: The Intelligence of Emotions*. Cambridge: Cambridge University Press.

Nyhan, B. and Reifler, J. 2010. When corrections fail: The persistence of political misperceptions. *Political Behavior*, 32(2), 303–330.

O'Hear, S. 2010. Germany to Outlaw Employers Checking out Job-Candidates on Facebook. *TechCrunch.com* [Online, 23 September]. Available at: http://eu.techcrunch.com/2010/08/23/germany-to-outlaw-employers-checking-out-job-candidates-on-facebook-but-googling-is-ok/

O'Sullivan, P. and A.J. Flanagin, 2003. Reconceptualizing "flaming" and other problematic messages. *New Media and Society*, 5(1), 69–94.

Oboler, S. 1994. Cultures of Resistance. *Novel: A Forum on Fiction*, 1, 204–207.

Olivarez-Giles, N. 2011. Facebook under Scrutiny for Face-Recognition Feature from Privacy Group, Lawmakers. *Los Angeles Times*. [Online, 8 June]. Available at: http://articles.latimes.com/2011/jun/08/business/la-fi-0609-facebook-faces-mobile. [accessed: 11 October 2011].

Opsahl, K. 2010. Facebook's Eroding Privacy Policy: A Timeline. *Electronic Frontier Foundation*. [Online]. Available at: http://eff.org/deeplinks/2010/04/facebook-timeline. [accessed: 10 October 2011].

Oreskovic, A. 2011. Facebook to Take Top Spot in U.S. Display Ad Market. *Reuters*. [Online, 20 June]. Available at: http://reuters.com/article/2011/06/20/us-facebook-idUSTRE75J5SU20110620. [accessed: 6 October 2011].

Paine, R. 1969. In search of friendship: An exploratory analysis in "middle-class" culture. *Man*, 4(4), 505–524.

Palmer, D. 2003. The paradox of user control. Paper presented at the Fifth International Digital Arts and Culture Conference, Melbourne, Australia, 19–23 May. [Online]. Available at: http://hypertext.rmit.edu.au/dac/papers/Palmer.pdf. [accessed: 1 October 2011].

Papacharissi, Z. 2002. The virtual sphere. *New Media and Society*, 4(1), 9–17.

Pariser, E. 2011. *The Filter Bubble: What the Internet Is Hiding from You*. New York: Penguin Press.

Park, N., Kee, K.F. and Valenzuela, S. 2009. Being immersed in social networking environment: Facebook groups, uses and gratifications, and social outcomes. *CyberPsychology and Behavior*, 12(6), 729–733.

Parks Associates. 2011. Parks Associates Sees Social Gaming on Track to Become $5 Billion Industry by 2015. Press Release. [Online]. Available at: http://parksassociates.com/blog/article/parks-pr2011-socialgaming. [accessed: 11 October 2011].

Parks, M.R. 2010. Who Are Facebook Friends? Exploring the Composition of Facebook Friend Networks. Paper presented at the annual meeting of the International Communication Association, Suntec Singapore International Convention and Exhibition Centre, Suntec City, Singapore. [Online]. Accessible at: http://allacademic.com/meta/p404726_index.html. [accessed: 9 September 2011].

Pash, A. 2011. Save Yourself from Weiner-Caliber Online Embarrassment with Internet Shame Insurance. *Lifehacker.com* [Online, 9 June]. Available at: http://lifehacker.com/5810453/save-yourself-from-weiner+calibre-online-embarrassment-with-internet-shame-insurance. [accessed: 1 October 2011].

Pateman, C. 1970. *Participation and Democratic Theory*. Cambridge: Cambridge University Press.

Patil, S., Page, X. and Kobsa, A. 2011. With a Little Help from My Friends: Can Social Navigation Inform Interpersonal Privacy Preferences? In Proceedings of the ACM 2011 Conference on Computer Supported Cooperative Work, 391–394.

Penenberg, A. 2010. Doctor Love: Social Networking Affects Brains Like Falling in Love. *Fast Company*. [Online 1, July]. Available at: www.fastcompany.com/magazine/147/doctor-love.html. [accessed: 1 October 2011].

Pettigrew, T.F. 1998. Intergroup contact theory. *Annual Review of Psychology*, 49(1), 65–85.

Pew Research Center. 2010. *Global Publics Embrace Social Networking*. [Online, 15 December]. Available at: http://pewglobal.org/2010/12/15/global-publics-embrace-social-networking/ [accessed: 1 September 2011].

Phillip, K. 2011. White House masters wild web. *Politico.com*. [Online 21, May]. Available at: http://www.politico.com/news/stories/0511/54063.html. [accessed: 19 October 2011].

Plummer, K. 2003. *Intimate Citizenship: Private Decisions and Public Dialogues*. Seattle: University of Washington Press.

Popkin, H. 2011. Facebook Loses 6 Million US Users, Continues to Conquer Globe. *MSNBC.com* [Online 13, June]. Available at: http://technolog.msnbc.msn.com/_news/2011/06/13/6848915-facebook-loses-6-million-us-users-continues-to-conquer-globe. [accessed: 1 September 2011].

Poster, M. 1996. Databases as discourse: or, Electronic interpellations. In *Computers, Surveillance, and Privacy*, edited by D. Lyon and E. Zureik. Minneapolis: University of Minnesota Press. 175–192.

Poteete, A.R., Janssen, M.A. and Ostrom, E. 2010. *Working Together: Collective Action, the Commons, and Multiple Methods in Practice*. Princeton: Princeton University Press.

Potok, M. 2008. President Obama? Many White Supremacists are Celebrating. *Southern Poverty Law Center Report*. [Online, 11 June]. Available at: http://splcenter.org/blog/2008/06/11/president-obama-many-white-supremacists-are-celebrating/ [accessed: 1 September 2011].

Powers, W. 2010. *Hamlet's BlackBerry*. New York: HarperCollins.

Preece, J., Nonnecke, B. and Andrews, D. 2004. The top five reasons for lurking: Improving community experiences for everyone. *Computers in Human Behavior*, 20(2), 201–223.

Preston, S. 2011. Movement Began with Outrage and a Facebook Page That Gave It an Outlet. *New York Times*. [Online, 2 February]. Available at: http://nytimes.com/2011/02/06/world/middleeast/06face.html?pagewanted=all [accessed: 1 September 2011].

Purdy, M. 2011. Improvements to Permissions for Address and Mobile Numbers. *Facebook Developers Blog*. [Online 17, January]. Available at: http://developers.facebook.com/blog/post/447/ [accessed: 1 September 2011].

Putnam, R. 2000. *Bowling Alone: The Collapse and Revival of American Community*. New York. Simon & Schuster.

Quan-Haase, A. 2007. University students' local and distant social ties: Using and integrating modes of communication on campus. *Information, Communication and Society*, 10(5), 671–693.

Raab, C. 2009. Identity: Difference and categorization. In *Lessons from the Identity Trail: Anonymity, Privacy and Identity in a Networked Society*, edited by I. Kerr, V.M. Steeves and C. Lucock. New York: Oxford University Press.

Rawlins, W.K. 1992. *Friendship Matters: Communication, Dialectics, and the Life Course*. New York: Aldine de Gruyter.

Rawlings, L.B, and G.M. Rubio. 2005. Evaluating the impact of conditional cash transfer programs. *The World Bank Research Observer* 20(1), 29–55.

Raynes-Goldie, K. 2010. Aliases, creeping, and wall cleaning: Understanding privacy in the age of Facebook. *First Monday*, 15(1), 4.

Reichelt, L. 2007. Ambient Intimacy. *Disambiguity Blog*. [Online, 1 March]. Available at: http://disambiguity.com/ambient-intimacy/[accessed: 9 September 2011].

Rideout, V.J., Foehr, U.G. and Roberts, D.F. 2010. Generation M2: Media in the lives of 8-to 18-year-olds. *Kaiser Family Foundation Report*.

Riesman, D., Denney, R. and Glazer, N. 2001. *The Lonely Crowd: A Study of the Changing American Character*. New Haven: Yale University Press.

Rilling, J.K. and Sanfey, A. 2011. The neuroscience of decision-making. *Annual Review of Psychology*, 62(1), 23–48.

Ritzer, G. 1993. *The McDonaldization of Society*. Thousand Oaks, CA: Pine Forge.

Roberts, N.C. 1997. Public deliberation: An altenative approach to crafting policy and setting direction. *Public Administration Review*, 57(2), 124–132.

Robinson, L. 2007. The cyberself: The self-ing project goes online, symbolic interaction in the digital age. *New Media and Society*, 9(1), 93–110.

Rogers, R. 2011. Facebook: How to Disable Instant Personalization. *TechRecipies. com* [Online, 5 January]. http://tech-recipes.com/rx/10622/facebook-how-to-disable-instant-personalization/ [accessed: 22 September 2011].

Rose, M. 1996. *Inventing our Selves, Psychology, Power and Personhood.* Cambridge: Cambridge University Press.

Rose, N. 1990. *Governing the Soul: The Shaping of the Private Self.* London: Routledge.

Rother, L. 2011. In Cuba, the Voice of a Blog Generation. *New York Times*. [Online, 5 July]. Available at: http://nytimes.com/2011/07/06/books/yoani-sanchez-cubas-voice-of-a-blogging-generation.html [accessed: 14 September 2011].

RoyalPingdom.com 2011. Internet 2010 in Numbers. [Online, 12 January]. http://royal.pingdom.com/2011/01/12/internet-2010-in-numbers/ [accessed: 28 September 2011].

Ryfe, D.M. 2002. The practice of deliberative democracy: A study of 16 deliberative organizations. *Political Communication*, 19(3), 359–377.

Saletan, W. 2011. Springtime for Twitter. *Slate.com* [Online, 18 July]. Available at: http://slate.com/articles/health_and_science/future_tense/2011/07/springtime_for_twitter.html. [accessed: 14 September 2011].

Salter, L. 2005. Colonization tendencies in the development of the World Wide Web. *New Media and Society*, 7(3), 291–309.

Sanson, A. 2008. Facebook and youth mobilization in the 2008 presidential election. *Gnovis Journal*, 8(3), 162–174.

Sartor, G. 2011. Legislative information and the Web. In *Legislative XML for the Semantic Web*, edited by G. Sartor, M. Palmirani, E. Francesconi and M.A. Biasiotti. Berlin: Springer. 11–20.

Sartre, J.P. 1956. *Being and Nothingness: A Phenomenological Essay on Ontology.* London: Taylor and Francis.

Schlozman, K.L., Verba, S. and Brady, H.E. 2010. Weapon of the strong? Participatory inequality and the internet. *Perspectives on Politics*, 8(2), 487–509.

Schmitt, C. 2007. *The Concept of the Political*. University of Chicago Press.

Schradie, J. 2011. The digital production gap: The digital divide and Web 2.0 collide. *Poetics*, 39(2), 145–168.

Schrage, E. 2010. Facebook Executive Answers Reader Questions. *New York Times Bits Blog*. [Online, 11 May]. Available at: http://bits.blogs.nytimes.com/2010/05/11/facebook-executive-answers-reader-questions/ [accessed: 19 September 2011].

Scott, J.C. 1992. *Domination and the Arts of Resistance*. New Haven: Yale University Press.

Selg, H. 2010. Swedish students online: An inquiry into differing. In *Youth Culture and Net Culture: Online Social Practices*, edited by E. Dunkels, G. Frånberg and C. Hällgren. Hershey, PA: IGI Global, 41–62.

Selwyn, N. 2004. Reconsidering political and popular understandings of the digital divide. *New Media & Society* 6(3), 341–362.

Sennett, R. 2003. *Respect: The Formation of Character in a World of Inequality.* London: Penguin Books.

Sennett, R. 1974. *The Fall of Public Man.* New York: W.W. Norton.

Shah, R.C. and Kesan, J.P. 2003. Manipulating the governance characteristics of code. *Info*, 5(4), 3–9.

Sheehan, K.B. 2002. Toward a typology of Internet users and online privacy concerns. *The Information Society*, 18(1), 21–32.

Shih, C.C. 2009. *The Facebook Era: Tapping Online Social Networks to Build Better Products, Reach New Audiences, and Sell More Stuff.* New Jersey: Prentice Hall.

Shih, C.F. and Venkatesh, A. 2004. Beyond adoption: Development and application of a use-diffusion model. *Journal of Marketing*, 68(1), 59–72.

Shirky, C. 2009. *Here Comes Everybody: The Power of Organizing without Organizations.* London: Penguin Group.

Sifry, M. 2009. Facebook's Truman Show Democracy. *Personal Democracy Forum.* [Online, 15 March]. Available at: http://personaldemocracy.com/blog-entry/facebooks-truman-show-democracy [accessed: 27 September 2011].

Simon, H.A. 1972. Theories of bounded rationality. *Decision and Organization*, 1(1), 161–176.

Slee, T. 2011. Blogs and Bullets: Breaking Down Social Media. *Whimsley Blog.* [Online, 4 March]. http://whimsley.typepad.com/whimsley/2011/03/blogs-and-bullets-breaking-down-social-media.html. [accessed: 19 September 2011].

Smith, J. 2011. The Internet, Tamed. *jehsmith.com* [Online, 9 January]. Available at: http://jehsmith.com/1/2011/01/the-internet-concluded.html. [accessed: 27 September 2011].

Smith, R.C. 2003. Diasporic memberships in historical perspective: Comparative insights from the Mexican, Italian and Polish Cases. *International Migration Review*, 37(3), 724–759.

Smith, S. 2010. Facebook Knocks Google off its Throne. *The Tech Herald.* [Online, 16 March]. Available at: http://thetechherald.com/article.php/201011/5381/Facebook-knocks-Google-off-its-Web-throne. [accessed: 11 September 2011].

Smith, Z. 2010. Generation Why: Review of the Social Network. *New York Review of Books.* [Online, 25 November]. Available at: http://nybooks.com/articles/archives/2010/nov/25/generation-why/?pagination= false. [accessed: 22 September 2011].

SocialBakers.com. 2011. Facebook Gains 80 Million New Accounts in the First Quarter of 2011. [Online, 4 July]. Available at: http://socialbakers.com/blog/143-facebook-gains-80-million-new-accounts-in-the-first-quarter-of-2011/ [accessed: 9 September 2011].

Sontag, S. 1977. *On Photography.* New York: Picador.

Sorkin, A.R. 2010. Facebook Tops 500 Million Users. *New York Times Blog.* [Online, 22 July]. http://dealbook.nytimes.com/2010/07/22/facebook-tops-500-million-users/ [accessed: 20 September 2011].

Stefanone, M.A., Lackaff, D. and Rosen, D. 2011. Contingencies of self-worth and social-networking-site behavior. *Cyberpsychology, Behavior, and Social Networking*, 14(1), 41–49.

Steinfield, C., DiMicco, J.M., Ellison, N.B. and Lampe, C. (2009). Bowling Online: Social Networking and Social Capital within the Organization. Proceedings of the Fourth Communities and Technologies Conference, 245–254.

Steinfield, C., Ellison, N.B. and Lampe, C. 2008. Social capital, self-esteem, and use of online social network sites: A longitudinal analysis. *Journal of Applied Developmental Psychology*, 29(6), 434–444.

Stern, S.R. 2004. Expressions of identity online: Prominent features and gender differences in adolescents' World Wide Web home pages. *Journal of Broadcast and Electronic Media*, 48(2), 218–243.

Stokey, E. and Zeckhauser, R. 1978. *A Primer for Policy Analysis*. New York: W.W. Norton.

Stone, B. 2011. Why Facebook Needs Sheryl Sandberg. *Business Week*. [Online, 12 May]. Available at: http://businessweek.com/magazine/content/11_21/b4229050473695.htm [accessed: 9 September 2011].

Subrahmanyam, K., Reich, S., Waechter, N. and Espinoza, G. 2008. Online and offline social networks: Use of social networking sites by emerging adults. *Journal of Applied Developmental Psychology*, 29(6), 420–433.

Sunstein, C.R. 2001. *Republic. com 2.0*. Princeton: Princeton University Press.

Surowiecki, J. 2004. *The Wisdom of Crowds: Why the Many Are Smarter Than the Few and How Collective Wisdom Shapes Business, Economies, Societies, and Nations*. New York: Doubleday Books.

Svensson, J. 2008. Expressive rationality: A different approach for understanding participation in municipal deliberative practices. *Communication, Culture and Critique*, 1(2), 203–221.

Tabuchi, H. 2011. Facebook Wins Relatively Few Friends in Japan. *New York Times*. [Online, 10 January]. Available at: http://nytimes.com/2011/01/10/technology/10facebook.html? pagewanted=all [accessed: 21 September 2011].

Tajfel, H. 1981. *Human Groups and Social Categories: Studies in Social Psychology*. Cambridge: Cambridge University Press, 1981.

Tajfel, H. and Turner, J.C. 2004. The social identity theory of intergroup behavior. In *Psychology of Intergroup Relations*, edited by S. Worchel and L.W. Austin. Chicago: Nelson-Hall, 33–48.

Tavani, H.T. 2008. Informational privacy: concepts, theories, and controversies. In *Handbook of Information and Computer Ethics*, edited by K.E. Himma and H.T. Tavani. Hoboken, NJ: Wiley, 131–164.

Taylor, M. 1982. *Community, Anarchy and Liberty*. Cambridge: Cambridge University Press.

Thaler, R.H. and Sunstein, C.R. 2008. *Nudge: Improving Decisions about Health, Wealth, and Happiness*. New Haven: Yale University Press.

The Economist. 2010. Mining the Social Web. [Online, 10 January]. Available at: http://economist.com/node/16910031 [accessed: 1 September 2011].

The Economist. 2011. From Pharaohs to Facebook. In *MoreIntelligentLife.com* [Online, 31 January]. http://moreintelligentlife.com/blog/pharaohs-facebook [accessed: 1 September 2011].

Thelwall, M., Buckley, K., Paltoglou, G., Cai, D. and Kappas, A. 2010. Sentiment strength detection in short informal text. *Journal of the American Society for Information Science and Technology*, 61(12), 2544–2558.

Thompson, C. 2008. Brave New World of Digital Intimacy. *New York Times.* [Online, 5 September]. Available at: http://nytimes.com/2008/09/07/magazine/07awareness-t.html?pagewanted=all [accessed: 19 September 2011].

Tilly, C. 2002. *Stories, Identities, and Political Change.* Lanham, MD: Rowman and Littlefield.

Todi, M. 2008. Advertising on social networking websites. *Wharton Research Scholars Journal*, May,1–34.

Tönnies, F. 1955. *Community and Organization.* London: Routledge & Kegan Paul,

Tufekci, Z. 2008a. Can you see me now? Audience and disclosure regulation in online social network sites. *Bulletin of Science, Technology and Society*, 28(1), 20–36.

Tufekci, Z. 2008b. Grooming, gossip, Facebook and MySpace. *Information, Communication and Society*, 11(4), 544–564.

Turkle, S. 1995. *Life on the Screen: Identity in the Age of the Internet.* New York: Simon & Schuster.

Turkle, S. 2011. *Alone Together: Why We Expect More from Technology and Less from Each Other.* New York: Basic Books.

Twenge, J.M. and Campbell, W.K. 2009. *The Narcissism Epidemic: Living in the Age of Entitlement.* New York: Free Press.

Vaidhyanathan, S. 2009. *The Googlization of Everything.* Berkeley: University of California Press.

Valenzuela, S., Park, N. and Kee, K.F. 2009. Is there social capital in a social network site: Facebook use and college students' life satisfaction, trust, and participation. *Journal of Computer-Mediated Communication*, 14(4), 875–901.

Valkenburg, P.M., Peter, J. and Schouten, A.P. 2006. Friend networking sites and their relationship to adolescents' well-being and social self-esteem. *CyberPsychology and Behavior*, 9(5), 584–590.

Van Dijk, J. 2005. *The Deepening Divide: Inequality in the Information Society.* Thousand Oaks, CA: Sage Publications.

Vance, A. 2011. This Tech Bubble is Different. *BusinessWeek.* [Online, 14 April]. Available at: http://businessweek.com/magazine/content/11_17/b4225060960537.htm [accessed: 19 September 2011].

Vascellaro, J. 2010. Facebook Founder in no Rush to Friend Wall Street. *Wall Street Journal.* [Online, 3 March]. Available at: http://online.wsj.com/article/SB10001424052748703787304575075942803630712.html.[accessed: 2 September 2011].

Villa, D.R. 1992. Postmodernism and the public sphere. *The American Political Science Review*, 86(3), 712–721.

Walther, J.B. 2007. Selective self-presentation in computer-mediated communication: Hyperpersonal dimensions of technology, language, and cognition. *Computers in Human Behavior*, 23(5), 2538–2557.

Wang, H., Lee, M. and Wang, C. 1998. Consumer privacy concerns about Internet marketing. *Communications of the ACM*, 41(3), 63–70.

Wang, S.S., Moon, S., Kwon, K., Evans, C. and Stefanone, M. 2010. Face off: Implications of visual cues on initiating friendship on Facebook. *Computers in Human Behavior*, 26(2), 226–234.

Wanta, W. and Hu, Y.W. 1994. The effects of credibility, reliance, and exposure on media agenda-setting: A path analysis model. *Journalism Quarterly*, 71(1), 90–98.

Warschauer, M. 2002. Reconceptualizing the digital divide. *First Monday* 7(7).

Wasow, O. 2008. The First Internet President. *The Root*. [Online, 5 November]. Available at: http://theroot.com/views/first-internet-president [accessed: 21 September 2011].

Wauters, R. 2011. Facebook Added Almost Eight New Registrations per Second in 2010. TechCrunch.com. [Online, 1 February]. Available at: http://techcrunch. com/2011/02/01/ facebook-averaged-almost-8-new-registrations-per-second-in-2010/. [accessed: 9 September 2011].

Wellman, B. and Hampton, K. 1999. Living networked on and offline. *Contemporary Sociology*, 28(6), 648–654.

Westen, T. and Madras, D. 2006. *A Digital Citizens' Bill of Rights*. [Online]. Available at: http://cgs.org/publications/articles/Digital_Citizens_Bill_of_Rights.pdf [accessed, 29 July 2011).

Whitchurch, E.R., Wilson, T.D. and Gilbert, D.T. 2011. He loves me, he loves me not. *Psychological Science*, 22(2), 172–175.

White, M. 2010. Clicktivism is Ruining Leftist Activism. *Guardian*. [Online, 12 August]. Available at: http://guardian.co.uk/commentisfree/2010/aug/12/clicktivism-ruining-leftist-activism [accessed: 11 September 2011].

Williams, C.B. and Gulati, G.J. 2007. Social Networks in Political Campaigns: Facebook and the 2006 Midterm Elections. Paper Presented at the American Political Science Association Annual Meeting, Chicago, IL, October 24–26.

Williams, C.B. and Gulati, G.J. 2011. Social Media in the 2010 Congressional Elections. Paper presented at the Midwest Political Science Association, Chicago, IL, April 2–5.

Williamson, E., Schatz, A. and Fowler, G. 2011. Facebook Seeking Friends in Beltway. *Wall Street Journal*. [Online, 12 August]. Available at: http://online. wsj.com/article/SB10001424052748703789104576273242590724876.html [accessed: 11 September 2011].

Wilson, J. 2009. Not Another Political Zombie. *New Matilda*. [Online, 25 February]. Available at: http://newmatilda.com/2009/02/25/not-another-political-zombie [accessed: 24 September 2011].

Womack, B. and MacMillen, D. 2011. Goldman Sachs Said to Invest 450 Million in Facebook. *Bloomberg*. [Online, 3 January]. Available at: http://bloomberg.com/

news/2011–01–03/facebook-valued-at-50-billion-as-goldman-is-said-to-invest-450-million.html [accessed: 19 September 2011].

Wong, Y. 2010. Does Mark Zuckerberg Believe in Privacy? *Quora.com* [Online, 30 April]. Available at: http://quora.com/Yishan-Wong/What-Does-X-Believe/answers. [accessed: 22 September 2011].

Wortham, J. 2011. Feel Like a Wallflower? Maybe It's Your Facebook Wall. *New York Times.* [Online, 9 April]. Available at: http://nytimes.com/2011/04/10/business/10ping.html?_r=1 [accessed: 7 September 2011].

Wright, K. 2008. Dare to be yourself. *Psychology Today*, 41(3), 70–77.

Wu, T. 2010. *The Master Switch: The Rise and Fall of Information Empires.* New York: Knopf.

Wysocki, D. and Childers, C.D. 2011. "Let my fingers do the talking": Sexting and infidelity in cyberspace. *Sexuality and Culture*, 15 (1), 217–239.

Yglesias, M. 2007. Global Test. *The Atlantic.com* [Online, 24 May]. Available at: http://theatlantic.com/politics/archive/2007/05/global-test/42380/ [accessed: 3 September 2011].

Young, I.M. 1990. *Justice and the Politics of Difference.* Princeton: Princeton University Press.

Zak, P.J., Kurzban, R. and Matzner, W.T. 2004. The neurobiology of trust. *Annals of the New York Academy of Sciences*, 1032(1), 224–227.

Zhang, C., Callegaro, M. and Thomas, M. 2008. More Than the Digital Divide: Investigating the Differences between Internet and Non-Internet Users. In *Annual Conference of the Midwest Association for Public Opinion Research*, Chicago, IL.

Zhang, W. and Storck, J. 2001. Peripheral Members in Online Communities. In *Proceedings of the Americas Conference on Information Systems.* AMCIS 2001. Boston, Massachusetts.

Zhang, X. and Zhu, F. 2011. Group size and incentives to contribute: A natural experiment at Chinese Wikipedia. *American Economic Review*, 101(4), 1601–1615.

Zhao, S., Grasmuck, S. and Martin, J. 2008. Identity construction on Facebook: Digital empowerment in anchored relationships. *Computers in Human Behavior*, 24(5), 1816–1836.

Zheng, Y. 2008. *Technological Empowerment: The Internet, State, and Society in China.* Stanford: Stanford University Press.

Zhuo, X., Wellman, B. and Yu, J. 2011. Egypt: The first Internet revolt? *Peace Magazine.* 27(3), 6–9.

Zimmer, M. 2011. Facebook's Censorship Problem. *MichealZimmer.org.* [Online, 21 April]. Available at: http://michaelzimmer.org/2011/04/21/facebooks-censorship-problem/ [accessed: 9 September 2011].

Zittrain, J. and Palfrey, J. 2008. Internet filtering: The politics and mechanisms of control. In *Access Denied: The Practice and Policy of Global Internet Filtering*, edited by J. Palfrey, R. Rohozinski and J. Zittrain. Cambridge, MA: MIT Press, 29–57.

Zuckerberg, M. 2010. Building the Social Web Together. *Facebook Blog*. [Online, 21 April]. Available at: http://facebook.com/blog.php?post=383404517130 [accessed: 14 September 2011].

Zuckerberg, M. 2010. Interview on *CBS 60 Minutes*. [Online, 5 December]. Available at: http://cbsnews.com/video/watch/?id=7120607n [accessed: 9 September 2011].

Zuckerman, E. 2010. Internet Freedom: Protect, then project. *My Heart's in Accra Blog*. [Online, 22 March]. Available at: http://ethanzuckerman.com/blog/index. php?s=psiphon [accessed: 14 September 2011].

Zuckerman, E. 2010. Overcoming Apathy through Participation. *My Heart's in Accra Blog*. [Online, 3 June]. Available at: http://ethanzuckerman.com/ blog/2010/06/03/overcoming-apathy-throughparticipation-my-talk-at-personal-democracy-forum/ [accessed: 19 July 2011].

Index